SHELLS FROM THE SANDS OF BOMBAY

SHELLS FROM THE SANDS OF BOMBAY

BEING

MY RECOLLECTIONS AND

REMINISCENCES-1860-1875.

SIR D. E. WACHA

GYAN

Published by

GYAN

Gyan Publishing House
5, Ansari Road
Daryaganj, New Delhi-110002
Phone: 011-47034999, 9811692060
E-mail: books@gyanbooks.com

Distribution Network
gyanbooks.com
India, USA, Canada, UK, Australia, France

ISBN : 978-81-212-9264-1 (PB)
First Published, 1920

2nd Impression 2023

Printed at: Gyan Press, Delhi.

SHELLS FROM THE SANDS OF BOMBAY
Author: SIR D. E. WACHA

Shells from the Sands of Bombay

BEING

MY RECOLLECTIONS AND REMINISCENCES—1860-1875.

BY

SIR D. E. WACHA.

AUTHOR OF

The History of Bombay Share Speculation (1863/4/5);
Life of Premchund Roychund; Life of J. N. Tata;
Rise and Growth of Bombay Municipal Government
and numerous brochures and papers on a
variety of Public Questions.

1920.

PRINTED BY SYED ABDULLA BRELVI, AT "THE BOMBAY CHRONICLE" PRESS, MEDOWS STREET, FORT, BOMBAY

AND

PUBLISHED BY K. T. ANKLESARIA, GENERAL MANAGER THE INDIAN NEWSPAPER CO., LTD.

To the Memory

of

My Dear Son,

Who

Was invariably helpful to me

In

My Literary Labours,

and who,

A little before his untimely death,

Revised the first proofs

With Loving hands and Filial Devotion,

I dedicate with Tears

This Volume.

LIST OF ILLUSTRATIONS.

CONTENTS.

INTRODUCTION.

CHAPTER I.

CHAPTER II.

CHAPTER III.

CHAPTER IV.

CHAPTER V.

CHAPTER VI.

CHAPTER XXII.

CHAPTER XXIII.

CHAPTER XXIV.

CHAPTER XXV.

CHAPTER XXVI.

CHAPTER XXVII.

CHAPTER XXVIII.

FOREWORD.

My Dear Sir Dinshah Wacha,

We have so often talked over the subject of these reminiscences that you will not need any assurance from me of the great personal pleasure which I have experienced in reading the pages in which you have gathered what you modestly call "Shells from the Sands of Bombay."

Bombay has changed so fast, and is still changing so fast, that without such reminiscences future generations will have no conception of the evolution of the stately city which has grown up under our eyes. No-one who did not know Bombay, as you knew it, before Sir Bartle Frere levelled the ramparts, can picture the narrow walled town which has blossomed into the second city of the Empire. My own memory goes back not quite a quarter of a century, yet Bombay is in many respects hardly recognisable as the city where I landed in July 1897. There were then no buildings on the Apollo Bunder estate save the White House. Where the Taj Mahal Hotel now stands was a boat basin, used by the rowing members of the Bombay Gymkhana, and many an evening have I taken a whiff there and sculled down the harbour to Mazagon. The house shortage was almost as acute as now, and there was no more familiar sight than the canvas settlement which sprang up every year on the Cooperage and in Marine Lines, each group of tents, true to the British tradition of isolation, being screened from its neighbours by fences of split bamboos. The Chartered Bank building, then in course of erection, was regarded as quite remote from the business centre and one often heard the remark that the directors of the Bank must be mad to think that people, were going into the wilderness to do business. The great centre of banking and commerce was Elphinstone Circle and Apollo Street and many of our leading firms were housed in ramshackle quarters, fit breeding places for the rats which spread the plague. Many groups of bachelors were driven to chummeries in Churchgate Street and Hummum Street, and I remember being implored to tread lightly when dining in Churchgate Street because of the insecurity of the floor. The old buggies had disappeared, but there were still one or two palkies in the streets and the bullock hackery was a familiar spectacle. The mail passenger who now lands in lordly comfort at the Mole little knows what it was to arrive in an outside steamer in the monsoon, and to be blown to Mazagon in a Bunder boat, as I was, before he could make the landing at the Customs House. It is difficult to realise that this was less than quarter of a century ago.

And these changes are as nothing in comparison with those which seem likely to fructify in the next quarter of a century. When Back Bay is reclaimed under the development scheme; the Fort is given entirely over to business purposes; the rice fields and palm groves which we have known in Matunga and Mahim are covered with tenement houses; and hundreds of thousands of people living in Salsette are borne swiftly to and from their work in electric trains, the Bombay of those days will bear little more resemblance to that of to-day than the city of our own times bears to that of the fifties, when the ramparts and gateways stood.

How then is a living picture of the Bombay of the early part of this century to be preserved for our successors? For those who wish to quarry in the past there is rich material in the letters of our forbears. The letters of Mrs. Postans and of Lady Falkland, to take only two instances, have enshrined for us vivid pictures of the life of the days in which they lived. Now-a-days no-one writes letters; our correspondence is made up of notes which are not worth keeping, even if any preserved them. The pages of a gazetteer, however rich, are a poor substitute for the untrammelled *vie intime* of the good letter writer. And amongst the busy migratory civil servants of to-day are we likely to find men of cultivated leisure like Sir James Campbell, who prepared the notes which Mr. S. M. Edwardes wove into his admirable Gazetteer of Bombay? We shall never see another James Douglas spending his leisure delving amongst the historical relics of the Presidency and recounting his discoveries in an English even more rugged than that of Carlyle, his literary *guru*. The files of the daily newspapers may record events in greater fullness than the records of the past; but they do not and cannot give a picture of contemporary life. Is it not true than to say that our hopes of maintaining the continuity of the living history of Bombay are bound up with the careful preservation of the reminiscences of all who have filled a considerable part in its activities, and in a more jealous preservation of the monuments of the past than has characterised the iconoclasts of the city?

It is rather dreadful to think of the completeness with which our architectural links with the past have been broken down. Bartle Frere's destruction of the Ramparts was no doubt a work of the greatest public utility, but how much more we should appreciate it if he had preserved one at least of the Gates with a section of the ramparts, which if they were never assailed gave to the citizens a feeling of security which was the foundation of its prosperity? The work of the town planners of Delhi has shown how an ancient wall can be adapted to the requirements of modern traffic. The only visible sign of these historic Ramparts is the fragment of wall which was part of St. George's bastion—such a poor fragment that few notice it. The historic heart of Bombay is the Castle, now given over to the base uses of a supplementary arsenal. Amid his tremendous work for the development of Bombay will not Sir George Lloyd spare a few moments to secure the Castle for the citizens, preferably as the home of the Bombay War

Museum? Sir Jamsetji Jijibhai's old town house has gone the way of many another and been converted into a shop. Will not the Parsi community see that at least one of these famous town houses—say that which you mention more than once, in Cowasji Patel Street, the family residences of the Dadys—is maintained intact so that future generations may see how their forbears lived during the making of Bombay? You record the conversion of the pleasant places of Byculla and Mazagon into an industrialism which is one of the most sordid in the world; the crumbling walls of Lowji Castle and of the old Manor House at Powai are amongst the last survivors of the spacious life of the fifties; they probably cannot be secured against the devastating march of bricks and mortar; but the Castle and one or two of our historic town houses surely should be preserved for the public for all time. Imagine what would be the feelings of Englishmen if the Tower were converted into a closed store house and every Georgian or early Victorian residence in

London was swept away for the erection of picture palaces and blocks of flats.

I have ridden my hobby horse so hard that I cannot say half the things I should like to say. But reading and re-reading these reminiscences of yours, I feel very strongly that there are few services more valuable than to preserve, as you have done, these vivid pictures of the life of Bombay in its great formative period. May you find many imitators. The re-creation of the past is however work half done unless it inspires in the present generation a quickened historic sense. We are citizens of no mean city. But the foundations of the city in which we live were laid by big men—Aungier, Elphinstone and Bartle Frere. The seeds of such intellectual life as we own were sown by Macintosh and the great missionaries and educationists—Wilson and Wordsworth and Grant. We live in days when materialism seems to be more and more rampant; everything is subordinated to the making of money, the churches are half empty and the Asiatic Society is a pale shadow of its former self, its library more a novel-circulating agency than a centre of learning. It seems to me that the one hope of arresting this tide of mere materialism is to quicken the historic spirit—to appreciate better the diversity and richness and real greatness of the lives of the men to whom the city owes everything, and to illumine our commercialism with the light of inquiry, rekindled by the memories of our forbears which you have blown into flame in the pages which follow.

Yours very sincerely,

STANLEY REED.

Bombay, August 16th, 1920.

PREFATORY NOTE.

The Recollections contained in this volume originally appeared, under the title of "Shells from the Sands of Bombay," in the form of weekly contribution to the columns of the "Bombay Chronicle", in 1914 and part of the following year, with the *nom de plume* of "Sandy Seventy," my having attained that age at the time.

Urged by kind friends, old and young, who found the reminiscences interesting, that I should give them a permanent place in our local annals, I resolved to have them collected and published, somewhat expanded, in bookform. Owing to the war and other reasons, the preliminary revision had to be delayed. It was, however, taken at last on hand and completed by my son, with his rare filial devotion and love of literary work, only a few short weeks before his untimely death.

(November 1919). The work has since undergone further revision; but some typographical and other errors have crept in for which I crave the indulgence of the reader. A list of the errors is printed.

Some interesting incidents escaped reference in the body of the book. These I now briefly relate. In the middle of the Sixties of the last century Dr. Livingstone, that intrepid and distinguished traveller, having arrived from Zanzibar, on his way to London, Sir Bartle Frere, the then Governor, invited him to give a short account of the principal events and discoveries connected with his travels in Central Africa before an audience of the citizens of Bombay in the Town Hall. It was a gathering of many enlightened and influential persons. Being one of the audience I should say, as my own personal impression formed at the time, that Dr. Livingstone actually took his hearers by storm, such was his thrilling and entertaining narrative. It was something to have heard first hand, from the lips of the great traveller and explorer, all about the wilds of Central Africa he walked on foot hundreds of miles, the mountains and rivers he carefully traced, the lakes he discovered as the sources of the Nile, the scenery that impressed him, and, lastly, the men and women of divers African communities he met with and who became his most excellent friends, thanks to his missionary character and his deep sympathy with the races. Dr. Livingstone seemed to me to be a personage of a wiry frame, well built, fine physique with next to no traces of the stress and strain of hundreds of miles that he travelled, often alone, but overcoming each and every difficulty as it arose. Of course, his face was "sundried." The lecture was made further attractive by many maps and other illustrations of the journey, as well as by a goodly show of quaint and archaic trinkets which the womanhood of Central Africa wore. Verily, the advent of the great traveller was a historic event in the annals of Bombay and needed a mention in this place.

Of minor interest may be mentioned, the visit in the very early part of 1864, of the then Commander-in-Chief of India, Lord Strathnairn and Jhansi, but more popularly known as Sir Hugh Rose, one of that most illustrious and heroic band of mutiny officers who saved India to the British when the destiny of the Empire was trembling in the balance. The other visitor was H. H. The Maharaja Dhuleepsingh who was in Bombay on his way to Lahore to perform the religious ceremonies of his deceased mother, the widow of the great Ranjeet Singh, "The Lion of the Punjab." Both attended the Convocation of the University in the Town Hall accompanied by Sir Bartle Frere as the Chancellor and Sir Alexander Grant as the Vice-Chancellor. The Maharaja, so far as my recollection carries me, looked a fine specimen of a brave Sikh. His bearing was noble as he walked down the aisle of the hall with measured step side by side with Sir Hugh. Of course, he was darkish in appearance but well built. Unlike, however, many of our indigenous Princes and Chiefs he had not bedecked himself with "pearls and parbaric gold" of the gorgeous East. Sir Bartle Frere's Convocation address was, as usual, full of brilliancy, culture and literary polish of which he was a master. Literary scholarship was in the family and the name of Sir Hookham Frere is well known as that of a great classic scholar. The visit of these two distinguished persons was also a unique event in the history of Bombay. The city was then at the zenith of her prosperity. The cotton lords of the day rolled in riches made in the cotton trade. The hum and buzz of hundreds of the madding crowd of brokers and speculators was in itself striking. Those were golden days; and they congregated in their thousands at their favourite trysting place in what is now called the Esplanade Road, under the grateful shadow of three or four large spreading trees, say, somewhere about the building formerly known as Treacher's and now owned by the Mercantile Bank.

Another omission which I feel I should supply is the catholic philanthropy of Mr. Rustomji Jamsetji Jeejeebhoy who was the recognised prince of cotton merchants.. Having amassed great wealth undreamt of by his legitimate trade in cotton, during the American Civil War, (1861—65) he magnificently emulated the benevolence of his venerated father, the first Sir Jamsetji Jeejeebhoy. He led the Lancashire Cotton Famine Fund in the city by donating a very princely amount. His name was as widely known as was that of his illustrious parent. Indeed it was a name to be conjured with for pure charity, not only in the city but in the whole of the Bombay Presidency, specially Gujerat. His philanthropy was unostentatious, and many are the stories of his charities to his poor relatives, friends, and strangers. The left hand knew not what the right hand did. This was *the* Rustomji Jamsetjee whose benevolence had spread far and wide, and I remember that in one of the weekly journals edited by Charles Dickens—"All the Year Round,"

—his name was funnily spelt as "Rumtomji Jumtolji," just as *Fraser's Magazine* had before travestied his father's name, when created a baronet, as "Jamramji." Verily, Mr. Rustomji was Bombay's Good Samaritan in those halcyon days. Bombay has not known of another such save the first Sir Cowasji Jehangir Readymoney.

Lastly, let me recall the Legislative Council of the early sixties under the governorship of Sir Bartle Frere. The first rudimentary Councils in the three Presidencies of India were established in 1862 or 1863. The nominations made by that liberal statesman were considered good in those days when the circle from which even to nominate was mostly limited to the merchant classes. Mr. Rustomji Jamsetji, Mr. Juggonath Sunkersett, Mr. Premabhoy Hemabhoy, Mr. Walter Cassels, and some of the Sirdars of the Deccan were the "additional members" during the first 3 or 4 years. The one important enactment passed by the early Legislative Council of Bombay was the Municipal Act of 1865, the very first, but a most elaborate and carefully considered piece of legislation. Thanks to the master mind and farsightedness of the very first aedile, or Municipal Commissioner, no other than Arthur Crawford, Bombay owes a deep debt of gratitude to him for all he accomplished. He was the first with his organising talents to develop Bombay on the right lines sixty years ago. But for him, I have not the least doubt in my own mind, that the future developments that have taken place would have not only been difficult of accomplishment but more costly than they are. It is much to be wished H. E. Sir George Lloyd may take a leaf from the book of Arthur Crawford. He was really a talented and farsighted Commissioner in advance of his age.

Let me, in conclusion, inform the reader that I do not claim any perfection for this volume of personal recollections. Let him take it for what it is worth. I have only essayed to link my own youthful reminiscences with the great history of Bombay prior to 1860 as I have read it, with a view that someone else may by and by give a faithful and graphic account of the rise and progress of Bombay generally for the last half a century so as to make it instinct with lively interest for the rising generation.

Meanwhile let me publicly express my thanks to the editor of the latest volumes of the *Bombay Gazetteer*. Mr. Edwardes, whose literary merit needs no praise, was entrusted with the editing of it on the basis of the mass of the most valuable papers left by the erudite Sir James Campbell. Many a hint and suggestion I have obtained from these interesting volumes I also express my thanks for the help I was able to derive from the Book of Bombay by the facetious and picturesque Mr. James Douglas. The book on the Origin and Early Settlement of Bombay by Dr. Cunha, antiquarian, historian and numismatist all combined, was also of great assistance. Again, I am deeply indebted to the Bombay Chamber of Commerce for the most valuable economic and commercial information I was able to glean from the many volumes recording the transactions of that body during the first twenty-five years of its existence. The men of the Bombay Chamber of Commerce, established 84 years ago, have been vastly instrumental in building up the greatness of the City. Few indeed are aware of the invaluable work the pioneers of commerce in the City had accomplished during the first twenty-five years.

Lastly, I am to offer my grateful thanks to Sir Stanley Reed, one of my most esteemed friends, of undoubted literary accomplishments in the journalistic line, whom I have known from the days of his first arrival in Bombay a quarter of a century ago. At my request he kindly undertook to write the "Foreword" with his customary alacrity and enthusiasm. In this way he has greatly lightened my task in respect of what I myself had first contemplated narrating in this Prefatory Note touching the marvellous transformation of Bombay. He has given a graphic portraiture of the evolution of the city, between 1895 and 1920, which is indeed unique. It is to my mind a perfect gem of the literary art of which Sir Stanley is the gifted possessor.

D. E. WACHA.

1st September, 1920.

BOMBAY FORT, 1670.

SHELLS FROM THE SANDS OF BOMBAY.

MY RECOLLECTIONS AND REMINISCENCES OF BOMBAY 1850 TO 1865.

INTRODUCTION.

" Time Rolls its Ceaseless Course."

THUS doth the tuneful bard of "Caledonia stern and wild" apostrophises Time which eminent evolutionists of the day regard as an "abstraction" pure and simple. According to these scientists it is only an invention of human ingenuity to mark its own progress. In the philosophy of Eastern sages, from days the most ancient, Time is "amitya" or immeasurable. It is without a beginning and without an end. Imagination has conjured it as "a mighty whirling wheel which none can stay or stem." Its spokes go round unceasingly. So we metaphorically speak of "the whirligig of Time." Unceasing in its revolution it is supposed to know no pause and take no breath. Generation after generation take their birth only to be swept away by the high returning tide in the great gulf of Eternity, leaving behind on life's sandy shore a few shells to bear testimony to their bare existence. These shells are patiently and laboriously picked up by a few faithful collectors, whom we call archæologists and historians. With infinite pains they endeavour to interpret their true significance.

Similarly, may not the present writer in his own humble way walk the ocean strand and pick up such stray shells from the sands as he may happen to stumble upon and evolve out of them his own narrative? In other words, may he not interest the present generation by relating his own recollections and reminiscences of the Bombay as he knew half a century ago and more? May he not string together a brief narrative of the marvellous transformation which the whirligig of Time has wrought in its ceaseless course, and the prodigies which have been accomplished by the race of yore on whose knees the infancy of two generation has danced?

Old "Bombain."

Throwing back the shroud of years, let it be revealed how it struck the boy of the early Fifties of the Nineteenth century that good old "Bombain" or "Mumbai," which two hundred years before was owned by "My Lady of the Manor," under a lease of £10 per annum, from his Gracious Majesty of Portugal, and which was so assiduously explored for drugs by Signor Garcia de Orta, that able scientist of botanic fame.

How did the "Killa" or Fort strike him? What were its environments? How many or few are the traces left of the old Fort for identification to-day? What were the ramparts or "Kote" and what the moats and ditches surrounding them which in the vernacular language were called "Chur"? How far did the "maidan" extend? Why a part of it was known as "Pavanchaki," and who were the good folk who resorted to the area to "eat the air" at even-tide and be refreshed by the balmy breeze blowing from the western sea? Where were the "Teen and Dao Durwazas" or Fort Gates, and where the "Dongri Killa" and the "Topekhana" (or artillery station)? And emerging from the "durwazas" or gates, which practically shut out the Fort or "Kote" from the native town in the north, what was understood by "Paidhoni," "Bharkote" or "Kotebahar," what by "Bori Bunder," "Fansika-talav," "Dhobighat," "Chandanwadi," and so

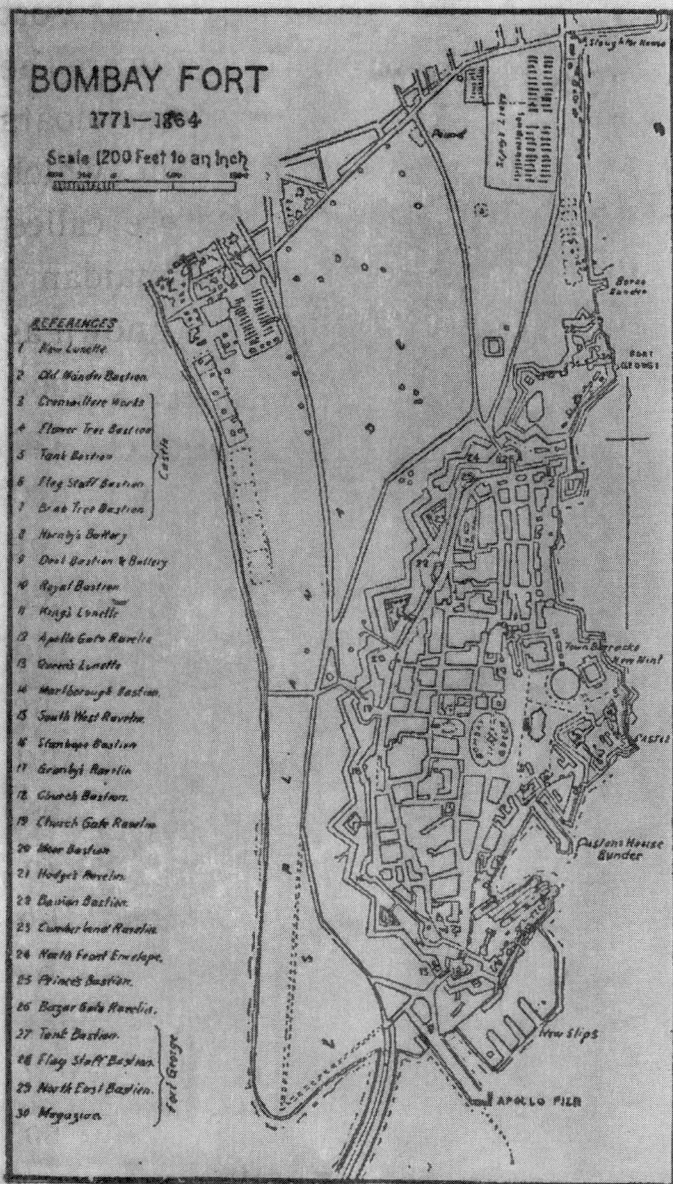

BOMBAY FORT
1771—1864
Scale 1200 Feet to an Inch
REFERENCES
3 Cremaillere Works
4 Flower Tree Bastion
5 Tank Bastion
6 Flag Staff Bastion
Castle
8 Hornby's Battery
10 Royal Bastion
11 King's Lunette
12 Apollo Gate Ravelin
13 Queen's Lunette
14 Marlborough Bastion
15 South West Ravelin
16 Stanhope Bastion
17 Granby's Ravelin
18 Church Bastion
19 Church Gate Ravelin
23 Cumberland Ravelin
24 North Front Envelope
25 Prince's Bastion
26 Bazar Gate Ravelin
27 Tank Bastion
28 Flag Staff Bastion
29 North East Bastion
30 Magazine
Fort George
FORT GEORGE
Town Barracks
New Mint
CASTLE
Custom House Bunder
New Slips
APOLLO PIER

FORT, 1711.

on? How were the suburbs of Mazgaon, Parel, Chinchpogli, and Girgaum, Mahalaxmi and Walkeshwar situated, where so many "wadis" or country house gardens were built for enjoying a holiday or spending a week-end?

What about the only "Godee" or dock and the great Wadia family who were known to be the hereditary master-builders of the mercantile marine and the Indian navy warships which navigated the Arabian and Red Seas and pursued the "buglas" and "dhows" of the piratical Arabs of Muscat, Socotra and Zanzibar, who bought and sold slaves? Where was the Custom House, the Post Office, the Supreme Court of Judicature? Where was the Secretariat and that impregnable "Bombay Castle," from which are still dated the Resolutions of His Excellency the Governor in Council, and the "King's Barracks"? Where were the offices of the Military Staff and the

Commissariat ? Where was the Mint ? It may also be enquired what kind of local government there was ? Who were the Municipal Commissioners ? What was the condition of the markets ? What was the source or what were the sources of water supply ? What about drainage and nightsoil ? How was Bombay lighted after dark ? What was the annual mortality ? What were the most fatal diseases ? Why were cholera and fever so rife ? How fared the foreign and inland trade ? Were there any banks and how were they managed and by whom ? What kind of scene did the harbour present with its serried phalanx of wooden vessels anchored in the middle ground, and the thousands of native craft of divers construction with peculiar names, Kathiawari, Arab, Bengali, and so on, in the Mody Bay, Carnac and other bunders on the eastern foreshore ? How did they pile cotton in warehouses ? Did the raw material take fire by " spontaneous combustion" and by other "unnatural causes"? And how did they manage to extinguish the big blazes? Where was the "Bombakhana" or Firebrigade station, and how did the firemen (lascars) work with their premitive handpumps? Whence did they derive their water supply for the extinction of fires? What was the *raison detre* of so many thousand wells, private and public, let alone the big tanks, built by the humane philanthropists of that generation, innocent of all thought of titles and other "honours"? Lastly, what was the state of education?

Thumb Nail Sketches.

The recollections and reminiscences which come crowding quite vividly to the writer's mind are so innumerable that they would fill volumes to narrate them with anything like amplitude. The object of these papers is only to give thumbnail sketches which will give in reality an outline of the Bombay of the

Fifties and Sixties—an outline which may be leisurely compared with the marvellously transformed city that is presented to the gaze of the generation flourishing at this hour. The change is wondrous and the gratifying metamorphose can only be done justice to by a born historian with the vivid imagination and the stately and sonorous style of the inimitable author of the "Decline and Fall of the Roman Empire." Such a writer alone can give a living and faithful picture of the marvels Time, in its ceaseless course, has accomplished in Bombay during the last fifty or sixty years. I can only scrawl in rude alphabet my own unambitious chalk-lines and passingly point to the distinguished persons who were contributory to the making of Bombay.

Chapter I.—"HEPTANESIA" AND THE HARBOUR.

As one attempts to trace the rise and growth of great cities, he is irresistibly reminded at every turn of the commonplace fact, which is so well crystalised in the lines of Sir Walter Scott quoted at the top of the Introduction. One generation in its own humble and primitive way erects a cluster of lonely huts, unconscious of the infinite possibilities and potentialities of the magnificent edifices, beautiful to behold and admire, which may be reared around it, stage by stage, by the hands of successive generations. The generations of men may be as the leaves of grass. They may live and die. But each has its own set of workers who do their appointed work which in reality is the earnest of what the next will do. Thus did the poet hold it truth, with him who sang to one harp in divers tones, that men may rise on the stepping stones of their dead selves to higher things. What is true of the progress of Humanity is also true of the rise and progress of great cities. Bombay is a striking example of the fishing village of centuries which now looms so large and grand in the eyes of an admiring world as the Second in the British Empire.

Early History of Bombay.

It is not the object of this book to narrate the history of Bombay. That history, in the sense modern historians of the day interpret it, is still to be written. But the writers are not a few who may be said to have faithfully and laboriously collected the dry bones which the genius of the coming historian will galvanise into life to interest and instruct those who may come after us. Divers have been the narrators from the days of the Portuguese. The local branch of the Royal Asiatic Society, which owes its existence to the erudite Sir

James Mackintosh, is a fairly good storehouse of divers texts about the earliest history of the city, long long even before the pirates of the Malabar Coast invaded the shores, and the fleet of the Habshi raided the nascent town. Those antiquarian authorities tell us how Bombay was a cluster of seven islands. Latinised, it is known as "Heptanesia." And the scholarly pen of Mr. S. M. Edwardes, the latest editor of the "Bombay Gazetteer," (now a retired Civilian) has given us a graphic account which the curious may read, mark and inwardly digest. And, if there be some who love the picturesque and the poetic, they may pour over the pages of that delightful Book on Bombay sketched by the graphic pen of our late veteran citizen, Mr. James Douglas, a Scotchman of the Scots but all the same a lover of Bombay which was the scene of his life long and energetic career. Or if one is so curious as to have a glimpse of "Society" in the early Fifties we may refer him to that bright little book, appropriately christened "Chow-Chow" by Lady Falkland, wife of the Governor who immediately preceded Lord Elphinstone. Perchance we should not be surprised if, fired by the example of this literary artist of local fame, the genial and vivacious consort of our late Governor, Lord Willingdon, were to emulate her, remembering also that she is the daughter of one who (Lady Brassey) gave us that sparkling book of the voyage of the yacht "Sunbeam" well nigh thirty-five years ago, called "In the Trade, in the Tropics and in the Roaring Forties." One point, however, in reference to "Bombain" may be made clear at the very outset. She has no mythological history of her own like the classic Delos where Phœbus sprung. There are no love stories of gods and goddesses extant; and there is no Byron to sing in rhyme; the "Isles of Moombai, the Isles of Moombai" to point a moral and adorn a

HARBOUR 1845.

tale. In short Bombay has no ancient pedigree and no aristocratic pride which the magnificence of the Great Mogul has imperishably associated with the city of the eternal Taj Mahal and the Motee Musjid. There are no Romuluses and Remuses to invoke and no Capitoline hill to worship, unless it be the latter day Moomba Devi and the magic stone of Walkeshwar.

The Harbour in the Fifties and Sixties.

With this preamble the writer begins his own parable. What may be, it will be inquired, was the outstanding feature of Bombay in the early Fifties and Sixties of the nineteenth century that struck his youthful gaze and interested him? The harbour and the Fort. The harbour is what it is. Nature made the harbour and the hands of the workers of each generation during the last two hundred years and more have improved it. The approaches were the same, but known to be full of danger for both skilled and unskilled navigators. The reefs near that beacon light known as Kennery were dangerous to a degree, and many a native craft and square rigged vessel had been lured to its fate on a dark and foggy night, more or less to be wrecked and seldom to be saved. There was, of course, another light nearer the harbour, the same which for years has become obsolete and known as the Colaba Observatory. Steam vessels had yet to come, albeit that tiny ferry launches plied between Carnac Bunder and Panvel and Oorun on the opposite side. Then there were two or three small steamers owned by private enterprise, which plied between Bombay, Surat, Gogo and Bhavanagar. In the era of pre-railways, these little vessels did yeoman's service to people going to and fro between the ports named for trade or other purposes. It was always difficult and somewhat dangerous to travel overland. The journey was long and tedious, and the vessels performed a useful service by sea. There was one known as the "Flox" and another as the "Elphinstone." In those days the medium of advertisement for vessels to ply backwards and forwards was not the "Times of India" and the "Bombay Chronicle" or the "Bombay Samachar" and the "Jame Jamshed." A Parsi-crier or two went round the native town, halting at centres where business men and women congregated. All the vessels were owned by Parsi shipowners, one of which belonged to the first Sir Cowasji Jehangir Readymoney of financial fame. There were a couple of criers with lungs of brass and stentorian voices. Each took his turn. The crier would stand at one of the recognised business centres in the native part of the Fort while all and sundry gathered round him. He then proclaimed the date on which the vessel would start, the name of the bunder from which the start would be made, the names of the ports at which it would anchor to embark and disembark passengers. These stentors always tickled my youthful ears, and methinks I imagine their voice still ringing. The programme of the departure of the vessel would be repeated in different market places, but it was never known that those sturdy criers ever got a sore or hoarse throat. The programme was a kind of stereotyped recitation, as much as that of the school lads, in fantastic clothes, who were made to recite their arithmetical tables in a chorus to the response of the Mehtaji or Puntoji of the indigenous "nishal" or "pathshala" (vernacular schools) generally held free of charge in the commodious verandahas of large houses. Those relics of indigenous primary instruction may still be seen in some quarters. Perhaps it would not be uninteresting to give a sample of the Gujarathi programme in English of the departure of the coasting steamers.

" Be it known as a public notice to the passengers going to Surat, that the steamer "Flox" will positively sail at.... o'clock on....the............instant. From Surat she will sail to Gogo, and from Gogo to Bhavnagar. Tickets may be had at the office of Messrs.......... in the Bazar Gate Street till the evening of........"

Vessels in the Harbour.

Of course, the local dailies, English and Vernacular, gave occasional notices of these ferry vessels; but the subscribers to those papers were to be counted as a handful. For the general travelling public this oral advertisement was the most convenient and useful. Apart from the ferries just referred to, the harbour was always full of wooden vessels of divers naval construction. There were ships with two sails and three sails called, " do dolee " or " teen dolee " vahans. ' Vahan ' meant ship, ' dolee ' meant mast. There were the Arab dhows and buglas, the Kattyawar "fattimars," "prows" and "battellas." Then there were the small native boats which plied in the harbour and drove a literally "roaring" trade. There were "dingees," "jollyboats" and "bunderboats," specimens of which are not yet defunct and not replaced by your modern steam and petrol launches. The native craft was allowed to be anchored in the centre of the spacious Mody Bay, the larger kind being moored in front of the then "Palva" (Apollo) Bunder. The line extended from say, where now stands the Ballard Pier to the extreme end of the bunder at Sewri. Between that there were bunders owned by private individuals on perpetual lease granted by the East Indian Company of which the one at Carnac Bunder, known as "Bhaoo Rusool" was most popular and well situated to bring a mint of money to the proprietor. All these intervening private bunders, streching as far as the Mahim foreshore, were eventually bought up by the Government of Bombay when the Port Trust was first established in the early Seventies. Foreign vessels of all kinds were moored in the deeper waters of the Middle Ground, while near the Cross Island were to be seen one or two of the vessels of the P. and O. Company which had for its earliest motto "*Quis Separabit.*" Lastly, there were the vessels of the Indian Navy, of just renown and distinction of which the East India Company were most proud, having braved many a battle and the breeze, which were moored more or less in the same area of waters where now anchor the Indian Marine vessels. They were steam vessels which, by the light of the Titans of to-day, may really be deemed so many minnows. The Indian Navy in those days had a senior naval officer who resided near the docks, about the same place where now lives the Director of the Indian Marine. He was generally called the "Commodore" and his band enlivened the citizens of Bombay at the Bandstand once a week so long as that Navy was maintained. The club known as the "Bombay Club" was most generally patronised by the officers of the Indian Navy. Standing on the Apollo Bunder of the day, which was not so far out in the sea as to-day, one could gaze and gaze at the thick forest of masts of foreign shipping and never get tired. They presented a picturesque appearance resembling the vessels to be seen to-day on the Hooghly from the Strand in Calcutta. It was a favourable resort for recreation as it is at present. Vastly amplified and improved, as we view it now, the old bunder would baffle identification without a plan of those days.

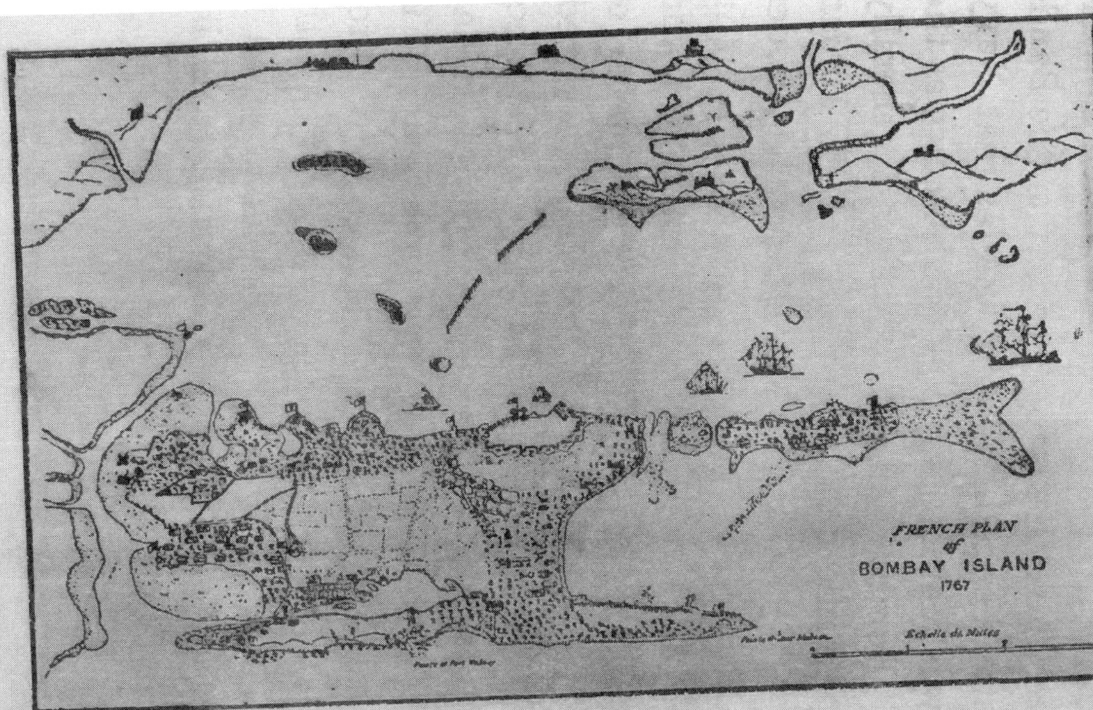

FRENCH VIEW, BOMBAY.

CHAPTER II.—THE HARBOUR AND ITS POTENTIALITIES.

FOR countless ages past has the trade in the deep Arabian Sea ebbed and flowed, and it is conceivable that long, long before "Heptanesia" had revealed its priceless value to inquisitive travellers and nations in pursuit of wealth and worldly glory, many a primitive mariner must have ploughed the tropical waters, while sailing past at no long distance by the seven islands set within the silvery sea, standing apart in their stately loneliness and unconscious of the great and glorious destiny which awaited them in times to come. They may have struck those ancient seafarers as the Islands of the Blest, after the manner of the fabled Hebrides. Anyhow it has not been recorded by historians and travellers of antiquity that those islands were known to the civilised world or that a capacious harbour lay where mighty argosies might float.

Though trade flourished between the East and the West, from times unknown, say between India and the Red Sea and the Persian Gulf, and merchant vessels used to ply between Musa, the modern Mocha, and Baragyza or the Sanscrit Bhrugugucha (Broach), Sorates (Surat), Kaliene (Kalian) down far south up to Tarprobane (Sansctit tambrapani) (Ceylon) neither the graphic and most faithful author of the Periplus of the Erythrean Sea, nor Pliny and later Western travellers have taken any notice of the Seven Islands. It was not, perhaps, till the seventh or eighth century of the Christian era that any mention of the fishing village of Colaba or Mazagaon was made. Kalian undoubtedly flourished for centuries as the great distributing centre on the coast of Western India for seaborne and inland trade, till Thana superseded it as the latter in turn has been superseded by Bombay these hundred years and more. But it is a curious circumstance that the islands so long remained unexplored, and the priceless value of the harbour which they form remained unrecognised. Perhaps no Crusoe stranded on the rocky shore to publish to the world a thrilling narrative of the island and its utilities and beauties.

Monsieur A de Perron's Record.

It was not till the advent of the early Portuguese and Dutch, in search of the wealth of the East Indies that "Bombaim" came to be known for its "good bay;" and later travellers, including Niebhur, left on record the potentialities of the harbour. It was during the eighteenth century that the value of the Bombay harbour came to be recognised, and Monsieur Anquaitel de Perron, the French scholar and traveller, in pursuit of a knowledge of the ancient scriptures of the Parsis at Surat, has left his own strong impressions on record of the value of the Bombay harbour. Perhaps until the early period of the nineteenth century none has rendered more invaluable service in connection with our harbour and its infinite potentialities both in times of war and peace than the Indian Navy, an incomparable service which the mercantile genius of the East India Trading Company organised. Many indeed were the explorers of, not only the harbour, but of the whole Arabian and Red Seas and the Persian Gulf whose names are now forgotten. But their deeds of valour and their hydrographic researches in navigation can best be read in the pages of the journals of the Bombay Geographical Society, afterwards merged in the Bombay Branch of the Royal Asiatic Society, while Eastwick Low and Chatterton may be consulted for a comprehensive history of this *really* "distinguished service."

As to the harbour itself it was related in 1845 that its capacity was such that, in case of a foreign invasion, the entire shipping could be anchored in a haven of safety in the inner waters of what is known as the Hog Island, where many years ago a hydraulic lift was erected to repair the battleships owned by His Majesty's Government. Such being the capacity of the harbour, it is no wonder that shipping from all parts of the world thronged there for the purposes of trade every busy season during the days of prewet docks and pre-Canal period. The crowded condition of the harbour had, as far back as 1845, engaged the attention of the Bombay Government. The construction of a capacious wet dock in Mody Bay was first mooted, and it is for the merchants and engineers of the day to say how far the Mody Bay docks might have daily proved more and more advantageous and how, as trade developed, those might have extended to the natural coast line of the Eastern foreshores. Of course, the difficulties in the way of importing all plant and tools and other hydraulic appliances available for the last fifty years must have been great. But labour and material were cheap, and it is no exaggeration to say that Mody Bay Docks might have been constructed soon after 1845 at a considerably less cost than the Prince's and Victoria Docks.

The Great Hurricane of 1854.

Speaking of the harbour, it may be interesting to recod the great hurricane that overtook Bombay on 2nd November 1854. It was slowly brewing on the evening of that unlucky day till the gales grew to a big cyclone, said to be unprecedented in the annals of the city. Its severity surpassed that of the one which the generation of 1837 had witnessed. So it was related by the men of the older generation. It was destructive storm of considerable magnitude. But the devastating elements might have done far greater injury, had it not been for the opportune heavy rain that fell in the raw early morning. The gale had abated by sunrise when it was possible to witness the appalling destruction that had been wrought overnight not only of the immense wreckage of all shipping in the harbour to the farthest extremity of Mazagaon, but of the havoc to all kinds of property on land, not to speak of the holocaust of those drowned in the sea.

As a boy of ten years I have a vivid remembrance of that stormy night and the scenes presented to me in the morning, living as I was in a house in old Mody Street which has both an eastern and western frontage. This eastern frontage faced the ramparts and the moat behind which lay the bay. All the livelong night, from ten till past two in the morning there was no sleep.

The waves lashed in all their fury every moment against the stony walls of the rampart moats, sending forth a roar which was indeed terrific and past all description. We sat cowering in our bed, while grandmamma allayed our boyish fears and tried to drive away our attention from the hollow moanings and groanings of the stormy bay by fairy tales from the Arabian Nights. She recalled the story of some previous storms and lulled our flabbergasted youth into a kind of semi-wakefulness. In the house itself the windows of the terrace were blown away in diverse directions, some falling with a loud noise in the "chowk." Terrific crashes of thunder were heard, while through the chinks of the wooden windows, there flashed every moment forked lightning which struck no little terror into our hearts, inexperienced as we were in this phenomenal physical disturbance. Our boyhood felt as if every minute the house would totter and fall burying us all!

Appalling Devastation.

Sleepless we arose in the early morning. On opening the windows to see what had happened we saw stretched before us the "Assaye" or the "Punjaub". It was a veritable leviathan afloat, on the brine which, having broken its anchor at its moorings, drifted along till the walled eastern foreshore and the battlements arrested its course and made a wreck of it. The bay was full of all sorts of native craft tossing on the still somewhat stormy billows while many had sunk, their topmasts alone being visible. Strewn in the bay were seen floating a variety of products, chief among which were thousands of cocoanuts and cotton docras. Emerging from my house a little later on in the day, and strolling for curiosity's sake in East Rampart Row, which is now known as the Mint Road, scores of bodies of the drowned brought to the shore were noticed, presenting a most ghastly appearance. It seemed as if they were so many tortured ghosts thrown up by the Evil Spirit in his demoniacal rage. Time-hallowed banian trees were uprooted and the entire road was full of scattered leaves and trunks and barks. In the town itself the same spectacle was to be seen at Mandvi and Mazagaon. West Rampart Row and Esplanade Road were one vast area of fallen trees, which floated in sheets of water, which the torrents of rain during the night had formed. The maidan from Bazar Gate and from Church Gate dazed our eyes, so complete was the havoc. Fallen windows, portions of back walls and so on intermingled, while it was afterwards reported that terraces had been so blown away and fallen elsewhere that it was impossible to account for how the velocity and the ferocity of the cyclone had done this work. Mahim foreshore and Mahim woods told the same tale. Coroner's juries wer held at temporary morgues impressed in certain centres of the Fort and the town beyond it. Crawling to Apollo Bunder, whilst on an inspection of other places in the Fort, we were greeted at every turn with similar scenes of rack and ruin. It seemed awhile as if Nature had done her work and only vestiges remained to tell the tale of woe and the aftermath of that eventful phenomenon. Of course, those interested to learn all about the hurricane may ransack the files of the local papers of the day to realise the enormity of the loss of life and property that occurred, and how Bombay only narrowly escaped almost total destruction by the mercy of Providence. That terrific storm recalls to my mind the description by the great classic dramatist of the fury of the winds which blew in his days on the northern coast of Europe:

So descends the fury of the storm,
The troublous breakers never rest;
Some from the chambers of the west,
Some from the chambers of the east,
Some from the short sun, or where,
At noon, he sheds his angry glare,
Or when the stars faint twinkling light
The gloomy length of Arctic night.*

---

* Eocylus—Adipus.

CHAPTER III.—EARLIEST MAKERS OF BOMBAY—THE BUILDING OF THE FORT.

THOUGH "Heptanesia," from days lost in the mist of ages, possessed a magnificent seaboard, it was not recognised till the whirligig of Time, in its ceaseless course, had, soon after its acquisition by the British, revealed to a growing and venturesome population, full of trading instincts, the priceless gifts with which Nature had endowed it. Its value was no doubt discerned by the Portuguese, the Dutch and their predecessors for some centuries before. But to the British must be awarded the credit of having recognised and appreciated its incomparable utility as a great harbour of infinite capacity for purposes of a well-organised and systematic trade. It was the genius of the race of the Drakes and the Frobishers who with a clear gaze foresaw the potentialities and possibilities of the dowry which a British monarch had received from the then navigators and the first maritime nation of Europe who had traded with the East Indies. Thus it came to pass that the imperative necessity of protecting the harbour from the periodical piratic invasions of the Sidees, the Moplas, the Angrias and others, was recognised. True it is that statesmen and warriors, soldiers and sailors, merchants and bankers, judges and scholars, shipbuilders and town-planners, each and all had contributed to the making of Bombay within their respective sphere from the days of Gerald Aungier to those of Elphinstone, Frere and Reay. And though the names of the latter three are household words in the Presidency and inscribed on the pages of history, it is sad to reflect that those of the earliest makers, the real founders of the greatness and prosperity of the town and island of Bombay, should have been forgotten. How oblivious are we of those memorable founders, the good men and true, who unobtrusively did their arduous, nay perilious, work, caring naught for name and fame at the close of the seventeenth and the commencement of the eighteenth centuries! In the illustrious roll of those men whose sagacity had been instrumental in the making of Bombay, their names should for ever stand in the front rank as pioneers.

Early History of the Fort.

Describing what has been called "the Fort" these two centuries past, as it presented itself to the gaze of the generation of the Fifties and Sixties of the nineteenth century, we are reminded of two such pioneers whose foresight and statesmanship are intimately associated with its construction wherever they landed. It was Gerald Aungier who, having recognised the incalculable value of Bombay as a great emporium of seaborne trade, embarked on formulating a project for the protection of the harbour and the safety of the population from those bold and intrepid marauders, the Indian Vikings of the Western Coast. They were most venturesome and troublesome during the occupation of "Bombain" by the Portuguese. The project of surrounding the eastern and western foreshores with ramparts was taken on hand by Aungier in 1685. It was, however, carried into execution by Charles Boone some forty years afterwards. Whatever may have been the military strategy of the times, it was in 1715 that he undertook to construct and complete the chain of fortifications from north to south and east to west in the town and island of Bombay, dilapidated vestiges of which may still be seen on the Sion and Worli hills, on the Mahim foreshore and elsewhere. The harbour thus came to be enclosed by high ramparts with bastions and moats and drawbridges. What is still called "Bombay Castle" was the pivot of those fortifications which extended from the Apollo Bunder to the eastern foreshore as far as St. George's Hospital and thence to the west, where now stand the Empire Buildings to the farther extremity where what is now christened the College of Science was enclosed. This large area, covering some two miles and more in length and about three quarter mile in breadth, was enclosed and called "the Fort." On these ramparts of great height and thickness were mounted guns at various strategic centres. The bastions, the last remnant of which is to be still seen on the eastern frontage of St. George's Hospital, on the Frere Road, were also mounted with heavy pieces of artillery.

Rumours of War.

War and rumours of war between the English on the one hand and the French and Spanish on the other were extremely plentiful. So much so that in 1739, owing to the trouble given by the Maratha pirates and rumours of war by England against France and Spain, the merchants were in a state of consternation. Bassein Fort had fallen. They subscribed Rs. 30,000 towards the expenses of constructing ditches all round the Fort walls. The work was fully completed in 1743 at the expense of 2½ lakhs. The war was actually declared in 1744, so that Bombay harbour and town were made quite safe from the invaders. But during the interval up to 1762, additions were being constantly made to the fortifications by means of bastions and buttresses. At the same time an old fortress which had stood on the Dongri Hill was demolished as being close to the town and therefore dangerous. It has been officially placed on record that by 1764 Bombay was made " fully impregnable." This was " the Fort " in 1743. The military strategy of the age might be guessed from what yet remains of the dismantled fortifications, east and west. It seemed as if the fortifications were so constructed on the Mainland that gun answered gun and fort replied fort ! Till the year 1862, these fortifications all round Bombay stood fast and the generation which flourished then had been able to realise what the makers of Bombay had achieved in matters defensive during the previous hundred years and more of threatened foreign invasion.

Trade follows the Flag.

Meanwhile, with greater security, the Fort, more or less a vast patch of green as viewed by many a traveller of the time, was fast built upon. Public offices and residences as well as business offices and houses of the wealthier class sprang up briskly within the area comprised. Trade literally followed the flag, which is still waving over "Bombay Castle." The "Castle" itself is described as a real bulwark of strength, strongly guarded by European troops who had their barracks in its vicinity, known as the King's Barracks,—that massive pile of buildings which still serves as a landmark to remind how well the defenders of the day had taken care of the possession of Charles II. Any day the curious may start northward from the Town Hall straight in the direction of Bazargate Street to view those barracks, now devoted more or less to peaceful storage of goods required by the existing troops, Indian and European, in the town. The massive buildings skirt the two sides of the southern end of the Bazargate Street and need to be closely inspected

FORT, 1811.

from within to gain a complete knowledge not only of the solidity of the buildings but their construction and accommodation from the military point of view.

"Bombay Castle."

To the present generation "Bombay Castle" is only a name, a legend. The antiquarian and the curious may still view it by permission of the proper military authorities. But it must have been for a century at the least a stern reality for the great object in view. It was the centre of the defences of the Fort as constructed by the genius of the Moltkes of the day who advised the Government. But he would in vain attempt to realise "Castle" in the sense in which we read descriptions of such in poems and novels or romance. Poetry there may have been, and romance also, but the piping times of peace which Bombay has enjoyed for a century and more have made "Bombay Castle" too prosaic and of little interest except to the historian or the curious. The gates are there, hoary with age. At any rate the writer had seen them in his boyhood. The moats and ditches and drawbridges were there though, perchance, they are mere curiosities at present. And one can say with Scott that though the castle gates have been flung open the drawbridges and other appliances have grown quite rusty and creaking or rocking and swinging about after the fashion of all things old of the kind. Viewed in my boyhood, it was even then an obsolete "place of arms." No doubt old guns and cannons and all sorts of shells were to be seen in abundance here, there and everywhere as one strolled leisurely over the entire castle ground, an exercise by itself of an evening. Heavy ordnance and small arms were all to be seen in a big hall safeguarded by English troops.

“ When we were Boys.”

To our boyish mind it was a striking place for recreation, while the sight of the soldiers, and their evening parade, to the tune of drums and fifes, were a constant attraction. Altogether, the “ Bombay Castle ” reality of my boyhood days has a vivid corner in my mind and now and again imagination carries me back to those days so that I may once more skip and roam and play the dummy soldier as I used to do. Though “ Bombay Castle ” inspired me and other companions with awe, we were neverfrightened by the heavy pieces of ordnance pyramidically arranged here, there and everywhere. Sometimes we strolled to the foot of the flagstaff to watch how the Union Jack, fluttering at the mast, braving many a breeze, was hauled down at sunset as the reveille beat. And sometimes we met with pleasing sights of domesticity which tickled and amused us, as we sauntered in the direction of the family quarters of the soldiers. The ruddy-looking lasses would call the poultry at eventime to their cages by whistling and offering grain, the little babies would play and sometimes we would join in the amusement. Perhaps those amenities in the midst of hard soldier-life in the Castle, were necessary to while away time. This was the way in which the Castle, the scene of our boyhood, now and again delighted and impressed us.

A Commander-in-Chief's Funeral.

One more incident may be related here in connection with the Castle. In the early part of the Fifties (it must be between 1851 and 1853) there was a great military funeral and the pageant was most impressive while the troops massed in front of St. Thomas Cathedral and the service was going on in the Cathedral itself. The funeral was that of a Commander-in-Chief who had died in Poona and who it was said, was connected with royalty. The coffin of the deceased was afterwards taken to "Bombay Castle" and deposited on a catafalque in the arsenal room pending its conveyance to England. Permission was given to the public to view it and batches in limited numbers were allowed to enter the room. But "Bombay Castle" was divested of all its military glory and ordnance in the sixties when the Kirkee factory was established, and the only thing which reminds us to-day is the customary "Government Gazette" which dates all resolutions of the Pro-consul from that locality. It was no doubt the seat of power and authority, while the head of the State resided in "Government House" on the opposite side of the road, the premises for years known as the old Secretariat, Jonathan Duncan of happy memory being the last of the Governors who ruled in

Bombay from that historic place. Thus it is that, though the gates of the Castle are still open, there is to be seen no "quivering drawbridge" which can rock or swing.

CHAPTER IV.—THE FORT AND ITS ENVIRONMENTS AND THE TRIPLE TRANSFORMATION OF BOMBAY.

You will not tell what chance will do
Within the next twelve months for you.

WHO has not realised the absolute truth of the reflection embodied in the lines quoted above? Nations, as much as communities and individuals, are for ever the sport of Chance. At this very hour the world of civilisation is tremulously watching the terrible issues which a chance* occurrence of a most tragic character has wrought on the battlefield of the European Continent. It was chance that led to the murder of the heir to the throne of the ill-fated Hapsburgs and of his consort. Ere the mournful tragedy was four weeks old, Europe has become the scene of a bloody war the like of which has not

*Now well-known to be a deliberate plan and not a chance.

been known in the history of the world. But what may be chance which brings forth at times momentous issues of a far-reaching character for a community or a nation? Your metaphysical philosopher explains that what we call Chance is a perfectly logical sequence of ancillary facts, seen or unseen. Causes have their origin in effects. "The effect defective comes from cause." This logical sequence is as inexorable as Nature's laws. Chance is but another name for this inexorable logic of events.

Chance.

Speaking of Bombay, it may be said with truth that it is Chance which has contributed to her present greatness. Chance made her in the first instance a British possession. Chance led to her humble beginning as an entrepot of trade and commerce. Chance was vastly contributory to her "making" during the last hundred and fifty years and more. Thus it came to pass that Chance unmade what it had made a century before. It was Chance that in 1862 levelled to the ground the fortifications built and completed in 1745. It is Chance, again, which at the present hour is entirely effacing her many old landmarks and erecting new ones which Time is certain again to demolish. The town-planner and the sanitarian are busy making a new, healthy and aesthetic Bombay. It is the dreadful outbreak of the plague that has afforded this chance of reconstruction and renovation. There is not the least doubt the Logic of Events has within the last three-score years transfigured the town and island three times. It is a transfigurement which was undreamt of by the generation which flourished in the Fifties. The first transformation was coeval with the levelling down of those stupendous Fort ramparts which had so well protected the city for well nigh a century and a quarter. It led to the uprising of a new class of buildings within its precincts, buildings handsome and substantial, the central piece of which is the University Clock (Rajabai) Tower, a thing of joy and beauty for ever, which we owe to the genius of Sir Gilbert Scott at the suggestion of Sir Alexander Grant, of Aristotelian fame and Sir George Birdwood of bright memory. We also owe to the same cause the Frere Road, which was the first one of its kind, constructed on a plan and of great width.

In the Eighties.

The Eighties next witnessed another radical transformation. Industrialism came to stay in Bombay and vie with the spindles and looms of proud Lancashire. Suburbs which were dedicated to the ruling hierarchy of Governors, Members of Council, Judges and other high State functionaries, for purposes of villa residences, were slowly appropriated by the new hierarchy devoted to the worship of King Cotton. The verdant groves and the sturdy and stately trees under whose graceful shadows nestled many a villa and country house of our local magnates and money lords were swept away with the rapidity of the prophet's gourd. Industrial capitalism drove out Civilianism who, therefore, planted itself thickly on the breezy Malabar and Cumballa Hills. The suburbs were appropriated by the cotton mills and the jerrybuilders of the day found chawls, now reduced to slums, for the accommodation of the growing industrial population. Ugly utilities displaced the verdant beauty of those fine suburbs of our youthful days where we now and again used to sojourn at week-ends and during holidays for a fine whiff of the bracing country air so salutary to our physical welfare. Trade also appropriated a part of the eastern foreshore and displayed its first pair of wet docks which the enterprise of the public spirited Chamber of Commerce, led by men of calibre like James Bythell, Kittridge, and others, secured from a too conservative Government, partly scared away by the unlucky Back Bay enterprise, and partly starved for want of the eternal pence, though the first prefatory process of decentralisation of finance was dimly discernible. Lastly, the generation now busy making Bombay witnesses the third great transformation. It is fast changing her face. It is the generation who in their infancy had heard from their ancestors many a thrilling tale of European hostilities first between England and France and later between England, France and Turkey on the one side and Russia on the other. "The Russians are coming," "the Russians are coming," was the cry we had heard in our own youthful days. It is well-known how Bombay was in a state of consternation and trapidation at the threatened invasion of India *via* Egypt by that warrior tyrant who had terrorised Europe at the close of the eighteenth and the commencement of the nineteenth century!

The Triple Transformation.

Thus has Bombay of the Fifties of the nineteenth century undergone three *avatars*, each surpassing its predecessor. Who, then, may venture to forecast what the Logic of Events will do when our little planet has gone the round of the glowing orb of day twelve months hence ? I hope to be able by that time to finish my own labour of picking shells from the sands of Bombay and construct my skeleton history of the Triple Transformation which unlike the Triple Alliance will only breathe Peace and Goodwill. Meanwhile the history of the Fort may be concluded. As already observed, the strongest bulwark was the " Bombay Castle." The ramparts with their moats and ditches, their drawbridges and sally gates circumvented it all round. The Castle stood on its own rocky base, an ever-watchful sentinel. The stranger who might have stood awhile on the top of either the Eastern (Bazar) Gate or the Western (Church) Gate might have beheld how lay the Fort of Bombay in the Fifties. The military eye of that age must have seized in a trice the conception of the strategist who planned the fortifications. To our boyhood gaze those frowning ramparts looked cyclopean in their dimensions and stately in their great solidity and impregnability. Two miles and more in circumference, they began in a somewhat broken line at the Apollo Gate, in or about the locality where stands the Wellington Fountain—a shabby memorial of the Iron Duke, an everlasting discredit to Bombay which it is to be devoutly hoped some aspirant to a baronetcy would wipe off—and circumvallated past the Mint and the Mody Bay where, debouching near a glacis, stood to the north what was known as Fort St. George towards the west, having the three-gated structure between, just about the locality of the "Victoria Place" (the old Bhattiabag,) till they ended somewhere about the present College of Science.

CHAPTER V.—A BIRD'S-EYE VIEW OF THE FORT IN THE FIFTIES.

THOSE to the east were called East Rampart and those to west, the West Rampart. The narrow streets passing by these were called Rampart Row, West, and Rampart Row, East. The western ramparts had a big stretch of the now abridged *maidan* behind them. Standing on their height, you could cast your eyes in a northerly direction as far as the present School of Arts and the Police Commissioner's Office, and in a southerly direction as far as the Floral Fountain and beyond it. The entire maidan was divided into two sections north and south. Where stood the Church Gate, we entered a fortified structure which had to be crossed by means of two massive gates till the foot passenger or the vehicle emerged on the other side, going either south or north. The northern road was the one now widened and known as the Esplanade Road, and the southern one equally widened as Rampart Row, West, commencing from the south-west corner of the Church Gate Street to the place where now stands the equestrian statue of King Edward VII. The western ramparts had at intervals a "sally gate" and drawbridge whence egress to the maidan was easy. At certain intervals there were also found many spring wells, the gift of benevolent citizens for the purpose of supplying water of which there was till 1865 a regular yearly famine in all parts of the city. During the summer months might be seen from early dawn to dewy eve, and even up to midnight bevies of women and girls of the different communities residing in the Fort, drawing water. The wells were crowded and such was the keen alertness to be early enough to get a turn to draw the water that querulous scenes occurred and choice Billingsgate was not unheard of. It was indeed a harrowing scene for a stranger to witness those crowds of robust women patiently waiting for a couple of hours to fill their *handas* or chatties. Drinking water from wells was dear enough and small casks loaded with the priceless necessary of life used to be drawn in bullock carts in the Fort to be sold from house to house at two and four annas for a single *handa.*

Weddings on the Ramparts.

Unavailable as these ramparts had become for their original military purpose, it was not infrequently the case that wedding *mandaps* on their top were allowed by permission of the proper authorities, to be erected by the wealthier Parsis and Hindus. That part of the rampart which was opposite to the town house of Sir Jamsetjee Jijibhoy (now occupied by Messrs. Evans Fraser and Company) was frequently in demand as being most eligible and convenient. Marriages in the family of the first Baronet were more than once celebrated there, and so also were dinner parties in connection with the weddings. Fairylike was the scene to be viewed on the top of this part of the western rampart from the level of the road below. The philosopher may reflect on the joyous use to which now and again the ramparts were put and descant on the vicissitudes of time! Did the stalwart engineers who erected those military structures ever dream that what was meant for purposes of offence and defence should come a century later to be used for purposes of revelry and merriment, and that the beauty and fashion of Bombay should occasionally congregate there and hold high jinks in which even Governors sometimes participated!

The Sally Gates.

As to the sally gates there was one for popular use, the exact situation of which was on the rampart opposite the present Alice Buildings. The other one, which led to the outer maidan, where is now the Mayo Road and the Oval, was just opposite the building of the old Commercial Banking Corporation that came to grief in 1866, the same as amplified vertically and laterally in the middle of the seventies, and now in the occupation of Messrs. Thacker and Company and where the late Sir P. M. Mehta had his chambers for well nigh forty years. The two gates known as Church Gate stood on the site where stands the Floral Fountain. There was a guard room at the north-west corner of the street, the same ground where is reared the big premises occupied by the Eastern Bank. There was also another small guard house in the space between the first and the second gate. Indian troops lived in this guard room and watched the gates. On the top of the first gate was the quarter of the regimental officer who commanded the guards and above it watch was kept by relays of sentry from evening till the dawn of the day. The statue of the Marquis of Wellesley, now, alas, relegated to an obscure corner of Elphinstone Circle Gardens, stood just at the north-east corner of the Post Office.

The eastern ramparts had three gates. Passing out of the second gate in a north-easterly direction, well protected by moats, was situated Fort St. George, where was located the force of the European Artillery. The entire area of the barracks has now been enclosed by the central and other blocks of the European General Hospital. Part of the Fort was the space now known as St. George's Street, commencing at the south-east corner of the administrative offices of the G. I. P. Railway and ending where it meets the Frere Road. One old landmark is yet to be seen—a narrow defile where stands a Mahomedan shrine. The remaining part of the barracks which faced the south, and where till late stood an old building, the previous mess house of the artillery officers, is now taken up wholly by the new Post Office. The glacis also was there and the Bazar Gate Native Guard mounted a sentry on the top while underground was a gunpowder magazine also well guarded. The exact spot was just opposite the curved road where the tram cars pass by near Mr. Vurjivandas Madhavdas's house. There commenced the eastern ramparts, an unbroken line, as far as the Mint, intersected with only one sally gate with drawbridge which gave access to the eastern foreshore.

A Vegetable Market.

Near this gate was a vegetable market for the Hindus. The general market for the sale of vegetables, fruit, fish, etc., was on the Mint Road, the exact locality being on the road where the tram rails are laid just opposite the footpath of the Fort Market. The eastern ramparts had on the basement cellars on its northern side which were, it is said, used at one time to incarcerate criminals. The cellars were really of a most barbarous character and suited only to the civilisation of the tenth and twelfth centuries. They were veritable black holes, with no light save that emitted from holes at the top of the ramparts covered with large inverted funnels. The only windows at intervals were fixed on the roadside. They were fit for the barbarities of a Spanish Inquisition but utterly unfit for the civilisation of the British of the early part of the nineteenth century. Here we may conclude the history of the Fort proper of Bombay.

New Factors.

The age which demanded those fortifications has passed away. Economic rivalry of the nations of the West, having for their principal aim and object, supremacy of the trade of the East, has long since been dead. But if the old order has passed away, a new age with new factors has ushered in. International commerce has introduced international rivalries. Wars of tariffs are common everywhere. These have sometimes led to other wars. India has herself been whirled into the vortex. Her trade and commerce have so expanded that their protection demands a new set of bulwarks and defences by land and sea. The piratical tribes who raided in the open sea on our western coast have disappeared, but a new tribe of pirates has arisen, and to defend Bombay against such is a supreme necessity. The titanic struggle now proceeding on the European Continent is destined to bring forth radical changes, political and commercial These would demand the highest exercise of foresight and statesmanship now to protect India. A new constructive policy of defence and offence in harmony with the needs and requirements of the country, must soon engage the attention of those responsible for the future safety of India.

CHAPTER VI.--SOME ENVIRONMENTS OF THE FORT. HOW INCIPIENT MUTINY WAS SUPPRESSED BY POLICE COMMISSIONER FORGETT

IT should be borne in mind that what is now known as the Fort was a real fort, in the military acceptance of the word, throughout the eighteenth century, specially since the construction of fortifications in 1739 as already described while the population was sparse. In fact, in 1803, the entire town and island of Bombay did not boast of even a hundred thousand persons. The Fort, of course, was only sparsely populated, the principal residents being members of the two Services, of the Admiralty, and mercantile gentlemen, European and Indian. It had not then expanded as a residential quarter. But there was a great fire in 1803. It originated in the northern part of the Fort and raged for several hours, the appliances for extinguishing it being of the most primitive character. I had heard from the lips of my grandmother in the Fifties what a terrible catastrophe it was. At the time the news of fire, large or small, was one to fill the citizens with extreme consternation, for it meant, in nine cases out of ten, total destruction of life and property. Naturally a fire, whenever it occurred, was greatly dreaded by the residents living in and around the locality. The ramparts, so it is said, served a most useful purpose as a signal station for giving news to the populace far and wide. The military were generally called in to render every possible assistance in the absence of any large body of policemen and anything approaching even the semblance of an organised fire brigade. Drummers scaling the top of the ramparts marched up and down and beat the drum. The warning thus given spread like wild fire and the city was thus apprised of the danger. I myself remember how as a youth I was filled with fear on hearing the occurrence of a fire which we were told in our infancy was to be regarded as something Satanic! Grandmamma used to explain to us the aphorism in Gujerati that, come what may, a burglary was to be preferred to a fire. Whereas the former swept away all the riches or stores of a household, the timbering and the roofing of the house were absolutely safe, the latter, in its flaming and furious course, did not even save the rafters and the roofing. Everything was burnt to the ground, sometimes burying alive innocent humanity. That was the moral firmly impressed on our minds as the consequences of a fire.

An Antiquated Fire Station.

In the Fifties there was only one fire appliances station within the whole town and island of Bombay. It was in the Fort, opposite what was then known as the Green,—a circular patch left unbuilt from the larger "Green" in the proper sense which Fryer and other travellers had seen and described as extending from the old Dockyard as far as Mazagon. Of course, as population grew a larger part of it came to be built upon. So the Bombay Green of the Fifties was a circular patch of turf left unbuilt, say commencing from Marine Street, where still stand the opium godowns, and ending with the boundary of Elphinstone Circle Gardens on the north, the easterly road along the Town Hall being the same and the western, just about the circumference surrounding it where there is a tamarind tree and a fountain, formerly a large well, with steps dedicated by a philanthropic citizen to quench the thirst of the wayfarers and of men of business and cotton brokers and others transacting business within the Bombay Green. The fire appliances were nothing but a large number of antiquated hand pumps. These were concentrated in a methodical manner in a large covered enclosure and watched by lascars who were the men who dragged the pumps to the seat of fire, wherever it occurred. The other set of lascars were those who worked the pumps. All round, and hung from the ceiling, were a variety of iron buckets, leather hose, and other petty fire appliances which the civilization of the days made available for Bombay. Its exact locality may be found out as the ground where now stand two blocks of buildings in the Elphinstone Circle, in the north-east corner. Those buildings, till some years ago, were occupied by their respective owners, the Chartered Bank and the Mercantile Bank. But more about the Elphinstone Circle and the Elphinstone Gardens later on. So also about the amenities of the Bombay Green in the Fifties.

The Maidan.

It remains now to describe the maidan. As already stated, it was a wide stretch of green behind the whole extent of the western ramparts, say from the spot where is now situated the College of Science to the Empire Buildings near Victoria Place. Beyond it was also the maidan, outside the precincts of the actual Fort, say, the big stretch in a northerly direction from the Cruickshank Road to the ground where stands the present office of the Police Commissioner. This northerly maidan was as now, used for a parade ground, but a portion to the east, say, from the buildings of the Bombay Municipal Corporation, to the School of Arts, was devoted to the dhobis. It was known as the Dhobi Lines. On the opposite side of the road, where now stands the entire block of the premises known as the Victoria Terminus and the administrative offices of the G. I. P. Railway Company was the Dhobighat for washing dirty clothes. And when washed and wet they dried them on the opposite side of the Maidan exactly as they now do on the Mahalaxmi flats skirting the Arthur Road, north, from Jacob's Circle. This northerly maidan had at least, four large wells whence water was raised to the level by the bullocks. Those belonged to the military for supply of water to the Indian troops located on what is now called the "Paltan" (regiment) road and the Marine Infantry on the other side. They were known as "Camp" wells and were surrounded by a small kitchen garden. In this garden were grown succulent Indian vegetables. As school boys, crossing the maidan to reach our homes every afternoon in the Fort, we often used to thrust our hands between the fences and pull up some of the vegetable especially the succulent bhendi. And sometimes our mischief led to the keeper turning out and driving us away from any more plucking the forbidden vegetables. Besides these camp wells there were half a dozen large wells, the gift of philanthropy to the city famishing for water, more or less used by the residents facing the western part of this northerly maidan. One or two were specially devoted to the use of buffaloes and milch cattle. There was one specially known as "Bhisti" (water-bearer).

The Troops.

This northerly part of the maidan has one special historical reminiscence about it which may be here related. Being specially devoted to the military for parade of the native infantry, it was not frequented by the population of the town. In those days, sanitary faddists had not invented the plea that morning parades for troops were more beneficial than afternoon ones. The soldiers, European and Indian, were inured to the tropical climate and did their manœuvring and other work as efficiently as those of this day in the afternoon. Perhaps, also, the exigencies of the cricket, the hockey, the golf and other sports had a great deal to do with the abandonment of the practice in the afternoon. There were generally three native infantries, besides the Marine Battalion. The full dress parade was a sight to behold, specially on Queen's Birthday. The European infantry in the Fort, as well as the European artillery from St. George's Fort, as well as the native artillery took part in the firing of the royal salute of 21 guns. The Indian troops had red tight fitting tunics and black breeches for purposes of ordinary wear and a pique cap. But on a field day, the breeches worn were white and the cap was a shako, either adorned with a white and red ball or plumes. Portraits in colours of these might be seen in some of those rare illustrated books about Bombay in some private library. I am not sure whether the local branch of the Royal Asiatic Society possesses some such of these interesting volumes. The troops carried a big black varnished pouch at the back waist and also wore white clayed leather belts slung cross-wise over the chest, with a small square brass plate in the centre giving the number of the regiment. They had a fine physique. The rifle gun was unknown, though it came in a little later. The funny way in which these soldiers repeated the words of command by their company officers was a constant source of merriment to us. Poor, unsophisticated soldiers, they knew no English. They caught the sound of the words and funnily reproduced them beyond all trace of the original. For instance, "Stand at ease" was transformed vocally into "Thunder Thhis." "By the left" was parodied into "Bai Jilabee" ! And so on.

An Incipient Mutiny.

Well, it so happened that in the darkest days of 1857 there was some serious apprehension of the Indian regiment in the city doing some mischief, if not exactly a mutiny. Every possible precaution was taken by the authorities at whose head was the calm, cool and sagacious Lord Elphinstone, who was popularly known to have been once spoken of in his early days as the possible consort of the good Queen Victoria. That was the legendary belief, whether right or wrong need not be inquired into. Luckily for Bombay there was a consummate, ingenious and resourceful detective in the person of Mr. Charles Forjett as the Police Commissioner. He was a stout, sun-burnt complexioned officer who was always seen sitting square and tight in his saddle. Fearless and brave, he was too alert to see that no mischief occurred in the city. He was known to be going *incognito* in a variety of disguises, even as a scavenger and a barber. Be the many stories of his disguises what they may, it is to his credit that he was long known as a Police Commissioner of surpassing ability, and born to command. In his days the efficiency and incorruptibility of the police were the theme of universal praise. The people vastly appreciated him and reverenced him as a veritable " Mabap " to keep them harmless from thieves, budmashes and all the criminals who were before a terror.

Mr. Forjett catches the Ringleaders.

" Farjett Saheb " was a household word. Wherever you went you heard of his wonderful feats in the detective line. Mr. Forjett was apprised of a secret conclave of some of the ringleaders of a proposed mutinous movement. He was able, with his large experience and shrewd sagacity, to catch the ringleaders. Lord Elphinstone was made fully aware of the plot which, in this instance, was to loot the town on Dhanteras Day, that is, the day two days previous to the Divali. It was arranged that the loot should be in the evening of the day when most of the people would be out to enjoy the Divali or feast of lamps. The plot was discovered and at once steps were taken to arrest the two leading conspirators, and hold a court-martial immediately. The sentence of the court was an awful one, but common in those dark days of sepoy revolt. The public were not aware, till the afternoon of the day (November) when the offenders were to be blown away at the cannon's mouth, from what grave danger they had escaped. It was an agreeable revelation but when we come to think of it, even at this hour, a feeling of cold shudder overtakes us and makes us tremble. What may have been the fate of Bombay had the plot succeeded? It is impossible to contemplate the tragic enormities the revolters might have perpetrated. But the precautionary military measures combined with the alertness and consummate detective ability of the Police Commissioner, saved Bombay.

Blown from Guns.

It was in the afternoon, just as we emerged from our school, the Elphinstone Institution, situated opposite the maidan, and which is now the Elphinstone and Anglo-Vernacular school, that a scene of the greatest bustle presented itself. The open maidan, the entire parade ground, was closely occupied by the military. Behind the military line vast crowds had congregated. Inquiring into the cause of the exceptional multitude, our boyish curiosity was satisfied by being told that two mutineers chained to two guns were to be immediately blown. With bated breath we ran to be as near the spot where the two were pinioned to the cannons. As far as my recollection goes, the guns faced the Esplanade Road, and were nearly in a line with the White Roman Catholic Cross, of ancient lineage, in the other maidan known as the Marine battalion parade ground. We made our way through the crowd till we had a good view of the prisoners. So far as my recollection goes, the European troops, infantry and artillery, took up a position by way of a square. The Indian regiments were located within the square. Some Indian Navy marines were landed and also there was a serried phalanx of the mercantile marine. They made an imposing but awe-inspiring show. There was a thrill of excitement all round and our pulse throbbed faster and faster till at a given word of command the cannons were fired and the pinioned criminals were blown. The burnt flesh sent an unpleasant odour which we all could easily sniff. All was over.

The tragedy was enacted in a trice and all Bombay on that eventful day heaved a great sigh of relief. I am here relating, of course, what are my own impressions so far as I am able to recall them after the long stretch of 63 years. The authentic history of the plot and all about the military trial and punishment and the part played by Mr. Forjett can be read in the authentic records of the Bombay Government. The Life of Mr. Forjett, written some years ago by his son, who was once commandant of the defunct Bombay Marine Battalion, gives a succinct account of that stirring incident. All that can be said in this place is that Bombay was primarily saved by the invaluable service that Police Commissioner rendered to the city—a service which, it is to be regretted, was never adequately rewarded by the Government.

Chapter VII.—THE MAIDAN DESCRIBED AS A POPULAR RECREATION GROUND.

THE northern division of the maidan, as already described, was chiefly devoted to military purposes. Not so the southern section which, being exposed to Back Bay, was naturally resorted to at eventide by the population residing in the Fort, mostly members of the Parsi community, for enjoying the cool and balmy breeze blowing from the western sea. This part of the Esplanade had a long undulating stretch from the bandstand (the original one) to the spot where is now seated, in calm but stately repose, the marble statue of the good Queen Victoria. The sally gate opposite the Alice Buildings was the means of ingress and egress and was crossed to and fro by a crowded population on any afternoon. Those, however, who chose to frequent the more distant but southern end of the maidan betook themselves to the sally gate opposite the premises of Thacker and Company. It was convenient to go to the Bandstand and the beach beyond it by that route which was guarded at each end by Indian sentries, furnished every two hours, by the larger guard at Churchgate Street. The other sally gate had only one sentry-go and that on the east. Emerging from the last a stranger visiting Bombay for the first time could at a glance view how the undulating stretch of the verdant meadow was dotted all over by groups of persons, young and old, but almost of the sterner sex, engaged in their daily social amenities of diverse varieties. He would view small groups of men squatted on China mats, either in a square or circle, averaging from six to ten. In the middle of the square or circle would be seen a large lantern with an oil *buttee* of double wicks shedding its white brown light on the "air-eating" company gathered. They were invariably Parsis who were immense lovers in those happy days of simplicity and plenty of all sorts of *al fresco* amusements and recreation. There could be easily counted fifty of such groups at short distances, while in the summer season as many as double that number might be found. A little further to the north might be seen parties of youngsters either playing the old but most popular game of "gilly danda" (a kind of Indian cricket still holding its own in villages outside the cities) or the game of "Asookh Mahasookh," a sort of physical exercise in which the feet were mostly in evidence, though the employment of hands was not less to be discerned when in the act of bowling and balancing on a single leg while the other was uplifted a few inches from the ground.

"Air-Eaters" on the Maidan.

The squatting groups would be seen merrily playing games of cards, the most exciting of which was that still known by the name of "Badshai" in which three players were invariably engaged. Others would be noticed playing either the *dam* (draughts) or the chess. A third set of groups would be your *goube-mouche* of the day, replete with town gossip and light criticism on men and things happening during the day. While a fourth, the most interesting and attractive, would be discovered listening with keen curiosity and bated breath to the thrilling legends of ancient Persian heroes, Rustom, Sorab, Afrasiab, Jamshid and so forth, or to the military heroines whom the poet Firdusi has immortalised in his imperishable Persian Iliad. The reader would be either a "Mobed" (priest) or a "Behdin" (layman) but well versed in Gujrathi and Persian. They were specially selected, first, for their great familiarity with legendary lore, almost committed to heart, and, secondly, for their loud singsong articulation, so as to be heard by those of the group sitting at the farthest distance. It was always agreeable and amusing to listen to their intonation which in its cadence had what is called the "Gregorian chant." These readings from the heroic. legends were exceedingly fascinating. while some of the readers so profoundly went into the spirit of the old Persian warriors themselves as to become animated and dramatic. A small crowd of passers-by, chiefly Parsi youngsters, with the blood of Rustom and Jal in their adolescent veins, would intently listen to some thrilling part of the narrative or be tickled by the intoned recital of the reader. Here and there the children, boys and girls, in their silk frocks, and quaint caps of *kinkob* from Surat, or embroidered in Berlin wool, would carry on their gambols all innocent in their happiness.

Popular Refreshments.

Refreshments were also vended but at these *al fresco* afternoons tea and cakes were unknown. The only refreshment was the sugarcane, stripped of its bark and cut into small cylindrical pieces which again would be subdivided into four. Cool and sweet as the pieces would be, the rage of the young and old after eventide was great. Nothing could be simpler by way of refreshment than this fruit of nature which Herodotus described second-hand as "honey reeds." A large number of vendors, also Parsis, selling this fruit, so health-giving and energising, moved from group to group, calling out "Ganderi, goolab ganderi." "Sugarcane, rosy sugarcane." Those Parsi vendors were the pioneers of the large Hindu and Mahomedan tribe of sugarcane itenerants whom one sees to-day tramping in the most populous streets of the town after evening, or squatting, at particularly favoured corners where the custom throws plenty of *paisas* in their trays. Daily every morning the passer-by across the maidan might see the scavenger sweeping away the chewed refuse. But those were not the days of the applied scientists and chemists. The energy contained in the sugar juice was unknown and saccharine was not yet invented for the soldier as much for the sweetmeat maker, the confectioner and the medical men. The art of converting waste products of sugar was hardly discovered or turned to profit. The early Fifties in Bombay, even at their best, were of a primitive character and what are now deemed necessaries were a luxury in those days. We had some ice brought by Tudor's vessels of American bottom. And one or two vendors in the Fort had learned from some Florentine or Neapolitan the art of ice confectionery. Morenas was a name to be conjured with for ice creams. He was an institution in Bombay, but the proprietor was a Parsi, a short black man of the amiable, sweet and obliging type of "Old Pallonji" of the Adelphi Hotel, at Byculla. But the ice cream was a luxury, aye, till even the end of the sixties, and a glass was worth eight or four annas. But this is a little delightful digression.

The Shettias.

Coming back to the southern section of the maidan, it should be related that that part of it which is now a road leading a few yards west ward from the Floral Fountain to Churchgate Station was included in the maidan. The grounds on which now stand the Post Office, the Public Works Office and the High Court were also utilised for recreation purposes. but evidently it was dedicated to the *Shettia loque* or the wealthier of the Parsi community. Members of this class, too, frequented the maidan and had their little groups—only these were a little more exclusive, though in other respect there was nothing to choose between them and the larger groups of the middle classes on the other side. These, too, indulged in the luxury of "gaṅderi" and also of confectionery made by a Parsi who had a bakery in Barrack Lane which adjoins in a easterly direction the office of Messrs. Graham and Co. He vended biscuits and cakes and such like sweets. There was also in Meadows Street a shop familiarly known as "Bahadurji's Bakery." This bakery had the custom of the rich and middle class Parsis, while the humbler confectioner of the Military Store Lane supplied the needs of the lower classes, among whom the favourite confectionery was called "Karakaree," a kind of crisp oval biscuit scooped out hollow with two crowed bits. The Shettias patronised on their own aristocratic ground the superior and more costly confectionery of Bahadurji. Their groups were more sedate. There was seldom seen any reader of legendary lore. But they were great chess and "chowpat" players. The last was an exhilarating game played on a square board, divided into four rectangles, each rectangle having twelve squares. In these squares the game was played by four or two pairs with the aid of dice and "sotkas," a kind of pyramidical pawns of either coloured ivory or wood. The trump of the game was the "Twelfth," that is, those who threw the largest number of dice representing twelve, or multiples of two three and four were the winners. It demands a good deal of strategic alertness and mental arithmetic to win with "honours."

A Brisk Trade in Toys.

It will be asked whether the maidan did not find any Hindu or Mahomedan air-eaters. The answer must be given in the negative. Outdoor recreation till late in the sixties was unknown among them. On holi-days like the Dewali or the Holi or cocoanutday they might be found emerging from their places to view the illuminations or go to the sea for throwing floral and other offerings or for having a stroll at fairs, which in those days were a kind of kindergarten. So many novel English and Swiss toys were exposed for sale with a variety of knick-knacks that toy sellers actually minted money. Primitive mechanical toys were in great requisition and fetched high prices. A little doll, dressed up, smitting "mamma" would fetch five rupees! A little accordeon with the most elementary tunes, about $1\frac{1}{2}$ to 3 rupees. All these toys were English. The variety of those "made in Germany" "were unknown," about this period. All fairs were held on this southern section of the large Esplanade. The stalls were most numerous and the wares were well displayed, though the art of parading them attractively was unknown to the unsophisticated vendors. The scene presented on a fair day was gala, though the crowds were not numerous. Some women of the poorer Hindus might be seen here and there in the crowds. But one would in vain cast his eyes on a female of the better class of Hindu or Mahomedan. The only women, and even those in a fractional minority, belonged to the Parsi community! Thus it was that the southern maidan was almost wholly monopolised by the Parsis. Again, the proximity of the sea, and the number of wells on the maidan were of attraction to the most devout and religious of the Zoroastrians. Numbers, before sunset, could be seen praying in the direction of the setting sun, some with a white towel on their turbans. On particular feast days (Aban and Adar) the priestly class were present in force. Even to-day a remnant of the orthodox school might be seen either of an early morning or at the time of the setting of the sun saying their prayers, the sun being the emblem of Light and Heat, same like fire. But we need not digress into the domain devoted to Zoroastrian theology and ceremonies..

"Sweet Auburn."

My youthful imagination conjured more than once the scene presented on an ordinary evening on this maidan as a kind of "Sweet Auburn" village but on an extended plain though equally "lovely" with a larger crowd than that so graphically and faithfully portrayed in his Deserted Village by Goldsmith. It was indeed a lovely sight and spot at the time where you met with faces ruddy and bright, full of cheeriness and contentment, albeit you seldom found any "labouring swain". Neither there were anywhere about the locality hawthorn bushes where loving maids and swains could whisper sweet talk in each other's ears. There were, however, veteran trees which gave a grateful shade in the cool of the evening where little children gambled in infantine delight and imbibed the free ozone wafted from the western sea. And as for "talking age" there was enough and to spare. The numerous groups which clubbed together had many a garrulous old man who delighted our youth with stories of the type of the grand father's clock or marvellous legends performed at land and sea by their grand progenitors when Bombay had scarcely put forth her budding blossoms. Gone are those rustic days and gone are the generations of men who fired our youthful spirits and invoked in us an admiration for all that was pure and noble, all that inspired high endeavours and higher hopes for our growing manhood. Glancing over the long tract of years that has intervened it seems to "Sandy Seventy" that this world is all a fleeting show. We meet with processions after processions flitting to and fro. Now there is leaden surge and next moment there is sunlit blue! To-day a glorious summer. To-morrow the sere and yellow autumn. Thus runs the world away.

Chapter VIII.—WEALTHY PARSIS AND HINDUS AND THEIR RESIDENTIAL QUARTERS IN THE FORT. ALSO THE BUILDINGS OF THE GREAT ENGLISH COMMERCIAL FIRMS.

IN the fifties there was a considerable population in Bombay. Though the first rudimentary census was not introduced till 1864, a crude guess had been made that, in 1850, Bombay must have had at the least a population of five lakhs. The Fort, since the great fire of 1803, already referred to, was also more largely crowded. Previous to the date of that catastrophe, it is recorded that the residential buildings were fewer, there being many business premises and buildings to accommodate public offices. As, however, trade expanded, the Fort necessarily was more thickly populated. The Custom House, the Dock, the Post

Office, the Court, all being situated within the precincts of the Fort, Indian traders naturally preferred to reside in its vicinity. And as the most important community which was engaged in the foreign trade was the Parsi, it is intelligible that the wealthier had domiciled in the Fort. Most of the English and Scotch firms had guarantee brokers who were all Parsis. The Dadys, the Readymoneys, the Banajis and the Wadias had scions in the family who pursued that avocation while the heads themselves carried on their own independent business which was chiefly confined to imports and exports—China and the United Kingdom being the principal countries. Thus it was that one of the scions of the Wadia family was connected with the eminent banking house of Messrs. Forbes and Company, a name still cherished with esteem and regard, though the firm has long ceased to exist. The house of the first Sir Jamsetji was intimately associated with that of Messrs. Remington and Co., the successors of Bruce Fawcett and Company, also highly esteemed, and which, too, long long since closed its business. Then the first Sir Cowasji Jehangir and his brother were connected with Messrs. Cardwell Parson and Company. The Banajis were brokers to the old and rich house of Messrs. Leckie and Company. The Dadys were brokers to the esteemed firms of Messrs. Grey and Company and Peel Cassels and Company.

Old Parsi Leaders.

The father of the first Sir Dinshaw Petit was engaged as a guarantee broker in the firm of Messrs. Dirom Hunter and Company and Rennie Scovell and Company. Again the eldest branch of the Wadias were master builders and pursued their avocation of naval architects to the East India Company who boasted of their great fleet manned by the distinguished Indian Navy which ended its brilliant career when the Royal Navy came to be the guardians of the Indian seas. The Vicajis were associated with the financing of the Nizam's dominions. Thus it came to pass that each of these great families had their residences in the Fort. Two houses still stand in all their obsoleteness, compared to your jerry-built houses of the day, in the street known as Cowasji Patel. Entering from its south end, near the Hongkong Bank, may still be seen a large house, on the left, with a broad verandah and three quaint looking floors. That house belonged to Ardeshir Dady, the founder of the family, a native of Surat. It is over 150 years old and worth visiting even to-day for its quaint disposition and structure of the interior. Just opposite, on the right, is another more imposing house, with arched verandah, till late in the occupation of the *Duftur Ashkara* Printing Press, which belonged to the rich family of Sorabji Readymoney. It is equally ancient. But a third house, only recently modified, is still standing next to it which belonged to the family of the original Cowasji Patel of heroic fame, who in the early seventeenth century is said to have repelled the invasion of the piratical Seedees who used to infest the town. This house, till recently, was a specimen of Portuguese architecture. It was low and had only a ground floor, and a kind of attic. For long it had Portuguese tiles on the roofing. Next again, to it, the master builders had a spacious house where, resided more than one branch of the prolific Wadias, specially the family of Mr. Novroji Jamsetji. It was partially burnt by fire and afterwards rebuilt. The Banajis gave the name to a lane still known which had a back entrance in the same Cowasji Patel Street. The premises, belonging to Messrs. Graham and Company, including the new annexe to the south, was long the property of Mr. Dadabhoy Pestonji Wadia, a millionaire before the halcyon days of the first Sir Jamsetji. The latter himself built a town house which is now occupied by Messrs. Evans Fraser and Company. Compared to the houses of the Dadys and the Readymoneys, it was modern and looked upon as of mushroom growth.

A Famous Hindu Banking House.

Thus it will be seen how men of the mercantile line came to reside in the Fort after 1803. But let us take the reader to another part of it. Up till now we have described the Northern Fort buildings and that mostly of the Parsi wealthy. The only well-known premises of the Hindus at that early time was that of Motichand, a merchant and a banker, in Bazargate Street. It is also over a hundred years old, and was once the pride of the caste to which

Motichand belonged. Opposite was an unpretentious house where the banking firm of Atmaram Bhookan carried on till 1866 its money-lending and hundi transactions. It was known commonly as "Kaka Parekh Pehdi." The name was a household word and even the child in the street knew it well. It was a sight to see an array of "Mehtas," banking clerks, sitting squatted, as is the custom even to-day in the Indian part of the town, and doing work, while the partners were engaged in selling and buying daily hundreds of inland Bills of exchange computed by lakhs. Indeed it was *the Indian* banking house and had continued for 150 years till the blazing fire of the speculation of 1864 brought it to grief. But such was the probity and integrity of the house that its bills passed clean in every part of India. And its commercial credit was so highly spoken of that there was a standing joke that each hair on the moustache of the partners was worth a lakh of rupees. This was the tropical figure of speech to represent the credit of the house.

In the north-eastern part of the Fort lived the well-known and wealthy forbears of Messrs. Varjivandas and Narotamdas Madhavdas and also of Sir Mangaldas Nathoobhoy. The street is named Rupjee Manordas after the name of the great founder of the Shett family of the Kapole Banias.

European Residences.

In the southern part congregated the official European population owing to the work of all the public offices being transacted in the Fort. And the European merchants also lived there, though the seniors generally resided in then fashionable suburb of Byculla. The business was carried on in spacious houses, some of which may be seen in their pristine architecture even to-day.

Their general features were alike. There was a ground floor and verandah and an upper floor reached by an easy flight of steps which had two or three landing places wide and well lighted. Some of them were approached by a compound and a yard. One of the specimens of the early business premises of a European firm may be seen in the one now owned by Messrs. Greaves Cotton and Company in Forbes Street from the east end of Marine and Apollo streets. It is quite in striking contrast with the later and more pretentious houses in the vicinity. Look at the gate itself. What an archaic appearance it presents! You enter it and walk down a few yards when a fairly good compound is to be seen and turning to the left you go up the first floor by steps divided into three stages. There was always a large roomy well-lighted hall in houses of this typical character. The building of the Forbeses in Apollo Street was similar. So too, the house in Marine-Street, where the Remingtons carried on business, the one which adjoins on the north the premises known as the Great Western Hotel.

Other old Landmarks.

The present office of the "Bombay Chronicle" itself is another example of identical character and gives one a pretty fair idea of the European business and residential houses combined, built a hundred years ago and more and which were to be seen in their old-fashioned condition, in a state of excellent preservation even in the Fifties and Sixties. The new era of architecture, first noticed in the elegant blocks of buildings in Elphinstone Circle, had not dawned till another ten years afterwards. There was also an old house called the "Admiralty," which till twenty years ago was also a copy of the one of the "Chronicle" Office on the opposite side, and till the Sixties was the office of

Mr. Bhavnagri, the father of the present Sir Muncherji. The old offices of Messrs. Volkart Brothers in Marine Street, before they were renovated, was another old-fashioned European building. And in the by-lanes abutting in Meadows and Apollo Streets, there still stand a premise or two of the character. Not to forget this class of office and residential premises, we should point to the house owned by Sir Sassoon David, at the westerly corner of Military Square. Before that capitalist overhauled it, it was a beautiful building in its quaint facade, windows and so forth. For many years the firm of Messrs. Manisty and Fletcher, solicitors, the successors of Messrs. Bowyer and Crawford, carried on their business there. Another firm of solicitors who also had had their offices of a like type was the late firm of Messrs. Dallas and Lynch whose present successors are Messrs. Byrne and Company. That house is situated in Tamarind Street, opposite the confectionery factory of Messrs. Mongini. But it was destroyed by fire some years ago and is in ruins. But enough of some of these old landmarks in Southern Fort. They are a study by themselves and the modern Engineering Department of the Bombay Municipality may as well derive some hints therefrom. Though we doubt not that the chief of the department would heave a deep sigh of relief and shake his head as to the impossibility of causing houses of this character created in any part of the town save, perchance, in the Mahim Woods or in the New Worlee, which the utility imagination of the Municipal Commissioner and other town planners have conjured. The fact is that Bombay, at the closing of the eighteenth and the opening of the nineteenth century, was, as stated at the outset, sparsely populated, specially the Fort which was more military in all respects than civil. There was abundant space to build roomy residences with sufficient light and air and free garden space. The land could be had cheap enough. Indeed, at that period the aim of the East India Company was to encourage the growth of the population for the sake of the expansion of the trade of the port. Land was given freehold on a nominal quit rent, so that sanitation, though not preached, came naturally and the old-fashioned Englishman of the period *knew how to live*. We of our days of high pressure, of railways and electric installations and æroplanes, have all forgotten it. The go-bye is given for ever. Still the Engineer, the Health Officer and the Municipal Commissioner, may derive not a few hints for their new fangled and expensive Bombay in the north by studying the internal structural arrangements of these buildings.

CHAPTER IX.—SOUTHERN FORT OF BUSINESS AND FOREIGN TRADE· RECOLLECTIONS OF GREAT ENGLISH MERCANTILE HOUSES.

WHAT a contrast the busy humming streets of the Fort present to-day compared to the comparative silence which was to be witnessed in the Fifties! Recalling those days one is apt to say that the Fort was a "sleepy hollow." All the immense congestion of traffic to be seen of any morning or evening to-day in Churchgate Street, Meadows Street and Apollo Street, in the entire length of the Hornby Road, was mostly absent. The old Hornby Road running parallel to the ramparts in the west, from the north of what is now known as Fort Street to the southern extremity of Colaba Causeway, was exceedingly narrow and least frequented. Instead of the stream of vehicles passing to and fro all along the day and up to midnight, you saw perhaps for an hour in the morning and a couple of hours between 5 and 7 in the evening only a few passing by. Those belonged to the wealthier classes of Parsis and Hindus or to the European members of the mercantile community. Hornby Road was in no sense the principal highway of business and commerce as it is to-day. The road itself was narrow, perhaps not more than 30 to 35 feet in width. Footpaths there were none. These came with the advent of our first aedile and founder of the new Bombay which sprang into existence after 1865. All houses were on the east of the ramparts. From the line of the existing houses there the breadth did not stretch beyond the first line of rails on which the tramways pass at present. The southern part of the road commencing at the corner of Churchgate Street, as far as the statue of King Edward, seemed more like a suburban area where might live the Arcadians rather than a busy haunt. In fact a few banks and English firms alone were to be seen in this quarter which, along with Meadows Street and Apollo Street, were specifically known as "Ingrez Bazar," that is, the business place of European mercantile houses.

Old Landmarks effaced.

This quarter no doubt has effaced almost all old landmarks. For instance, at the corner of Churchgate Street, say up to the showrooms of Ditmar, there was a conglomeration of half a dozen ground floor shops, mostly of Memon booksellers, who drove a roaring trade in a variety of old and rare books. They were the largest purchasers of these at auctions where officials and others leaving Bombay for Europe used to send up all their household furniture. Thus the curious collector of old books was sure to find on the shelves of these "old Haji" shops many a rare book which could be purchased at an exceedingly moderate price. Their owners also used to send their shopboys as hawkers who went about offering to those well-known to take interest in intellectual enjoyment of odd volumes. They hardly knew English and used to have the assistance of a clerk who could write and speak broken English. It was amusing to hear their own "patois" about books of intrinsic worth of which they knew next to nothing. But by familiarity and by constant handling they could pick up at any time a book a buyer wanted. Often they would commit ridiculous blunders, but on the whole they mechanically knew the books and their worth. Old editions of cyclopedias and ponderous dictionaries they knew by sight. A Johnson's Dictionary in English was then greatly prized and for some of us students in rudimentary Latin, Ainsworth's dictionary, King Edward VI's Latin Grammar, or an odd volume of Cæsar, Horace or Virgil, were prized highly, and much was the haggling to get these "Haji" bookwallas to part with them.

Time's Changes.

There was a photographer's shop, too, next door, known as Harichand Chintaman. He was the pioneer among the Indian photographers and his photos were greatly in requisition. Only two or three houses in south Hornby Road still stand almost in the same condition as they were in the Fifties. The chief of these is the premise now in the occupation of Messrs. Ralli Brothers. The ground floor was then occupied by the old Bank of Bombay which came to be established in 1841, with a level headed, capable and cautious Scotch manager in the person of Mr. John Stuart. In the Fifties the directors had resolved upon having bank premises

INNER CHURCH GATE, 1864.

of their own. That was the cyclopean looking granite building which is now known as the Currency Office. But in the middle of the Fifties the Bank occupied the premises now in occupation by the Rallis. All round there have been vast changes since that period, but this house, so imposing in its own early nineteenth century style, stands almost unaltered save for a second floor put up some years ago and the outer glass windows which the necessities of a European shopkeeper have from time to time demanded. It belongs to that philanthropic Parsi, the late Mr. N. M. Wadia, whose charities are so ably and judiciously administered by the Trustees of his crore rupees' worth estate, and are so beneficently showering their fragrance all round, near and far. Another house, next to the offices of Messrs. Currimbhoy on the north, is a very old house, albeit a little more changed than Wadia's. This still belongs to the family of Byramji

Jijibhoy. Every other building has undergone transformation demanded by the modern conditions of business in the locality. The opposite row of buildings of some architectural pretensions did not exist till the ramparts were pulled down some years afterwards. In fact those rows of new premises rose only after the Hornby Road was fresh laid out by Arthur Crawford almost in the same condition in which we see it today broad enough, with wide foot-paths and arcades. But these elegant piles of new Bombay will be described later on.

The Story of John Treacher.

But one little house which stood in the old Rampart Row, west, must be referred to, seeing that there was carried on for years, say up to 1860, the enormous business of the thriving house of Mr. John Treacher. It was afterwards bought by the Oriental Bank, that prominent building which juts out between Hornby Road and Meadows Street.

It was an old ground floor building with thatched roof. Here John Treacher began his calling as chemist and druggist, vending medicines and making soda water. It was the purity of that liquid which made his name famous and enriched him immensely. There was no other soda water manufactory in Bombay in the Fifties. Treacher was a household word, and that short man, so unassuming, yet so keen in business, was the architect of his own fortune. He never moved out of his original place of business till having made his pile he converted it into a limited company. Mr. Jivanji Hormasji, the late proprietor of the hotel now known by the name of Great Western, was his chief factotum. Hence he was generally known till his death as "Jivanji Treacher." He became the manager of the new company which then removed its business to the ground floor which had been vacated by the Bank of Bombay.

There was another old landmark on the opposite side. A shop belonging to the Palkiwalas was situated, where members of that Parsi family carried on the business of building carriages on English models and palkis which were the principal mode of conveyance in the Fort for solicitors, barristers, doctors, and merchants, Indian and European. The palki was indeed a cherished institution for years and many were the old residents who regretted their almost total disuse after 1874. These useful conveyances, along with the antiquated bullock hackeries, need a chapter by themselves to recall to the memory of generations to come how well did they serve the purpose of locomotion in days gone by when the tram car and the motor car were only a dream.

Meadows Street.

But we are still on the streets, the streets which were crowded with men of business. Meadows Street, from end to end, from the shop of Messrs. Dunnett to the old building now in the occupation of the "Bombay Chronicle" was the busiest as it is to-day. But in the Fifties Bombay Green and Apollo Streets surpassed it in point of mercantile activity and mercantile wealth. Meadows Street, was dedicated as at present, to English shopkeeping. In the premises occupied by Dunnett was St. Andrew's Library which has been absorbed in the thriving business of Messrs. Thacker and Company, the successors of Thacker Vining and Company. Next door was a highly patronised silk shop owned by a respectable proprietor of the Borah community known as "Myaji." It was the only Indian shop in the Fort where a variety of silks and other fashionable requirements for the sartorial decking of European ladies was to be procured. The prices were stiff and "Myaji" never receded from his fixed price by even eight annas, proud as he was of his monopoly and prouder still of his wealthy custom.

It was no shop for humbler folk unless dire necessity made it necessary to resort to it. The Myajis were indeed most polite and courteous and every way helpful. Messrs. John Watson and Company, the founders of Watson's Hotel (now known as Esplanade) was a great rival and ultimately the Myajis had to wind up their lucrative business. Further on, exactly opposite the westerly end of Hummum Street was "Morenas," another institution, but in the confectionery line, where ices and cakes in the Fifties were vended as a luxury. The shop where the Parsi proprietor, one Mr. Merwanji, made his fortune, is the one now in the occupation of Messrs. Dhanamal Chellaram, Jewellers. Here of an evening, specially in summer months, might be seen draw up on the road half a dozen carriages and pair, in which were seated the "burra beebies" wives of officials or merchants, sipping their glasses of ices, while humbler customers thronged the shop, dingy and unornamented as it was. But in those days the art of dressing up shops and shop windows was unknown. That, too, was brought into vogue by the "Ingrez" and foreign shopkeepers to whom Bombay was a rich colony to carry on shopkeeping since the days of the great share speculation of 1863-64. During that feverish period Morenas minted more money than he had ever done in his life career. Morenas, they say, was an Italian with whom Mr. Merwanji was a partner. When the Italian retired he became the sole proprietor. Meadows Street on the whole, has not changed much. But its pride was gone when the high rentals there fell owing to the big buildings which came into vogue with the rearing of Watson's Hotel, the Bombay Club, Treacher and Company and so on.

Old Mercantile Houses.

But in the Fifties the part of business Fort where wealth rolled was, of course,

Apollo Street, and also Marine Street. In those areas were crowded the busy merchantmen. Those eminent and enterprising houses, now only names to recall the foundation of Bombay's greatness in foreign trade, of Messrs. William Nicol and Co., Messrs. Ritchie Steuart and Company, Messrs. Peel Cassels and Company, Messrs. Forbes and Company, Messrs. Rimington and Company, Messrs. Edward Bates and Company and others, were all congregated in these two once most busy streets of the Fort, long before the Elphinstone Circle, which the utility imagination of Mr. Forjett, the Police Commissioner, brought into existence after 1860. Where are they? The new order of merchants knows them not, and the old residents of the Fifties, are more or less gathered to the majority. Some came to grief after the aftermath of 1865-66, some struggled for a few years more, and some voluntarily wound up and bade a long and lasting adieu to the scenes of their great mercantile activity. Who is now aware of the great house of W. Nicol and Company whereof the two Flemings, John and James, were the most active and enterprising spirits. That was a name to be conjured with. It was that firm which was the pioneer of a gigantic private enterprise, the pioneers literally of the present Bombay Port Trust. It was they who launched that scheme known in the monetary circles as the Elphinstone Land and Press Company. It was they who first began to reclaim the eastern foreshore from Carnac Bunder northward. The scheme was launched in the piping times of peace and mercantile steadiness, when none of those, wild, fantastic and ambitious schemes which came into vogue with the meteor rise of that speculative star of 1863-64, Mr. Premchand Roychand, were dreamt of. The history of that enterprise can be read in the monograph issued under the authority of the Port Trustees in 1905, on the occasion of the laying of the foundation stone of the Alexandra Docks by King George V (then Prince of Wales). Bombay owes a deep debt of gratitude to Lord Elphinstone, the Governor, who gave the concession and to the firm of Messrs. Nicol and Company, who brought it to a head in 1864. Similarly may be mentioned the name of Messrs. Ritchie Steuart and Company who were the promoters of the gigantic Backbay enterprise, in every way sound but which came to grief by the ill fate which overtook Bombay in 1865. The names of Messrs. Tracey and Michael Scott are inscribed on the pages of the commercial history of Bombay. They were mighty builders. One firm alone now remains, which must not be omitted to be mentioned. That is of Messrs. W. and A. Graham and Company. They were indeed the largest

OUTER CHURCH GATE, 1864.

importers of Lancashire piecegoods and yarns long before the Rallis, their great rivals being Messrs. Peel Cassels and Company, the head of which was that personage of massive intellect, Mr. Walter Cassels, and Messrs. Grey and Company who senior partner Robert Hannay of financial renown in connection with the old Bank of Bombay, was the most prominent. Gone are those distinguished members of those old firms with their rich and honourable traditions the like of whom we shall never see again. If Bombay has undergone a great physical transformation since 1850, not the less has she undergone a radical change in the strength and ability of her old sturdy Englishmen of trade, the founders who flourished some 60 years ago and more.

CHAPTER X.—THE OVERLAND MAIL AND THE POST OFFICE. THE OLD SECRETARIAT IN APOLLO STREET.

THE itinerary of the Fort in the Fifties would be incomplete were no mention made of the situation and condition of the great public offices. Of course, it goes without saying that in those quiescent days the work of the administration in all parts of the country was not so circumambient as it is to-day. In the first place there were no sea cables to carry on hourly communication with the Chairman of the Board of the great East India Company. They called themselves the Court of Directors and their office was in the historical Leadenhall Street in London. The Chairman occupied the position of the Secretary of State and communications between him and the Governors

POST OFFICE.

and Governor-General of the day were regular, both official and private.

The Overland Mail.

The "overland mail" as we called it was bi-monthly, when we are to-day agitating for a bi-weekly. That alone tells us of the strides which both the administration and the mercantile community have taken. Things were done leisurely which carried the unique advantage of greater concentration of thought, and greater length of time to study the grave problems of administration from all points of view. Necessarily in India of the time there were not so many multiplications of public offices as there are to-day, be they at the seat of the central authority or at the seats of the two important Presidencies of Madras and Bombay. "Efficiency" may have been known to the Honourable the Court of Directors and to the great pro-consuls carrying out their instructions in obedience to the periodical

Despatches of grave import. Still it was not a word that connoted in the minds of the various administrations of the time the same standard with which the great "Efficiency" Viceroy made them familiar during his eventful septennate. The overland mail was not regular. It could not be expected with that clock-like punctuality noticed at the commencement of the twentieth century. Navigation had not been so perfected. The P. & O. Co.'s vessels from Suez to Bombay were still in their infancy and their commanders had to learn many a lesson from those gallant officers and scientific geographers of the Indian Navy of which not only the Honourable the East India Company but all India and the United Kingdom should remain proud. The Company's officers had to undergo a vast training to mark out the routes and they had to greatly depend on what the geographers of the Indian Navy had then accomplished. Those curious about the history of the navigation of the Red Sea, the Indian Ocean and the East African Coast, would find ample pabulum of the scientific efforts of those officers in the papers read by many of them before the then Geographical Society since merged in the Bombay Branch of the Royal Asiatic Society.

The Postal Service.

Apart from the overland mail, the postal service was also in its infancy. The reader should remember that there was no post office in India in the acceptation of the term till 1837 and it was not until 1854 that anything like an organised effort was made by the Government to carry on what may be called primitive postal work. Inland mails were few and far between in the fifties. They had to be carried by staglike postal runners, a race by themselves. Before 854, on the recommendation of the

Commission appointed in 1850, there was no such thing as a postage stamp! Between 1837 and 1854, private service or enterprise did all the work under Government protection. These private postal agents levied cash for a letter. There is a history by it of how they distributed letters in the city which must be related in a subsequent chapter. Suffice to say, that in the Fifties a letter from Bombay to Calcutta cost one rupee per tola, and a letter from Calcutta to Agra 12 annas! What a fortune postage stamp collectors might make by searching for Indian postage stamps of the year 1854!

Administrative Work.

But such being the conditions of communication, it would be readily realised that all administrative work was not only slow and leisurely, but hardly considerable quantitatively. The "Covenanted Clerks" of the East India Company, must have had a fine time of it, and we can well imagine how the Indian Civil Service of to-day would sigh for those blessed days of the Arcadian era of the Fifties when reports by tons and miles were absolutely unknown and did not worry the District Pasha smoking his hooka of quietude, with none of the petty tyrants of the Secretariat to vex his peaceful soul and to remind him of the belated character of his divers reports! Well, then, it might be said that public offices were few and far between in the Fifties. Of course, they were all located in the Fort. Save the Secretariat and the Military Staff Office and the Custom House and the Post Office all carried on their appointed work in buildings rented on hire.

The Secretariat Building was the building which has long been called "the Old Secretariat" in Apollo Street, once the residential quarters of the Governor of Bombay. The last of such a

Satrap, it is said, was Jonathan Duncan who died of cholera in the beginning of the nineteenth century and was buried in the outer churchyard of St. Thomas' Cathedral, till that space by the Municipal Act of 1865, was closed for all purposes of burial. The tombs there were removed and taken elsewhere, while some of the prominent ones were relaid on the inner floor of the Cathedral, that of Duncan included. Of course, the Cathedral was in reality, next door to the Governor's residence. So that in the days of the eighteenth century, all through, the European section must have realised in concrete what was meant by Church and State.

The Old Secretariat Buildings.

The Church stood under the shadow of the State. Each edifice stood in its solitary glory surrounded by large shady trees. Even in the Fifties the Old Secretariat Building was standing alone amidst a large square with trees and gardens, having a caretaker who had a house at the back, say in Tamarind Lane, or Dean Lane. It is quite conceivable that there was no building during the greater part of the eighteenth century, between the area enclosed by the Secretariat and the one which surrounded the Cathedral. Bruce Lane which now divides them must have existed later on and thereafter the Forbes's must have reared their stately offices there. The name Bruce belonged to a partner of an old firm which carried on its business as Bruce Fawcett and Company whose successors were Messrs. Remington and Co. There are yet many traces which recall how nice, cool and elegant the edifice must have been as a gubernatorial residence, till the official vandals at the commencement of the 19th century converted it into the Secretariat office, and till the exigencies of the State prompted it to dispose of the building many years ago to "Raja Bahadur"

Shivlal Motilal of Indore, a shroffing celebrity. Further vandalism overtook the historical building after this titular Raja converted it for ordinary business offices to exact his ecomic rent on the capital invested in the purchase. However, Bombay of to-day must feel thankful to him that he has preserved intact the largest portion of the garden, facing the west, where we can imagine many an interesting function must have taken place in the early days and where no doubt the fashion and beauty of Bombay occasionally met and kept up dignified revelry till the small hours of the morning. It is perfectly conceivable that all the buildings in the front on the west were non-existent and the wind of the western sea blew sweet and low straight from the Back Bay over the western ramparts.

The New Secretariat Building.

The Old Secretariat served its purpose till the multiplication of administrative work urgently demanded a new building enough spacious and boasting of some architectural pretensions, to be erected on the Mayo Road in the Seventies. Thus the edifice was shorn off all the old historic glory of the hundred years and more where so many governors of the eighteenth century had resided, and where the affairs of the Presidency were administered by the "Covenanted Clerks" of the Honourable the East India Company, the immediate predecessors of the new Covenanted Service, and issue their august decrees by way of "Resolutions" of His Excellency the Governor in Council, after the manner of the Doges of Venice. A marble tablet at the south corner recounts the history of that State Building. But the present writer is not aware whether similar tablets have been placed elsewhere n old Government buildings either sold or utilised for other purposes. They of London are better every way in their historic instincts and historic perception. For there one sees a large numb er of tablets which remind him of old places of historic interest. But we in India are yet a century behind in all kinds of progress. The only matter in which there is a progress is in writing the history of India whereby a large number of old idols have been white-washed, faithfulness and absolute accuracy having been a minus quantity for the older official historians. Let it be hoped that some Councillor or Civic Father will rise in his place and plead for the sad omission of civic amenities which while satisfying the true historic instinct would teach the rising generation to cherish the honoured places of the past with the accumulated wealth of their traditions. The Old Secretariat is the only relic preserved intact to recall many an act of the Bombay Administration for over a century. There is even a greater reason to give selected records of that century, so brimful of many a local and provincial event, to educate the public which, alas! in these days of high pressure confines all its attention to the present, following the example of that Persian Prince or Princess to whom the Past was a perfect blank, and the Future a vast sheet of mist. I would rather sing with that inspired genius of the French Revolutionary period, no other than Andre Chenier, and recall the colours of the past by the thoughts of the present.

> "Let us change to golden honey flowers,
> Whose fragrance, aye, will last;
> Paint the thoughts that throng the present,
> With the colours of the past.
> Let us kindle our torch at the old poetic fires,
> Sing as songs to the tune of ancient lyres."

Chapter XI.—THE CATHEDRAL.

"Oh ! sometimes when the solemn organ rolls
Its strain of sounds down the grey historic aisles" !

The other public edifice of importance which attracted greater attention in the Fifties than it does at present was St. Thomas' Cathedral. It was indeed a solemn and stately public building in those days. Our boyish curiosity and reverence combined, often prompted us to stand at the entrance of the western portal of this stately shrine, with its grey towers, the solemn tolling of the bell, attentively listening to "the man of God" in the distant pulpit, while within the historic aisles and all around was solemn silence, inspiring us with an ineffable ecstacy of the divine worship. Noiseless was the street on a Sunday evening and none of the myrmidons of the police patrolled it, making signs "chip, chip" to the

THE BOMBAY GREEN, 1864.

drivers of vehicles passing by to drive slowly. Neither any European constable superintended that patrol. The worshippers within the sacred hall said their prayers with devotion unmixed with any alarm or consternation. All that new-fangled order of vigilance was the consequence of those dark days of 1857 and the atrocities which the sepoy mutineers had perpetrated in sacred Christian places at Delhi, Lucknow, Cawnpore and other cities where the revolt was most rife. Though the desecration of the churches by the "heathens" could in no manner bear comparison to the ruthless vandalism of those "Christian" barbarians, purporting to be civilised and cultured, and deep in the lore of the humanities taught in their higher seats of learning, who during the late war destroyed the architectural beauty of the great cathedral at Rheims. The cathedral in Churchgate Street filled our youth, ever mindful of the creed of our ancestors with solemn reverence. It may be interesting to learn how many of the congregation of the day assembling weekly for worship there are aware of the fact of the near approach of the bicentenary of this historic pile on the Christmas day of 1918!*

History of the First Chapel.

The curious may learn from Mr. Edwardes' account in the revised Bombay Gazetteer of the beginnings of the cathedral and of the vicissitudes which attended the first attempt to build God a church in the city two hundred years ago and more. The very first chapel ever thought of for the spiritual ministration of the Christian officers of the Government of Bombay, the seat of which was then at Surat, was in 1665! The chapel was a mere room in the Bombay Castle. Ten years later Gerald Aungier's devout

* The Jubilee now past and gone was unostentiously abbuted.

entreaties to the honourable directors at Home brought the cheering news of the construction of a church on the Bombay Green, then fully open to the Backbay sea, and monies to the extent of Rs. 50,000 were collected. Then suddenly after the foundations were laid, there was a long lull, some one ungodly had violated the decalogue and the funds were spirited away! It is ever so in human affairs. Man's cupidity never fears to lay hands on the most sacred things.

The history of the Christian churches for well nigh seventeen centuries is not innocent of such profane dishonesty. But to come to the history of our local church. It was during the governorship of Mr. Charles Bocne, a most energetic pro-consul, full of practical ideas which he was able to carry out, after Gerald Aungier, the earliest to lay the foundations of Bombay, that the unfinished chapel was completed, the funds having been provided by means of a lottery. One chaplain, Mr. Cobb, was most instrumental in its completion and it was on the Christmas day of 1718 that it was opened with an imposing ceremonial. But till 1835, it may be observed in passing, Bombay episcopate was subordinate to the see of Calcutta. It was in that year that by a legislative enactment, Bombay was raised to the dignity of a bishopric with the Reverend Mr. Carr as the first Bishop. The Cathedral was found somewhat incommodious and in 1865 a chancel was constructed to the east with another State ceremonial by Sir Bartle Frere of which I was one of the spectators.

"Cowasji Cross."

The ever philanthropic Mr. (afterwards Sir) Cowasji Jehangir donated it with a beautiful fountain, costing

Rs. 35,000, which stands at the entrance of the Western gate. For this catholic benevolence, for Sir Cowasji was nothing if not catholic in all his philanthropy, his orthodox community of 1864, was in revolt! It was a profanity of profanities for the scion of the rich Parsi house of the Readymoneys to erect a fountain in a place of worship devoted to Christianity! And some of these Zoroastrian fanatics of the day, a remnant of which class still exists, nicknamed the donor "Cowasji Cross" as the structure is surmounted with a cross. The fanatics are dead and their names are steeped in oblivion, but the beautiful fountain still stands, a work of art as much of charity, for at any day and at any hour one may see troops of the poorest Indian humanity residing in the vicinity, filling thence chatties of water for their domestic use. The Cathedral was also enriched by a magnificent organ, at a cost of Rs. 15,000, made by the well-known makers, Messrs. Bishop and Starr. The slow and solemn chimes, however, of the Cathedral clock, which in the silence of the night were heard at a long distance remained till late. The structural alterations and other exigencies of the sacred edifice led to some changes. But gone, gone are the solemn, slow and rythmical chimes of the Cathedral clock which used to ring in our ears during the Fifties. They struck all quarters, and the deep toned hours as they rang filled our young hearts with infinite joy. The change in the chimes may have been necessary by the utilitarianism of the day but to us it is a change which we regret. It has obliterated all old memories. It has dissociated our old associations with the historic Cathedral. The iron age of the twentieth century has for ever destroyed the one utility which had so well served the Fort of Bombay for a whole century.

Architectural Grandeur of the Cathedral.

But it is interesting to relate that in the Fifties the Cathedral was the only edifice of any architectural pretension in the Fort, save the Town Hall. As such it was a thing of joy and beauty, of reverence and dignity all through till the first lustre of its architectural glory was dimmed by the Rajabai Clock Tower and its musical chimes. And modernism has completely put this hoary edifice into shade since. For how many are there of the reverential spirit to be found in the city who care much for it, though on great State occasions it is yet the only suitable and majestic place of worship within whose four walls "Te Deums" and universal prayers for our country and sovereign are heard. It is to be presumed the devotees now congregating there go more for the music there than for prayers or sermons. But, perchance, a non-Christian is entirely wrong in his surmise. It may be that the Cathedral is very well cared for spiritually, and that there is no fault to be found with men of the State who dispense the patronage of the Church. An eloquent preacher who could send a thrill through the hearts of the worshippers has been somewhat wanting for many a year. No learned divine and scholar preaches now from the old pulpit. A Manning or a Vaughan alone can revive the spirituality within the Cathedral. Or it may be, as many allege, and as the rationalism of the day teaches, that the creed itself is decaying and dying. Whatever may be the cause the Cathedral is not the Cathedral spiritually which Sandy Seventy occasionally used to visit to hear the preachings of the chaplains of the Fifties. Still it stands out in the midst of all mundane things surrounding it as the landmark of the beginnings of Bombay. The Town Hall is simply modern compared to it. And one can hardly point out to a single stately edifice erected by Government two hundred years ago which can be fairly associated with it. There have not been wanting local vandals with the suggestion to raze this historic pile to the ground, but the historic spirit of our citizens has never listened to the voice of these unhistoric folk. And it is to be presumed were the suggestion to be revived Bombay to a man would revolt against it. So few and far between are the public edifices which may count a couple of centuries and whose memories are dear, that it would be a day of general mourning when the ruthless hand of the vandals levels it to the ground. It is to be devoutly hoped that no such fate will await this building which is so intimately associated with the early beginnings of Bombay.

Chapter XII.—OLD BOMBAY GREEN. THE TOWN HALL ANTIQUITIES AND LITERATURE.

NEXT to the hoary Cathedral in Church Gate Street, the object of the greatest delight and curiosity was the Town Hall, vulgarly pronounced "Tondal." Even in the fifties every school boy knew where was the "Deval" (the Cathedral) and where the "Tondal." The cockney of the Fort may not know "Baharkot," Kalbadevi, Girgaum or Walkeshwar, but he knew these two popular edifices. Our youthful imagination was no doubt struck by these. The Cathedral was a place of solemn worship only open on service days. Not so the Town Hall. It was a place free of access to all at certain hours of the day. Strangers visiting the "Killa" of Bombay, cannot return to their homes without seeing the great civic

BOMBAY GREEN, 1860.

hall, the only one of its kind and architecture in the city. The Green, now the Elphinstone Circle Gardens, was the favourite resort of almost all Parsi boys and girls residing in the Fort for evening recreation. Owing to the circular character of this playground it was named *chakri* in Gujrathi, *chakar* being a circle. It was exceedingly attractive, for two or three reasons. In the first place, it was exposed to the soft breezes from the Bay on the West. So far the green was health-giving, and really served as a lung for the recreation of children residing in the northern Fort, the big Maidan, being too distant for them. Indeed. it is absolutely a fact to say that whereas the two Maidans already described were the resort of adults, chiefly Parsis, the Green opposite the Town Hall, was the recreation or playground of the children, also mostly Parsis. There were no high buildings around it. In the south at some distance were those large godowns smelling of "Afim" or opium. Great activity was to be seen in the buildings and warehouses which owed their existence to one enterprising European employee of the East India Company, rejoicing in the name of Henshaw. Marwaris and some Jews trading in the drug flocked here and inspected opium. So that after office hours a large quantity of opium or poppy leaves dried, were seen strewn in that part of the green.

Fine Statuary.

At this south end there was a group of fine marble statuary canopied containing a statue of Lord Cornwallis surrounded by other emblematic figures. It was evidently raised somewhere in 1805, if my memory serves right. It was a memorial in honour of Lord Cornwallis, who was the Governor-General when the battle of Seringapatam was fought. There was a group which related the glories of the E. I. Company, including a bag of shining rupees by the side of a female figure. It was a most excellent work of the marble sculptor, and if furbished up to-day and placed in a conspicuous part of the Oval, say somewhere near the bandstand, would be greatly admired. But the custodians of this statuary—the best we have yet seen,—have allowed it to lie as a lumber in some corner or other, Heaven knows where. In all probability it will be allowed to slumber there until, some day, our Sovereign again revisits the city, and opens the Museum, which has taken already nine years to build, and the public is once more afforded a perennial inspection and appreciation of the statuary with the ejaculation of "Wah! Wah!!" Facing the west, the green boasted of a nice well of spring water which served day and night to quench the thirst of wayfarers, either cotton brokers or opium brokers, or clerks or strangers. The exigencies of the place and its new amenities after the Elphinstone Circle was built, demanded that the well should be filled and closed. In its place they have erected on the identical spot a handsome fountain bearing the name of the original donor of that most serviceable well. Here seated under the grateful shade of the old tamarind tree, which still exists, there was to be noticed groups of all kinds of men at noon or in the afternoon taking recess and otherwise refreshing themselves. There were always seated sweetmeat-sellers and others to satisfy the inner man. These itinerants served a useful purpose in those days, and for many years after, till at last the Irani tea shops and the Hindu Upahar Grhas studded the city. Curiously enough the landmark of the old Bombay green may still be noticed, somewhat modified. One can visit the place at any hour be tween 12 noon and 4 p.m. to find that a similar class of people who resorted there in the Fifties still visit it. It is just like modern Londoners resorting to the taverns where Johnson and Garrick, Goldsmith and Joshua Reynolds passed their time in intellectual and other bouts. But this particular spot on green was an *al fresco* refreshment place.

Music on the Green.

The other attraction of the green for us young boys of the Fifties was the music that was played there every evening after sunset. It was a custom which had continued from the days when the Governors of Bombay resided in the Fort in the building which is known as the "Old Secretariat." Those august administrators ceased to occupy it after the death of Jonathan Duncan. But the practice to regale Government House continued till it was given up in the Sixties when the Elphinstone Circle came to be built and the Military Staff offices, opposite the Cathedral, were levelled to the ground. The staff offices extended from the south end of Cowasji Patel Street, where stands the handsome pile of the Hongkong Bank, to the end of Kemp and Company's premises and into Parsi Bazaar Street, as far as the godown of Mr. Hasanalli, the stationer. They pointed out a low yellow house, at the east end of Humam Street opposite the old Secretariat, where for years together medical stores were kept. This houses was for years the official residence or office of the "Town Major". So from that office up to the end of the Military Staff buildings at the corner of Kemp's, a band, sometimes consisting of drums and fifes, and sometimes of musical instruments, played airs. In fact, the brass band of an Indian infantry regiment went up and down promenading this part of the green, and our boyish delight at hearing such music was great. We "ate" the fresh air, and tickled our ears with the regimental music!

Coming to the Town Hall, let it be said that the flights of steps in the Fifties were daily thronged at eventide by scores of children for purposes of "eating the air" and playing. It was an excellent pastime going up and down the flights of steps till one was tired, unmindful of the call of timid servants who feared lest we should have a fall and our parents upbraid them at home. My servant "Jivan," I remember very well, was one of those extremely nervous fellows whom it was a cruel pleasure to tease by increased efforts at running up the steps and climbing down the bannisters. The verandah also served as a kind of playground. The large number of Buddhistic, Assyrian and other idols at the foot of the north-eastern staircase, the property of the Royal Asiatic Society, or Geographical Society, was a constant source of curiosity, and I suppose it was my constant gazing at those Assyrian and other antiquities which led to my devouring all literature about these and caves in Western India and elsewhere at a very early period of my college life. These antiquities unearthed by many an antiquarian were my earliest inspiration, and I owe my love of all antiquities to the inspiration first imparted by these figures. I distinctly remember that in 1856 Mr. Layard, of Nineveh and Babylon celebrity, paid a visit to Bombay and presented some of his excavations to the Royal Asiatic Society, and I also remember having seen him in person when on a visit to our Elphinstone Institution in company with Dr. Haines, then Educational Inspector of the Central Division. Mr. Layard was a stout personage, with large whiskers which were the fashion of the period. But these are a few personal digressions which I daresay will be excused by those who read these scrappy recollections.

The First Town Hall.

It is said that Bombay did not boast of any kind of a Town Hall, small or great, artistic or inartistic, spacious or confined, during the first few years of British rule. It is recorded that in 1665 a room in the law courts of the day where judicial administration was carried on was occasionally allowed for the purpose of a meeting by the citizens. Two years later a small hall was set apart in Aungier's Court, which was situated in Mapla's *pol* (Mápla was a Malabar merchant and great landowner) in the street known as Gunbao in the Fort. The *pol* with a large courtyard in the centre still exists, and may be inspected any day by the curious. The part where the hall was situated was burnt down in the Eighties, but there is a tablet there which informs us how 200 years ago Gunbao Street was almost unbuilt upon, and therefore open to the sea, with no buildings whatever in front to obstruct the scene of Back Bay in the west. Curiously enough my very first school class was in the Mapla's *pol* for a time. It was the first Anglo-Vernacular school endowed by a philanthrophic Parsi, the late Mr. Dhunjibhoy Nusserwanji Cama. It was commonly known as Ayrton's school owing to the fact of Mr. Ayrton being the person who first suggested the foundation of the school. He was a solicitor in good practice but rose on his return to London years afterwards to be the first Minister of Public Works in the Ministry of Mr. Gladstone in 1871. It was in 1849 that I went to this school, a boy of 5, and later on the late (Sir) P. M Mehta was my school fellow in that seminary, and I am rejoiced to say that the friendship first formed there continued till the day of his death in 1915. The Camas were the earliest social and educational reformers in the Fifties, and it was owing to their encouragement that Mr. Dadabhai Nowroji eventually became a partner in their London firm in 1855. One more fact in connection with the Mapla *pol* may be related here. It was an extensive building running south and east: in the east was a range of shops and at the central part there was also a vernacular school known as Mehtaji Tamakram. The school flourished for years till transplanted by the latter-day primary schools. In reality it was a kind of covered court-yard with stone seats erected parallel to each other and a central gangway between. Beyond it there was the office of Mr. Ruttonji Edulji Bottlewalla a wealthy merchant trading with China in opium, pearls, etc. He had as an assistant in the Fifties, a distinguished alumnus of Elphinstone College, a contemporary of Mr. Dadabhai Nowroji and S. S. Bengalee, in the person of the late Mr. Cowasji Edulji Khambatta. He rose to be the Chief Manager in the Seventies of the Port Canning Reclamation

Company in Calcutta which he brought up from a most depressed condition to the very meridian of prosperity. This venerable business man, scholar and publicist died about three years age (1917.) But Bombay knows not some of its past literary men of distinction.

The Present Building.

Turning again to the history of the Town Hall, it may be observed that in 1720, what was known as the Town Hall was a large room leased in the house belonging to one Rama Kamati. Here it continued till 1788 when accommodation was provided on a floor of the house in Marine Street, known as "Hornby House," the same where the High Court was located for years together, and which till late was in the occupation of the Great Western Hotel. Yet a further wandering took place while the citizens remained without a permanent hall of their own suited to their growing wants and importance of Bombay as a commercial city. That great builder, Henshaw mooted the erection of such a permanent edifice, but evidently there was no response. They slumbered, the Arcadians of those days, till 1811, when the two most influential and wealthy firms of Messrs. Forbes and Company and Messrs. Bruce Fawcett and Company moved the Government in the matter. Sir Charles Forbes, the head of the firm, was a name to be conjured with and commanded the regard and esteem of the entire Indian and European population. It was resolved to raise the funds by a lottery, which the Government readily sanctioned. A lakh and ten thousand were raised but the cost was a great deal more. It was resolved to raise a second lottery, but it failed. A third attempt however proved successful. At last plans and estimates were framed. The edifice was designed by Colonel

Cowper, R. E., and was completed in 1832 at a cost of six lakhs. Lastly, it should be mentioned that in the Fifties and Sixties, many a lecture on literary and scientific subjects was delivered by learned professors, scholars, divines, engineers and others, which were of a highly interesting and instructive character. First and foremost in this literary activity were two Protestant Missionaries of note, namely, Dr. Wilson, whose name is associated with the great, thriving college at Chowpatti, now under the principalship of that other divine and scholar, so full of eloquence, the Revd. Dr. Mackichan, and the reverend Dr. Murray Mitchell. Both were eminent scholars and linguists, and have left a mine of knowledge on Indian subjects which may be diligently quarried in the Library of the Royal Asiatic Society, itself founded by a distinguished man of literature and European fame, no other than Sir James Mackintosh who, in the early nineteenth century adorned our High Court as an erudite Chief Justice.

Mechanics' Institute Lectures.

Almost all the lectures which I had heard in my youth at the close of the Fifties and the early part of the Sixties were in connection with the Bombay (now Sir Sassoon) Mechanics' Institute, which was *the* literary society of Bombay, where scholars had abundant opportunities to unfold to the uninitiated knowledge's ample page "rich with the spoils of Time." Besides the two eminent Missionaries, there was the Rev. Dr. Fraser, who was for long the distinguished principal of Sir Jamsetji Jijibhoy Parsi Benevolent Institute, then located in a hired house, first in Borah Bazar Street, belonging to the great Mapla, next door to the Shravak temple, and later in subsequent years in the spacious house in Church Street known as Vicaji House, Vicaji being the great financier and banker of the Nizam during the first half of the nineteenth century. It was here that the late Mr. Dosabhoy Framji Karaka, first, and the late Mr. Mahipatram Rupram later on, read interesting papers on their travels in England and elsewhere. The lectures of Dr. Fraser were exceedingly finished and ornate. He was the father of the late Sir Andrew Fraser, who rose to be the Lieutenant-Governor of Bengal in the viceroyalty of Lord Curzon. There were lectures on scientific subjects from the pen of the professors of Grant Medical College, Dr. Giraud being very prolific. He had an excellent delivery, and was most popular with the young schoolboys and college students of the Fifties. Among professors of Elphinstone College, Sir Alexander Grant, the Principal in the early Sixties, was most famous. As the author of Aristotle's Ethics he had a European fame, and the

Town Hall was always thronged to hear his lectures. Dr. Sinclair, Professor of Mathematics, was another. Then there was Mr. Craig, a handsome-looking personage, very coy and dandy, who then edited the "Daily Telegraph and Courier." His lectures, too, were exceedingly finished and ornate. Lastly, one can never forget the lecture on "Thall Ghat" delivered by that great genius, Mr. Berkley, among the early railway engineers of the Fifties in the service of the Great Indian Peninsula Railway Company. I have a very vivid recollection of that talented engineer and of his eloquence which was the theme of universal praise. It was a thrilling narrative of what that great railway engineer had accomplished in the way of tunnelling the two Ghats and the innumerable difficulties he had to surmount. Those tunnels are a permanent monument of his engineering skill and ingenuity. But he was also a most accomplished literary artist. Where are men of such intellectual calibre and talents to-day, and where may be the literary activity of a high order in these utilitarian days? Alas, nowhere; the professors are all for saving money so as to retire to their native homes on good pensions in the very prime of their lives. As we have boy civilians, we have mostly boy professors at our art colleges. No doubt there are exceptions. But gone, gone, is the generation of those stalwart literary men under whom we had our instruction in and out of the college. The worship of Mammon has smothered all literary activity in Bombay, which, though first in commerce and industry, is the very last in scholarship.

CHAPTER XIII.—THE HISTORICAL PROCLAMATION OF 1858 AND THE UNIQUE DIWALI OF 1864. THE BEGINNING OF HEALTHY SOCIAL REFORM AMONG PARSIS.

ONE important historical fact in the Fifties in connection with the Town Hall should not be omitted from mention here. The Queen's gracious Proclamation of 1858 was proclaimed on the 1st November of that year from the topmost steps of the great civic hall. Immense crowds had gathered on the road, while the steps were thronged by a variety of officials and notables. Lord Elphinstone, the Governor, who had steered his bark through the troublous days of 1857 with consummate statesmanship and unceasing watchfulness, was on the topmost steps surrounded by his Council, the judges, the great civil and military officers and almost all the well-known citizens, European and Indian. The proclamation was read amidst all the pomp and pageantry of state then available. Being an eye-witness of that great historical ceremonial, it much impressed my youthful memory. Methinks I recall even to-day as vividly as I can the scene that presented itself to my gaze on the evening of First November 1858. There was the temporary flagstaff planted at the foot of the steps on the road on the south which leads to the Custom House. The ceremony began with a magnificent flourish of trumpets. Who read the English part I cannot say ; but I have a vivid remembrance that Mr. Vinayak Wassooe dev, the Oriental Translator, whose face was not unfamiliar to me, read the vernacular translation. As soon as the reading was over a salvo of royal salut-thundered forth from the adjacent battery, while the Union Jack was hoisted.

Unfortunately it happened by some inadvertence to have been hoisted upside down, which created quite a loud murmur in the crowd of which I was an humble unit, and scarcely conscious of the great political evolution in British rule that, that ceremony presaged. But the elderly crowd was heard to say that the hoisting of the flag the wrong way was a sign of ill-omen. But ill-omen or good-omen the flag was immediately lowered and was up in a few seconds on the topmast in the right way, midst the thunderous clapping of hands, and the hurrahs and the huzzas of the crowd, the soldiers, mingling with the crowd to the solemn but stately strains of "God save our Gracious Queen."

An Evening of Rejoicing.

The evening was an evening of great rejoicings. There were brilliant illuminations in the town. The effect was doubly heightened by reason of our being then in the midst of our Diwali holidays. But nowhere was there a more blazing show than in Churchgate Street, and at the town residence in the Fort of the first Indian baronet, Sir Jamsetji Jeejeebhoy, of great philanthropic renown. In Churchgate Street, in the absence of gas, which was not visible till eight years afterwards, it was one vast festoon, at short intervals of huge chandeliers, lighted with thousands of candles interlaced with Argand and a large variety of globe lamps, the largest stock, perhaps, ever exhibited between Churchgate and the Cathedral. Thousands upon thousands of persons, men, women and children, moved about in crowds, a perfect sea of all kinds of turbans, saris of rainbow colours, and what not, to view the illuminations. It was indeed a rare sight which was greatly enjoyed. And the enjoyment seemed to have been greatly heightened by the fact that the old order of the East India Company's Raj had passed away, and a new order of "Rani ka Raj" had that day been firmly established through the length and breadth of the land. And next to the name of good Queen Victoria (she was not yet Empress) the other which was heard most loudly was that of the great Earl Canning, than whom no other Governor-General had borne the brunt and heat of the troublous eighteen months during which the fate of the great Empire trembled in the balance. "Lat Canning" was a household word and associated with everything that was calm, patient, sober and merciful. The few vernacular papers of the day published in the town had made his great career as a statesman known to the populace, and there was nothing but unstinted admiration for him as the Governor-General who was the saviour of India. "Clemency" Canning may be the name he eanred among a section of the hot-headed and unrestrained class of Europeans, but it was a name of the deepest reverence, esteem and regard among the Indians.

Queen Victoria's Long Reign.

But who thought among the vast crowd that had gathered on 1st November 1858, before the Town Hall, that there would be celebrated twice in the same place, with even greater pomp and parade, with a higher consciousness of the beneficence of British rule, twenty-nine and thirty-nine years afterwards when the Jubilee and the Diamond Jubilee of the brilliant and most prosperous reign of Victoria, the Queen-Empress, the "Maharani." were respectively celebrated. Such indeed is the whirligig of time, and such sometimes are scenes of great historical events repeated. A Diamond Jubilee of a reigning sovereign is indeed the rarest of rare episodes, and happy is the nation and the people who are fortunate to witness it. In the long roll of English Kings and Queens the reign of Victoria alone lasted 64 years to enable her people to rejoice in her Jubilee first, and her Diamond Jubilee ten years later. By a lucky and happy incident it happened that I was in London on the occasion of the Diamond Jubilee in 1897, and had the satisfaction of participating in the rejoicings there, apart from having a glimpse of the great Queen for the first and last time in my life. But that glimpse had been a long and lasting one, as the long, long and brilliant pageant slowly passed in its stateliness by London Bridge. But no more of these recent recollections.

The Diwali.

As already stated, the Diwali of 1858 happily came in the midst of the Proclamation rejoicings. But it need not

crowds not so numerous and enthusiastic as we have been accustomed to since those days, when, thanks to the railways, thousands sojourn in this great city, of commerce and industry from all parts of the Presidency. Bombay has established the reputation of being the facile princeps of all great Indian cities in the matter of Diwali illuminations. None can approach her; not even the "City of Palaces." No, the "City of Palms and Palaces" is the only city in all India which presents such picturesqueness on a Diwali day, and adds to the brightness and joyousness of the occasion. Nowhere is the Hindu new year celebrated with such eclat. As such it is a unique presentation, this Oriental illumination to the Occidental.

The Finest Diwali.

But Bombay went on vastly improving since 1858, so that when the share speculation was at its giddy climax in 1863 and 1864, all Bombay presented a wondrous-sight to the stranger. Never was she so widely ablaze from Colaba to Mahim as in those halcyon days when Premchand Roychand was the King of that speculation, the Idol of multitudes, and the Great God of Gold, at whose shrine European and Indian alike paid puja. The Diwali of 1864 surpassed all. It remains unsurpassed. Nevermore could the brilliant scenes then presented be revived. Illuminations there have been on the occasion of the visit of the Duke of Edinburgh, of King Edward VII, as Prince of Wales, of King George, as Prince of Wales and King-Emperor, but never shall Bombay witness the peculiar Diwali illuminations of 1864 without gas or electricity. They were unique and had a brilliancy and originality of their own. Each owner of a shop or house illuminated his belongings according to his ability, but the pervading religious sentiment was at the bottom of them all. The sentiment of purity—purity in thought, purity in action, purity in all social relations, especially between trader and trader and merchant and merchant. Interchange of trading courtesies were common and are still continued. Indeed such amenities in trade as custom and usage from times immemorial have directed are still with us. They will continue so long as the sun and moon endure.

Inner Meaning of the Festival.

This conservative ceremonial, of the purest ray serene, is indeed a glittering gem of holidays and is admirably symbolical of the New Hindu Year. The poor, the middle class and the rich, all are pervaded by the all-inspiring and all-arresting sentiment that once a year, as Diwali comes, there should be a clean sweeping of accumulated dirt and dust, that the shop or the house should be washed and painted, so that the Goddess of Purity and Prosperity may have welcome entrance. The humblest would rejoice in having his illumination with a couple of red earthen saucers of the primitive type (called *kodia*) as the potters of thousands of years made and are still making. There should be ghee only for the purpose. The next in point of money would have oil butties in pure cocoanut oil, sometimes coloured with green or red, thus giving a diversity and shade to the glaring blaze all round. He would have *handees* or glass globe lamps, the earliest foreign importation of luxury. The *handees* if not available would be borrowed from some rich neighbour or patron. And the house would be illumined for four days with these cocoanut oil butties, white, red or green. The next higher strata would have portraits or pictures of gods and goddesses, side by side with those of Napoleon or Nelson or Queen Victoria or some great mythological hero or heroine. The gods of the Indian pantheon would be there. And midst a profuse medley of such decorations there would be Argand lamps besides globe lamps.

"What a Tamasha."

And the highest strata of society, the wealthiest, would have in addition to these, large mirrors in gilt frames, a better style of picture decorations and last though not the least, all shades of chandeliers. The Bohemian or Venetian glassware was the pride of the rich, and he who hung in his hall or *pedhee* the largest number of these decorated by the glittering prismatic drops, was esteemed as a man of great riches. There would be also by way of foreign novelty a musical or dramatic clock with soft chimes and other mechanical devices. Mechanical toys, too, of foreign origin would be exhibited with the greatest gusto. Crowds would stand

and gaze at the blazing illuminations, and hear the music so novel to their ears. You could read on the face of those innocent persons, a bewildering amazement. And when they would reluctantly move on they would be heard saying "Waha, waha, kia tamasha." As commerce increased the richer classes imported Brussels carpets and many other knicknacks to adorn their halls. In the Fort, Bazargate Street was literally ablaze with thousands of lights from globe lamps, Argand lamps and chandeliers, and the most notable and famous place of such illuminations were the *pedhies* of Jewraj Baloo, Khatao Makanji, Goculdas Tejpal and Ebrahim Nooroodin, a rich Borah trading with China. The old and venerable firm of Atmaram Bhookhan, the great bankers in inland exchanges, otherwise known as "Kaka Parakh" as also one of such places. Next was the Holee Chackla and the old Mody Street.

All these three were streets where resided the wealthiest Bhatias. The Parsi shopkeepers and those wealthy people who had houses in the street were not a whit backward in their illuminations, and no house was better admired in Bazargate Street than that of "Homla Pastagia," opposite the old Manockjee Sett's Agiary, now adorned with winged Assyrian bulls. Messrs. Pestonji Hirji and Company were rich China merchants, and had some excellent Chinese pictures which were unfurled during Diwali and the better class of the crowd allowed an entrance to the house to have a view of them. Next Borah Bazar and Parsi Bazar, with their large number of Bania shopkeepers were in evidence. And as to Kalbadevi, Mandvi and Sheik Memmon Streets, they were almost as impassable in the Fifties as they are to-day. But the Dewali of 1863 and 1864 remains to this day unsurpassed in magnificence. People literally rolled in wealth, and that wealth was seen in the streets and on the persons who thronged the streets. Silver and gold were to be seen by way of ornaments in profusion, so that really even a Belshazzar might have envied that Diwali. And though all illuminations were put off after 12 midnight, it is an absolute fact that the sightseers, even from the distant mofussil, were so many that they tarried long during the Diwali of 1864 till 3 a. m. of the next morning. Indeed night was turned into day, and that without the aid of gas or electricity.

A Social Consequence.

One social consequence of that memorable Diwali specially dedicated to the financial genius of Mr. Premchand Roychand was the number of women of all classes, specially the Parsi, who turned out in their hundreds in the streets, either on foot or in open carriages! That was a phenomenon which was not allowed to pass unnoticed in the vernacular Press, notably the *Rast Goftar*—which was the special organ of the social reformers and founded by Mr. Dadabhoy Nowrojee and his friends, with those pioneers of social reform, the Kamas. Parsi women of the better class used to go about in their carriages, mostly shigrams with the venetian windows closed. They used to peep, like their purdah sisters, through the venetians. But the Diwali of 1864 changed it all. They went about driving in open carriages, a movement first faintly witnessed on the day of the illuminations celebrated on the great Proclamation Day. Thus it sometimes happens in India that a signal auspicious event, like the Proclamation or the advent of a Royal personage, or a special Fancy Fair, has the mighty influence of breaking through old, obsolete and conservative custom, and that spontaneously without the artificial crutches of leaflets, sermons, and what not from the social reformers. Such events break down the barriers of old customs as not even the greatest of reformers could possibly break. But the long, long and glowing Diwali processions of 1864 have faded and receded into twilight. They have, however, not faded from the memory of the writer, who sighs and yearns for another bright hour of that golden and picturesque era. Long live the Diwali of our Hindu friends. May it ever shine bright and bring peace and prosperity to all. Christmas like it comes once a year, but brings with it not only good cheer but Peace and Goodwill. May the Diwali of 1919 be the glad harbinger of joy to the entire civilised world, and may it usher in an era of prolonged peace to afflicted and mourning humanity.

Chapter XIV.—THE CUSTOMS HOUSE. THE TOWN BARRACKS. THE FIRST MUSEUM ESTABLISHED BY Dr. BUIST AND Dr. BIRDWOOD.

A Customs House is the most essential auxiliary to a government. We may trace its origin to the most ancient usage of levying tolls at *naka* or radiating centre, for purposes of obtaining revenue. No organised government, however primitive or rude, can exist without raising the wind from those who must trade or barter and be afforded protection of their commodities. He must have been a man of resource who first devised the toll system which if closely looked into, is based on equity. The trader or the rudimentary barterer has to dispose of his cattle or food-stuffs or commodities, be they for domestic utility or for the purposes of indulging in luxury. He must have means of communication for conveying them from the place of production to the place of distribution or market. That communication, be it a road or some kind of a ferry, has to be built or maintained. It has to be kept in a condition of tolerable repairs. More, when the goods enter the village or town they have to be protected from thieves, which demands watchmen. Thus expenses have to be incurred. And it is but fair that the user of the road and the trader whose goods have to be safeguarded should pay for those expenses. Accordingly it came to pass that tolls came into vogue almost everywhere. In India the toll system has been exceedingly old, and no prince brought it to greater perfection than Chandragupta over 2,000 years ago. Of course as population and trade grew, specially with foreign countries, the tolls became more profitable. At the same time the collection of goods brought in from abroad or exported outside, became essential. The levy of the customs dues rendered it summary that goods imported or exported or both should pass through a single door where the toll could be collected. There could be no ingress or egress without paying the dues. The place or house where the dues had to be paid came to be called "Customs House." It was obvious that it should be cheek by jowl with the harbour or landing place.

The Bombay Customs House.

Our own Customs House, where it is presently situated is at least 150 years old. In the main its features have not altered since it was first built. There is a little history of it. In 1668, the Customs House of Bombay was situated in the Town Barracks, in the Fort, near the Mody Bay. But by 1714, that is 50 years afterwards, it was found incommodious and a house had to be built.

It was brought near the very edge of what was called the "Town Bunder," a name still in vogue. There is a very old marble slab proclaiming the construction. The bunder itself, however, has undergone three improvements during the nineteenth century, the first having taken place as early as 1802. In the Fifties the Customs House was a large straggling place, but was always crowded by a variety of persons, the lascars of the boats which came alongside the bunder, the coolies who hauled goods up and down, the muccadams who cleared the goods, the chittiwallas who properly made out import and export manifests, the middleman and the smaller class of traders. Entering the main gate and reaching the edge of the bunder you saw hundreds of native craft hustling each other and the crew toppling or vociferating. The same scene is presented to-day except this that, despite the docks, the crowds are larger. All the clerical offices were situated below while the chittiwallas drove a roaring trade. And most of the half-a-dozen Assistant Commissioners had also their respective offices on the ground floor.

Popular Officials.

The Assistant Commissioners were most popular and well-known. There were Messrs. Faulkners Silva, Mehrjibhoy Bapuji Vicaji and Ramchandra Laxmanji of the Bhau Rasool family. Sometimes my youthful curiosity prompted me to accompany my father who, in connection with his Aden business, had a good deal to do with those amiable and obliging officials. Mr. Faulkner was a man of great humour, very courteous and evidently bent on pleasing those who came to him on business. He made it a point that no needless friction existed between him and the traders. Faulkner, it is said, made his " big pile " during the prosperous days of the share mania. Being extremely canny, he soon after retired, being one of the few Assistant Commissioners who escaped the aftermath. Messrs. Souza and Silva were equally amiable and did their work so well as to elicit the praise of their superiors. So, too, Mr. Meherjibhoy, who was a son of the great Bapuji Mehrji Vicaji, banker to the Nizam. His firm came to grief in 1848 and had to go into insolvency. So Bapuji's sons had to seek employment. Mr. Mehrji joined the Customs, while another brother, Mr. Hormasji, was provided with an assessorship in the Municipality in 1865 Mr. Mehrji was not only popular and obliging with the traders, but also with the members of his own community, He was a bit of a dandy, and the only Parsi who used to wear gloves of an evening at the Bandstand where he was a regular frequenter. Indeed he seemed to us younger folk quite an institution there. He was go-ahead, and a social reformer. In the Fifties there was one Mr. Spooner, a Civilian, who was Chief Commissioner of Customs—a middle-aged personage, somewhat short, lame, but keen in stimulating trade and devising facilities for helping commerce. In the olden days, at the commencement of the nineteenth century, the Covenanted Clerks of the East India Company who lived in the town had been accommodated with apartments on the first floor of the Customs House. Even Mr. Kinloch Forbes, the talented author of "Ras Mala," who rose to be a distinguished judge of the Appellate Side of the Supreme Court of Judicature, was said to have lived in one of the apartments during his early career.

Older than the Town Hall.

In 1895 the Customs House underwent some outward transformation by way of a good stone porch. Another storey was added to accommodate other under offices connected with the growing work of the Customs House. Some good changes were made during the Commissionership of Mr. (afterwards Sir Charles) Pritchard. Thus the Customs House may be said to have stood where it was a hundred and fifty years ago. It was a fine specimen of an old-fashioned public building constructed for the special purpose designed. As such it is older than the next door Town Hall, though not so old as the Town Barracks which are, indeed, a monument of the skill of the architect and builder of the seventeenth century. Your "sanitary" barracks of the day may be better in some ways, but it will be readily recognised that nothing can approach these barracks even to-day, though they have been for the last seventy years put altogether to a different purpose. The Castle and the Barracks are twins and the oldest relics of the Bombay of the seventeenth century after its acquisition which, as antiquarians tell us, was not acquired without much travail some seven years after the date of the marriage of Charles II. The Portuguese administrator of the day was so unwilling to part with the island, that he brought forward a variety of objections when the Earl of Marlborough in 1662 first came with his warship, and four other ships, to demand the cession of the island in the name of his sovereign.

The Town Barracks.

But a few words more may be said about these Town Barracks. They are a solid piece of masonry, exceedingly rare and hardly to be found in the city, save the earliest basin of the Bombay Dockyard, which the Portuguese had built in the middle of the sixteenth century. These barracks are approached by their main westerly entrance, fronting the Bazargate Street, and you stand at once in the midst of a spacious quadrangle. On the right and left of the entrance gates are a flight of steps which lead to the top floors. The ground floor on its three sides within the quadrangle has many rooms where one European regiment, generally belonging to the East India Company, was located, it being unsuited to the soldiers of British force, who were always lodged at Colaba. It may be observed here that the European soldiery all over India was divided in the fifties, prior to the Queen's proclamation of 1858, into two, the troops exclusively recruited by the East India Company in this country and maintained at its expense, and the troops brought here on service from the United Kingdom. The E. I. European soldiery was mostly of Eurasians, or " half-caste " as they were called. These were allowed to marry Eurasian or even Indian women. The married were generally accommodated in another block, equally substantial on the opposite side of the road. These barracks for the married soldiers had thus its facing eastward and its back to the west over-looking Homji Street, better known as Byramji Homji Lane which turns into Gunbow Road in the north.

East India Company's Soldiers.

These E. I. Company soldiers of all branches, infantry, artillery and cavalry, were fine men, but they were in marked contrast with the ruddy, sturdy folk on service from Great Britain. One vice was most prominent in them—insobriety! In my youth, in the fifties, I used to witness many a drunken brawl in Bazargate Street, almost once a week. And when these kept company with the jolly fraternity of the mercantile ships "on a spree" in the town, it was a sight to terrify all timid folk, specially the small bania shopkeepers in Gunbow and Bazargate Streets who vended groceries, including tea, sugar and coffee. In a brawl one had to run up for protection to these shops, for they always ran amok, these tipsy soldiers, among the passers-by. In those days the police was scarce, and more or less the one patrolling would take to his heels. There were a few sturdy Parsi shopkeepers, licensed liquor sellers. These were the men who were brave enough to intervene, and bring to an end the quarrel and carry the besotted soldiers home peacefully. There were two such young fellows of great intrepidity and courage who would seize the strongest brawler by the neck and tame him down as a bear-leader could tame his playing bear. One of the two brothers is still alive and living in retirement at Deolali and is still known by the name of "Makoo Sailor."

Old and Venerated Names.

They are talking of lofty and ventilated rooms in modern barracks, but one had just to look at the ground floor rooms of the Town Barracks in the fifties to be convinced how fairly lofty they were, and how cool and pleasant they must have been. There was adjoining the married quarters in the south a mess house, a fine one-storied building which for years served as the "Shipping Office" after the Town Barracks were put to a different use. This building also may be said, along with another of the same character used for stores in the adjoining lane, still known as Military Store Lane, to be old, possibly co-eval with the Barracks themselves. I remember well that in 1856 Dr. Buist, the well known scientist and editor of the "Bombay Times," had with great efforts opened a "museum" the very first of its kind in the city, and I had, with my other school fellows, the pleasure of being sent out to view it. If I remember rightly the late Sir George Birdwood was the co-adjutor or lieutenant. One heaves a deep sigh when recalling such old and venerated names of our early youth. The name of Dr. Buist was well known in the literary and scientific circles of Bombay, and was everywhere respected till his rabid diatribes against the whole Indian community in the columns of his paper during the darkest days of 1857, alienated the sympathy of all good men and true, European and Indian. The proprietors of the "Bombay Times," who were almost all Indians, had had to ask him to resign the editorship which then passed into the hands of that " Bayard of Anglo-Indian Journalism," Robert Knight, of the greatest journalistic purity and sterling independence. Dr. Buist later on started on his own hook, the " Bombay Standard," but for want of support it was eventually amalgamated, after a brief existence, with the " Bombay Times." The paper was then called "The Bombay Times and Standard" which was eventually christened The "Times of India." Sir George Birdwood whose death at a great ago occurred in June 1917, was very active with his unceasing literary penchant. Perhaps, none was more competent to write a local history of Bombay of the latter fifties than he, who was then Professor of Materia Medica in the Grant Medical College. Sir George was a personage of the strongest likes and dislikes. But be his opinions on Indian problems what they may, Sir George's deep and abiding sympathy for India, and his warm love for the Indian people, were too well known to require any eulogy here. He was one of our few Indian antiquarians, and many are they who have profited by his antiquarian contributions on India to the pages of the Journal of the Society of Arts. His scholarly and illuminating writings deserve a niche in the Indian temple of fame, and no place is worthier to cherish and preserve those writings than the Bombay branch of the Royal Asiatic Society, of which he was a most conspicuous member, and for many years its indefatigable secretary. But one again sighs and inquires where are men of the type of Buists and George Birdwoods ? Echo answers "Where" ? It is, however, gratifying to add that a few short years before his death Sir George himself published his writings selected by himself, entitled 'Sva' which has had such a great run in London among scholars.

APOLLO GATE, 1864.

CHAPTER XV.—THE DOCKYARD AND THE WADIAS—THE GREAT PARSI MASTER-BUILDERS.

THE Castle and the Cathedral, the Custom House and the Town Barracks are not the only landmarks of old Bombay beyond a century. There is the Dockyard, a venerable edifice which, perhaps even better than the Customs House, is an admirable monument of historic evolution. The Castle and the Cathedral do not give us evidence of the entire chain of old history, linking three centuries almost as the Dockyard. The two former have a past of their own, but that past is in no way linked with the living present. The sacred edifice in Church Street has now only a purely antiquarian interest. And the history of the Castle also suffers from want of modernity. Not so the Customs House and the Dockyard.

From a mere insignificant toll-place in an eastern corner of the Fort overlooking Mody Bay, the Custom House has by slow degrees taken giant strides till we can step by step trace how it has kept pace with the march of our foreign trade. It has a continuous history of its own from 1662 to date, and one can clearly mark each stage of its progressive development. It links the trade of the Honourable the East India Company in the seventeenth century with that of His Majesty King George V. by the Grace of God, King-Emperor of India, at the opening of the twentieth century. So, too, the Dockyard in the Fort. In a way, it has even a more ancient lineage than the sister Customs House, seeing that we owe its first rudimentary or protoplasmic existence to those sturdy navigators who in the West founded under the intrepid Columbus, what we call the "New World."

First Portuguese Anchorage.

It is recorded that as far back as the sixteenth century the Portuguese had selected the Eastern Mody Bay as a place of safe anchorage not only for the native craft but for all foreign vessels from Europe and elsewhere. In 1531, the Portuguese Viceroy of Goa, Nuno de Cunha, selected it as the rendezvous of his fleet against the island of Div. Since that date, now nearly four hundred years, the little basin has extended and extended till to-day it forms a magnificent maritime area for naval and mercantile vessels for a variety of purposes. It is the only dry dock in Bombay, but of supreme value and importance to the British Government. The original place of the tiny dock is said to have been a mud basin situated on the present site known as the Middle and the Lower Bombay Docks. But for nearly two hundred years little or no improvement by way of extension and equipment was known, though the early administrators of Bombay, after her acquisition in 1666, had often emphasised the importance and expediency of such. At last in 1748, the first step was taken towards the construction of a proper dock on the original site of the mud basin and 1750 saw its completion. It was an historical event, this construction, as it was the first dry dock built in India. It is known by the name of the Upper Bombay Dock. Thereafter extension after extension proceeded from time to time as the exigencies of the E. I. Company and the Home Government demanded. These various extensions taken in quick succession from 1750, have each a name of their own, which thus brings to one's mind the diverse stages of the evolution of the historic Bombay Dockyard. Mr. Edwardes, in his description of it in the revised "Bombay Gazetteer," speaks of it as "the boast of Bombay and the wonder of travellers" at that period. Things went on slowly afterwards, though Admiral Hornby is said to have urged a most extensive construction in 1784.

A Man-of-war Ordered.

Circumlocution and dilatoriness, the bane of all administrations, were, however, in the way, and it was not till 1804 that the Court of Directors sanctioned the building of a man-of-war of 74 guns. They had to look round where else a ship of that magnitude, a great one in those days, could be well built. They surveyed Butcher Island and Colaba, but eventually came back to the same old and safe anchorage first selected by the Portuguese Viceroy. Lieutenant Crozier was ordered to build a new dockyard, and at the same time a second new one was also ordered. Captain Cowper brought about their completion and they were christened after Governor Jonathan Duncan. They are even to-day known as the Upper Duncan Docks. In the middle, however, of the eighteenth century the docks were so far growing in space that marine officers, seamen, etc., were quartered in the enclosure. and even a jail was erected.

In the fifties the Dockyard was a very important place and one of the sights of Bombay, which neither a local citizen nor a stranger from without could omit to view. The entrance gate originally built in 1798, along with the clock tower, was the same, the one fronting Marine Street just opposite "Hornby House," now the Great Western Hotel. I remember well having in company with some of my college fellows paid a visit in 1858 to the then dockyard which took nearly three hours looking round here, there and everywhere.

Extensive Improvements.

But the Dockyard of to-day had during the last half a century undergone many extensive improvements and additions at a cost of several lakhs of Rupees. New exigencies of the State and the opening of the Suez Canal have been most instrumental in bringing about these. Modern naval warfare has been steadily progressing and the progress of the Dockyard has excellently kept pace with it. It is really a first place of naval arms. The southerly part of the docks has undergone the greatest changes, so much so that one hardly is aware that the present Sailors' Home and the Yacht Club once formed part of it. Similarly, it should be remembered, that what is now known as the Cooperage formed part of the area of the old dockyard. Here coopers used to do all the needed work in connection with shipping appliances, and so forth. Similarly, the place known as Ropewalk, in Rampart Row, west, was a large place where all the work in connection with the ropings of the naval fleet were done from the earliest days of the E. I. Company in the seventeenth century. It is lucky that these names continue to recall to our memory old sites used for specific purposes, but which know them no more, and the whirligig of time has made other dispensations. It may be truly said, therefore, that there is no place in the entire island of Bombay which is as old as the Dockyard and which is such a connecting link between the dead past and the living present. In the fifties there was Commodore Sir Henry Leeke as the senior naval officer, and our youthful glee was always great when it was announced in the papers that the Commodore's band would play at the Bandstand—not the same place where it has been re-erected since 1867—

but just near the spot where the College of Science now stands.

The Managing Committee of the Yacht Club can show the place where former Governors and other distinguished personages were landed on their arrival. And we distinctly remember that even so late as 1872, when Lord Northbrooke arrived in Bombay to assume his exalted office of Viceroy and Governor-General, he was landed at the historic landing place, and was driven thence by the road which reaches the western gate of the bungalow, for many years in the occupation of the Director of Indian Marine for the time being. Here also was landed King Edward VII when he first visited India as Prince of Wales in 1875. Perhaps no public building in Bombay has so long been associated as many as four hundred years with the many momentous and historical events, whether in connection with India herself or with Great Britain and Europe, as the Bombay Dockyard. From His Excellency Nuno Cunha, the Portuguese Viceroy of Goa, to the days of His Excellency Lord Hardinge, it has a glorious history by itself, of which Bombay should be proud.

Parsi Master-Builders.

Here began the career of the construction of the naval men-of-war, not only on behalf of the E. I. Company, but the Admiralty itself. And luckily for the Company they found in the Wadias a succession of master-builders, Parsis, such as no other part of India has ever known. It was in 1735 that the first master-builder, Mr. Lowji Nusserwanji Wadia, was engaged, having been brought down from Surat. The family seemed to have a genius for the art of building ships, and that of a most durable type, many of them having survived 100 years. This Mr. Lowji Wadia was highly respected, and such were his valuable services that when he retired in 1773 the grateful E. I. Company richly pensioned him and showered many favours including those of royalty, which are still the heirlooms of that distinguished family of master-builders. An immense area of ground at Parel, near the old Government House, was presented to him, and the family mansion on the summit of the slope still bears the name of "Lowji Castle," where in days of yore there used to be given brilliant entertainments whereat all the beauty and fashion of the city assembled together. The family was well-known for its hospitality, and the last dispenser of it was the late Mr. Ardeshir Hormusji Wadia, who so successfully carried on the firm of Messrs. B. and A. Hormusji and Company till the exchange speculation of a colossal but heedless character by his second son brought the highly esteemed firm of a century's standing to inexplicable grief. But it is a satisfaction to notice that two younger brothers have greatly retrieved the fortunes of the family by their connection with the cotton industry, namely Messrs. Jamsetji and Pestonji. Next to the founder of the family he who was most popularly known to the generation of the fifties was Mr. Nowroji Jamsetji Wadia, who was a contemporary of the first Parsi baronet, Sir Jamsetji Jeejeebhoy. Every Parsi child knows Nowroji Wadia's house in Cowasji Patel Street. He died full of years and honours and was succeeded in the post of master-builder by his son, the late Mr. Jehangir. Another distinguished one was Mr. Jamshedji Dhunjibhoy. Indeed he was the last of the master-builders as the office was abolished in 1880 or thereabouts.

An Extensive Family.

But the Wadias are an extensive family, each branch of which has its own talented scion. For instance, there was

Jehangir Wadia, he who extensively traded with France and assisted that country after the time of the intended invasion of India by Napoleon Bounaparte. His grandson was the late Mr. Nowroji Manekji Wadia, C.I.E., the millionaire who has bequeathed his whole fortune for purposes of catholic philanthropy, the like of which was never before known in all India. Mr. Hormusji Bomanji Wadia was also a name to be conjured with in his business relations with the great banking firm of Messrs. Forbes and Company, at whose head was the distinguished Sir Charles Forbes, whose statue adorns a conspicuous niche in our local Temple of Fame, the Town Hall. Lastly, there was that great merchant prince, the late Mr. Dadabhoy Wadia, who once owned more than half of the suburbs of Parel including the most valuable property, still known as 'Lal Bag,' which is now in the occupation of the Jamsetji

Nusserwanji Petit Parsi Orphanage. His father, Mr. Pestonji, was a most influential personage at Government House, and highly respected, and whose loyalty had made him markedly conspicuous in a riot known as the " dog riot." This Mr. Dadabhoy Wadia owned that magnificent house in Parsi Bazar Street which, since he came to grief in 1851—was purchased by the firm of Messrs. Graham and Company. Mr. Dadabhoy lived to a good old age, and died about twenty-five years ago. Both politically and commercially the Wadias have carved out a name and fame in Bombay which is associated with her early history and development.

The First Indian Expedition known as the Malta Expedition.

Coming back to the Bombay Dockyard, it may be useful to know that it was as much a scene of busy activity as it is at the present juncture, in the year 1878 when the first expedition of Indian troops to Europe was sent. It was during the sanguinary hostilities between the Turks and the Russians in 1876—78 that Benjamin Disraeli, ever oriental in imagination, astonished the world of Europe by sending for an Indian contingent to Malta to assist in the demonstration which was then contemplated to take place at the Dardanelles. Indian troops had no doubt been sent to Egypt in 1798, during the Napoleonic tyranny, and when that country was threatened. And a contingent of ten thousand was sent in 1867-68 to Abyssinia under the command of Sir Robert (afterwards Lord) Napier of Magdala, of Sind fame, to bring to book King Theodore who had absurdly and capriciously imprisoned her Brittanic Majesty's Consul, Mr. Cameron. Three Indian officers, Dr. Julius Blanc of the 15th Native Infantry, Capt. W. F. Priedaux of the same regiment and

Mr. Hormuzd Rassam, the First Assistant Political Resident at Aden, were sent on an embassy to that King to release the Consul from his captivity. But the infatuated King imprisoned the whole mission. But till 1878 no Indian troops had been despatched beyond Suez in European waters till Sir Richard Temple organised the expedition. It was a sight to see the bustle and activity at the Dockyard during that eventful period, and how thousands used to throng from day to day before the Dockyard entrance in Marine Street to see the cavalry and infantry which were then being embarked. The Prince's Dock was under construction and not completed till 1880 when Lord Lytton opened it, sailing in the "Himalaya" just as on 21st March 1915 Lord Hardinge sailed in the "Lhassa" to open the Alexandra Docks. But in 1878 Sir Richard was the very personification of a civilian Governor and chief military administrator rolled into one. He was proud of his great achievement, specially as he always, likened himself to Louis Napoleon, as the dictator or Caesar in his palmiest days at the French capital. So here we bring to a close the history of the Bombay Dockyard, which is so intimately associated with the civil, military and naval history of England and India from the seventeenth century downwards. May the Dockyard ever flourish as the historic naval yard for all India till the sun and moon endure, and may the Union Jack ever flutter in the breeze at the summit of the great clock tower, itself a century old and more.

CHAPTER XVI.—THE EVOLUTION OF THE POST OFFICE.

THE Post is an ancient institution and History points to the Persian Empire of old as the original seat of conveyance of correspondence with post-haste or celerity from town to town and country to country by means of foot and horse messengers. The art of riding was certainly one of the established military institutions of that ancient and historical kingdom over which once ruled Darius and Xerxes. Riding and shooting went together as physical exercises, while truth was inculcated as an indispensable moral lesson for each and every Persian from infancy. Thus riding being as the breath of their nostrils, it is quite intelligible how those once masters of all Asia, were keen to establish from the military point of view what we may call the primitive postal organisation. A relay of swift horses could achieve wonders in a military campaign. Ambassadorial missions to distant royalties, even to "Chin" and "Maha Chin" that is, Hither China and Thither China where, reigned "The Son of Heaven" would inform us how from the military post grew the civil post. In India it may be said that the post as an institution was well organised by the Great Mogul. It is well known how correspondence to distant Kabul and Bamian and even to Aleppo and Smyrna used to be carried by *Kasad* (messengers) for purposes of trade. The earliest merchant traders who humbly sued at the Court of the Great Mogul at Delhi, in the sixteenth and seventeenth centuries, for the establishment of trade relations between Western India and Europe, knew well how post was essential for purposes of commerce. Thus in the seventeenth century and even earlier, letters used to be despatched from the factory at Surat and elsewhere to Europe *via* Leghorn and Marseilles. The excellent exchange of commodities between Venice and Aleppo, thence to Cambay, Broach and Surat is well known. So the first merchantmen of the East India Trading Company of the time of Elizabeth and her successors knew well how to carry both their commerce and correspondence.

First Inland Post in India.

The first elementary inland post was established in 1688, and orders were given by the E. I. Company to their agents at Surat to have a small post office built in Bombay. Some land *paks* and ponies were ordered from Surat. The instructions of the Court of Directors were to have the letters to and fro distributed or despatched by means of confidential persons of position and property, so that no venal betrayal might occur, and that the job should be farmed out for a valuable consideration, say, £500 a year. But there was no well-ordered or well-equipped organisation till the middle of the eighteenth century. The first post office of its kind was established in 1787. The E. I. Company appointed an agent in Egypt to supervise the interchange of all letters between England and India. An armed cruiser used to be annually despatched from Calcutta, halting on its way at Madras to carry letters to Bombay and thence to Europe. The route was by the Red Sea to Suez and Alexandria. In the same year (1787) a regular Postmaster was appointed in Bombay for the purposes of establishing a periodical service between the city and Madras. He had no salary, but was remunerated for his services by being authorised to levy fees on all private letters. A delivery fee of one anna was charged on every letter delivered at the Post Office. For further transmission to Europe there was a regulated scale, single letter Rs. 2, double letter Rs. 4, treble letter Rs. 6. The charge on parcels was 4 annas per ounce. The letters were carried by messengers, four pairs of whom were posted at each Presidency Town.

But a regular General Post Office was not established till 1794, under the superintendence of one Mr. Charles Elphinstone. Fees were regulated and a closer and careful service instituted, but commanders of country vessel- were enjoined to receive no letters from Bengal or Madras save through the Postmaster. Letters from Europe were charged a fee of 4 annas for each on account of the service of the messengers employed for their distribution.

A Regular Monthly Mail.

The Napoleonic wars, however, quickened the activity of the East India

Company, and in 1798 a regular monthly mail was instituted between Bombay and London *via* the Persian Gulf. The letters of private individuals were then to be handed to the officer appointed in the Secretariat Office with a note specifying the identity of the writer. There were limits designed as to the width and length of the letters. Postage at the rate of Rs. 10 was levied on a letter weighing ¼ tola, Rs. 15 for tola and Rs. 20 for one tola.

Evolution of the Mail Service.

Thus it will be seen from the brief history of the Post Office, for which we are indebted to Mr. Edwardes' invaluable "Gazetteer," how private letters were despatched and received from Europe, how inland service was carried on and what fees were levied. The fees may appear heavy and "intolerable," to the person who has only to pay an anna now, and who gets his mail letters regularly week after week. What a revolution the century has made with the establishment of penny postage by Sir Rowland Hill and extension and universality by the late indefatigable Henniker Heaton. But it is of no use further discoursing on the narrative of the evolution of the Post Office in India Suffice to say that in 1837, the year in which Queen Victoria ascended the English throne, no general system existed. An Act was passed in that year for the establishment of public post office. Yet there was no central postal authority or uniformity of system. Even there were no postage stamps. A Commission was appointed to report on a complete organisation of inland post offices throughout India and in 1854 an Act was passed on the basis of which we are now receiving the benefits of a daily correspondence and the regularity first of fortnightly and later on of a weekly mail. And it may be taken for granted that after the great War of 1914-18 is over. India will witness the establishment of a regular bi-weekly mail service with added conveniences every way to the millions of the population who are now sending to and fro over 1,000 million letters and post cards per annum. Again. we are already on the highway to a system of aerial navigation which will practically establish a regular daily postal service. But we need not speculate on the glorious gains of aerial science, for as the poet has said, men's minds are daily widened by the process of the sun.

The Bombay Post Office.

In the fifties the Bombay Post Office was a ground floor building sandwiched between the Custom House on its north-east and the Dockyard on its south-west. In reality it was a congeric of small mean buildings. To those who have seen them and are still living to compare it with the stately and imposing structure in Fort North, near the junction of the Mint and Frere Roads, it may seem marvellous the progress in Bombay in this direction. And to tell the truth those humble congeries of small buildings never gave us the slightest idea of the world service of the Bombay Post Office even in those days. It inspired us with no lofty speculation, neither did it stimulate our imagination as to the vast strides the modern Post Office may reach. While the next door Customs House has remained almost conservative and ancient in every way, it seems a wonderful transformation the magnificent pile in Mint Road with its domes, and other architectural merits, from the straggling ground floor buildings of our youth in Marine Street in the fifties. The Dockyard, too, though internally transformed to serve all the useful purposes of a perfect place of naval arms and utilities has in the year of grace 1919, hardly undergone any radical change. It preserves outwardly its own landmarks of the fifties and the years before the eighteenth century. But the Post Office has not only changed its habitation twice, but has shot out like a gigantic or mammoth edifice within the short space of sixty years. The internal accommodation for receiving and despatching letters in those days was also so primitive as to be called antideluvian. Indeed, in those days the Post Office was deemed such a negligible public office that little or on thought was bestowed on its extension and development. How could it be when it was only a modern structure of rudimentary growth brought into existence by the first General Post Office Act of 1854? How could it be when, as already observed, we had no postage stamps, and all our letters were delivered or despatched by a farming agency? For it should be remembered that even in the fifties the farming system established one hundred and fifty years before had hardly undergone any change. In our youth we knew that a tall ruddy-looking Parsi wearing the white priestly turban, well proportioned and born to command or control, was the farmer of all inland letters on which he received the fee prescribed, in his place of business in the Fort, in the Bazargate Street, just within a stone's throw of the Wadia Clock Tower. There our post farmer used to sit squatted, as is the wont of all oriental men of business, with spectacles, perusing his own *dak* and giving instruction, to his clerks. His name was Mr. Merwanji Nowroji Postwalla, a fine type of the old stalwart Parsi priestly caste who was a near relative to the family of the great Murzbans, who had established the *Duftur Ashkara* Press and were spreading in Gujrathi excellent translations of some interesting works in English literature. The Post and the Press go together, and these twins, the Murzbans and the Postwallas rendered no mean service to trade and literature in their days. Of course, in the native town outside the Fort, there were other farmers to serve the needs of that part, but I have, not been aware of their names to rescue them from oblivion. One or two however of the tribe may still be seen plying their work at Mombadevi even now.

Sparse Letter-Writing.

Letter-writing in those days was exceedingly sparse, and the delivery and despatch could not have been extensive. Things were done leisurely, and people had hardly begun to understand the significance of the word "post-haste." The post may come of a morning, or at noon or at dewy eve. We may hand over our letters for inland towns at any hour quite innocent of the exact day when they might reach their destination. Neither were people in the town accustomed to the use of English stationery, ordinary indigenous paper or strips cut off from thin French foolscap paper served the purpose of note paper. Of course English officers and those Indian firms who had business relations with them used note paper and envelopes. But to the illiterate mass, of whom perhaps not one per cent. knew English, note paper and envelopes were taboo. The thin country paper served for writing a letter. It was rolled up like a cigar and closely gummed. And one blank space on the surface served to write the address in Gujrathi or Marathi. But the address was given superscribed with astonishing minutiæ, so that there might be no mistake as to identity of the addressee when the letter came to be delivered. It must have been an effort for the scribes employed by the postal farmer to make out the addresses correctly, for even the vernacular superscription was oftener than not written in such crooked letters that great difficulty was found in deciphering the hieroglyphics. It is not an exaggeration to observe that only one in hundred could read or write so that readers and writers on hire were not uncommon and they eked out a fair subsistence. Sometimes these men themselves had great difficulties in making out the signatures or the places whence the letters were written. Altogether the fifties was a period of visible darkness in point of reading and writing.

Hunting for the Addressee.

But what a colossal difference sixty years of education, thanks to the great Charter of 1854. have made all throughout the land. The postal delivery peon was no more than a common coolie and knew not how to read and write. If he delivered letters it was because of his familiarity with the residence of persons generally in the habit of correspondence. Otherwise it was a regular hunt to find out an addressee,—a chase which sometimes baffled those rude illiterate servants of the Post Office—itself in the embryonic stage. Bangy and parcel post were an innovation which, however beneficent, were rarely used. The sender had such a fear of using those means for the transmission of something or another to a person at even a short distance. Many indeed were the moans and groans over a miscarried bangy or parcel. The mode of transmission was for years looked upon with suspicion and considered to be almost wholly unsafe. Then, again, the Postal authorities themselves were obliged for safety's sake to issue instructions how a bangy could be made up. The meticulous directions were too much for the illiterate. It meant two or three days preliminary going up and down the Post Office to thoroughly understand the right and proper way of covering the parcel with white oil cloth, sealing it and the rest of the postal abracadabra. Indeed it was a kind of travail for the sender to undergo all the worry of despatching a small parcel.

Mails Provokingly Slow.

The Chamber of Commerce was in this respect far in advance of official opinion, and was constantly urging the authorities to reform the post office in many directions and have a fortnightly instead of a monthly mail. Many indeed were the objurgations of the commercial community in this respect, for locomotion by land and sea was provokingly slow, and during the monsoon they never could rely on any kind of punctuality in the hour and day of the arrival of what was called the over-land mail" Navigation had not been brought to perfection and the speed of the mail boats was nothing compared to that now prevailing. It took in fair weather eight days to reach Bombay from Aden and 16 or 17 from Suez! In the monsoon it might take from 15 to 16 days. The arrival of each fortnightly mail was looked forward with the greatest eagerness. On the day that it was expected, the office peons of the English firms, with a pass for early delivery at the postal window, thronged the outskirts of the Post Office, and were often detained for hours together to get their letters, since there was a weary waiting till past 9 or 10 in the night. In the monsoon it was so unsafe for the mail to be piloted, the beacon lights were not complete and the pilots had to take the greatest care to bring the boat to a safe anchorage. The mails were of course, landed at the jetty behind the Post Office, it being an extension of the adjoining town bunder. And what a long time it took to sort mails for delivery! It was only when the Apollo Bunder was improved and reclaimed and the Port Trust came into existence that the mails began to be landed there till the Ballard Pier was constructed in 1897. In short it may be said that the present day people can have no idea of the primitive organisation of the Post Office in the fifties and the immense number of difficulties it had to contend with, apart from popular inertia and the customary official redtape and circumlocution. They must consider their good fortune that, thanks to a new departure since 1880 in the matter of postal reorganisation, they are to-day so well satisfied with the efficiency of our General Post Office. Indeed no public office in India serves the people more efficiently and intelligently than the Bombay General

Post Office with its veritable "Imperial" functions. It is verily the "Literary Gate of Asia" and no mistake.

Post Office Buildings.

One more fact needs to be noticed in connection with the Bombay Post Office. From 1854 to 1866 it was located in Marine Street, sandwiched between the Custom House and the Dockyard. But it was completely burnt down in the latter year and was temporarily located on the premises now occupied by Messrs. Ralli Brothers. Meanwhile the Government had sanctioned a new Post Office building in Church Street, the same which is now converted into a Telegraph Office. It was in every way a most convenient and central place and equipped with all the postal modernities. The new premises were occupied in 1869 till the extensive requirements of the Imperial Bombay Post Office demanded vaster space and even better equipment and conveniences in harmony with the expansion of the population, the trade, and the manifold State purposes. Thus in sixty years, perhaps, no public office in Bombay, has undergone such vast strides demanded by the progressive times, as our Post Office. The evolution is indeed phenomenal and I have nothing but unqualified admiration for the great department of the State and the invaluable service it renders to all India with its 310 millions of population.

CHAPTER XVII.—THE SUPREME COURT OF JUDICATURE, SOME OF ITS MOST DISTINGUISHED JUDGES SPECIALLY SIR ERSKINE PERRY, SIR MATHEW SAUSSE AND SIR JOSEPH ARNOLD.

AMONG the great public institutions of the fifties we should not forget to make mention of our High Court. Though it is located since 1876, in its own handsome palace in Mayo Road, it had a history of its own for place prior to 1824, when for the first time it really obtained a local habitation, and the ideal of a Palace of Justice in concrete was presented to the denizens of this city. But the history of the wanderings of the judicial administration between 1670 and 1824 may be briefly noticed at this stage. That great Governor, who must for ever be credited with the honour of the earliest maker of Bombay, Gerald Aungier, intuitively apprehended during his proconsulship that Justice, in order to be administered with serenity and dignity, demanded a suitable house. But where was it to be had? At first, with Bombay a vast green, only a small room was allotted to the Justices in the Custom House buildings. The judges, in the sense we understand them, had yet to come, and nominated from Home. But there were local justices, and for a long time we had the King's Judges as distinguished from the judges appointed by the Honourable the East India Company. An account of the great war between these judiciaries may be read with interest in the life of Chief Justice Sir Edward West, published a few years ago by Mr. Drewett.

The Court's Wanderings.

The first Judge of the King was appointed in 1675, and held his Court in a hired house somewhere in the Fort. Later on a house belonging to the then Deputy Governor was bought. Part of this building is still said to exist in the Castle. As such it ought to be for ever enshrined, and an annual pilgrimage in State made to it by the whole phalanx of our judges in their robes of State. But as the fates would have it, the house was never used. So justice continued to be administered in a hired building till 1677 in what has already been described as "Mapla Pole" in Gunbow Street. The rooms set apart were also used as a Town Hall where the Court of Petty Sessions was held. There was also a prison-house attached to this place, but one cannot now identify it. Thus for well nigh half a century, say till 1720, all judicial administration was carried out there. Then a shift was made and the famous house, known as Rama Kamati's, was let for the purpose. This house was situated in Bazargate

Street, the identity of which is also unknown. In 1786, another move was made. There was the house known as "Hornby House," called after a great admiral of that name, the same which is now owned by the Great Western Hotel. In this house some rooms were provided for justice which had to flee from Bazargate. The Court was then known as the "Mayor's Court." It was two years later suggested that the Court might be removed to the unjudicial Custom House buildings; the mayors considered it as highly derogatory to their dignity that justice should be administered in a place where so much of the noise of the busy traders and the *dingi-valas* of the bunder was rife. Then came the Recorder, the first of that dignity being Sir William Sayer, who transferred his sittings to a house in Marine Street, the same where are now the bonded warehouses. Yet another transfer had to be made in 1800 owing to the great inconvenience felt by "My lords." So Hornby House came to be again occupied at a rental, and our poor wandering Justitia found a final haven in that well-known house, specially after 1824, when was established what was known as the Supreme Court of Judicature. Some of the richest traditions of law are associated with this century-old building, which by a curious fate serves now to find shelter for globe-trotters from all parts of the world! Alas! What a fall! From an awe-inspiring and solemn Court of Justice to an hotel! But such are the vicissitudes which the whirligig of time brings forth.

Great Judges.

In the fifties it was no doubt the rendezvous of all Bombay litigants. Our youthful imagination had associated it with great awe as the place *par excellence* where criminals were placed in the dock before the highly learned judges, and sentenced to long years of imprisonment in the jail or at Singapore and "Buttom Bay," a vernacular corruption of Botany Bay in Australia. Persons sentenced to penal servitude for life were all transported there. Those for a term of 14 or 20 years were sent to Singapore, and our youthful mind was greatly appalled when the news was heard in the town that the son of a highly esteemed Parsi was transported to Penang on account of some cheque forgeries for defalcations while in the fiduciary position of cashier or shroff at the now defunct Oriental Bank. He was connected with the family of the great "Shroff," of whom the late Mr. Manekji Cursetji was the most conspicuous as a judge of the Small Causes Court. In the fifties we used to hear of the names of the big judges like Sir Erskine Perry, Sir Mathew Sausse and Sir Joseph Arnold, each distinguished for his rhadamanthine impartiality in administering justice. Indeed to our young minds they struck us as the very personification of Minos and Rhadamanthus, of whom we had been reading so much in the history of ancient Greece. Sir Erskine Perry was a household word. Not only did he make a stern judge who mixed his justice with mercy. He was also known as the great friend of Bombay citizens, in whose social and educational welfare he took a deep and abiding interest. He had closely associated himself with all Indian reform movements, but the extra-judicial work by which he was chiefly known, and for which he has left a name to be remembered for generations to come, is that of education. To this he had devoted himself with a zeal, enthusiasm and singleness of purpose which are beyond all praise. In the early fifties, education in Bombay was administered by a Board or Society, of whom Sir

Erskine was no doubt the most active and independent member. Fully free from bureaucratic traditions he was able to move the springs of the educational car with courage, indefatigable energy and great sagacity. His interest in the development of higher education was unbounded, and he rejoiced as each year the Elphinstone College sent forth a handful of young men, Hindu and Parsi, as well finished scholars, able to hold their own in the world of practical life.

Mr. Dadabhai Naoroji.

Of one such we may make special mention. He was our late venerated nonogenarian, Mr. Dadabhai Naoroji. It is superfluous in this place to refer to his youthful academic career, which was brilliant. His attainments in mathematics had earned for him the professorship in that branch of science in his own college, and Mr. Dadabhai was thereafter known as "Professor" Dadabhai, a name by which he is still recalled to memory to some of his contemporaries. So great an impression was made by him on the mind of Sir Erskine Perry, and such was his broad and generous sympathy for the social and educational advancement of the Indians, that somewhere in 1853 or thereabout he had recommended some of his wealthy Parsi friends to send Mr. Dadabhai to London to qualify himself at the bar. The suggestion was soon taken up by the reforming Kamas of the day, who were great patrons of education and the pioneers of social reform; but the orthodox party were not in favour. The conversion of three or four Parsi youths to Christianity at the time had greatly alarmed the more conservative of these, and so the suggestion had to be dropped. All the same Mr. Dadabhai in 1855 found the opportunity to proceed to London as a partner in the firm of Cama and Company, the first Indian firm established there and managed purely by Parsi members. So that it happened that on his retirement to London Sir Erskine had the great satisfaction of seeing his young Professor of Elphinstone College at the counting house. They became great friends, and when Sir Erskine was made a life member of the India Council he proved of invaluable assistance to Mr. Dadabhai in all the great efforts he put forth there for the greater moral and material welfare of his countrymen. At the India Office, all through Sir Erskine's career there, Mr. Dadabhai was the most welcome Indian, such were the mutual esteem and regard in which each held the other. As a boy of seven or eight, I still remember that it was at the hands of Sir Erskine Perry that I took my first school prize as a pupil of the "Ayrton" Anglo-Vernacular School to which reference has already been made. The prize distribution took place on the floor of one of the blocks of "Punchayat Wady" as it was called, in the Fort, where the school house was situated. Perhaps no Chief Justice of the Bombay Supreme and High Court of Judicature had so closely identified himself with the educational progress of this great city as Sir Erskine, and the present generation has hardly any idea of the lasting interest he took in the matter of educational reform. His name, however, is still cherished with gratitude and is well preserved in the Professorship of Jurisprudence which was established, to perpetuate his memory, by the wealthy citizens of Bombay in the fifties. The Perry Professorship of Jurisprudence must remind our law graduates of the great name and recall to their mind with gratitude what they owe to his initiative.

Sir Charles Jackson and Michael Westropp.

Speaking of the Judges of the Supreme Court of Judicature, as was the

High Court called prior to the date of the Letters Patent of 1861, one is reminded of Sir Charles Jackson who acted as a judge for a short time. He had made himself extremely popular. And it is related that Mr. Westropp, afterwards Chief Justice Sir Michael Westropp, owed all his rise and distinction to this shrewd judge who had perceived in him in embryo all those high judicial qualifications which are now so well known. It is said that the seniors had so far monopolised the Court work that Westropp was on the point of returning to London to seek his chance there. But Sir Charles was his good fairy and pressed him to persevere. Sir Charles was a good prophet, for Michael Westropp soon after began to get good briefs and his eminent forensic talents began to be known and substantially appreciated. He rose to be Advocate General, Judge and Chief Justice of our High Court, the bench of which he adorned for many a year with his brilliant judicial qualities. Sir Charles Jackson returned to Bombay in 1869, but not to revisit the former scenes of his judicial labour. He came as the President of the old Bank of Bombay Commission, to thoroughly investigate the causes of the failure of the unfortunate institution subsequent to the great aftermath which took place on the Black Day of Bombay, *viz.*, 1st July 1865.

Sir Mathew Sausse—A Stern Judge.

In 1856 Sir Mathew Sausse was the Chief Justice. He was the very personification of all that a stern British judge of downright impartiality is and was held in awe by all practising before him. Well versed in law and equity, Sir Mathew led the even tenor of his judicial life which, it might be fairly observed, was one of self-imposed ostracism. He never mixed in society and was hardly ever seen at Government

House. His Court and his home were the two places to which he was endeared. You will not have seen a finer and nobler example of a British judge, albeit he was Irish by birth. He was unmarried, but had a fine stately figure quite befitting the solemnity, dignity and sternness of a judge. One could readily recognise him by the phaeton and pair in which he used to drive to the Court House. The carriage had a white quilted cover on it which was the distinctive sign whereby the child as well as the man in the street knew that the carriage conveyed the great Lord Chief Justice of Bombay. In those days they maintained not a little the dignity of the judge and some of the obsolete Court traditions of England. Chief Justice Sausse, as well as his puisne, Sir Joseph Arnold, had each an aide-de-camp known as the "Tipstaff," a kind of household steward. His tipstaff was one Mr. Malins, who rose afterwards to be the

Deputy Sheriff of Bombay. In the days of the old Supreme Court, and till the High Court was established in 1863, there were only two English judges, appointed directly by the Crown. The Appellate Court or as it was known as the "Sudder" Court, was located in a different building with three Civilian Judges. The Appellate Court continued to transact its judicial business in Byramji Hall at Mazgaon for many a year till the new buildings of the High Court were completed in 1879.

Sir Joseph Arnold.

Sir Joseph was a Puisne Judge in the fifties—a stout-looking gentleman, with an aldermanic paunch, a beaming and beneficent countenance, and an air and dignity which informed us that every inch he was a judge. But he was not a judge only. He was an erudite scholar, a brilliant Fellow of Wadham College, a contributor to the "Saturday

Review" of the salad days of the early fifties, a friend of the Brownings, and, last though not least, the author of a standard law book on Marine Insurance. As a judge Sir Joseph was as well-known for his stern sense of justice and impartiality as his senior and Chief. It happened that the great libel case known as the Maharaja Libel Case was heard before him. The judgment he delivered was not only just and impartial, but brilliant for the scholastic and historic lore it revealed, and otherwise so full of the spirit of social reform. And it also happened that he heard what is called the Aga Khan case. His scholarship and literary brilliancy were even more marked and those two judgments remain on the records of our High Court as a great monument of his legal and forensic ability and literary culture. He met with a domestic misfortune and afterwards shunned all society. He declined the office of Chief Justice on the retirement of Sir Mathew Sausse and himself left the Bench in 1869 midst the universal regret of the people who had revered and adored him as no other judge had been. In his latter days he used to take long walks in the Oval and afterwards at sunset to stretch himself on one of the benches on the bandstand till the chimes of the great Cathedral clock tolled 8. But he was a great admirer of the Parsi youths then much in evidence in the Oval playing cricket, long before the cricket game became popular and an institution in the city. And such was his love for the game, and such his sense of justice, that when a brawl took place between a party of Eurasian lads and Parsi youths, enraged at the way in which the police interfered, he wrote a letter to the "Times of India" upbraiding the latter and vindicating the Parsi youth in whose veins he observed ran the blood of the old Persian heroes Rustom and Jal!

Such was Sir Joseph Arnold, a type of the thorough English gentleman, polished, cultured, of high scholastic attainments, of stately dignity, broad sympathy and above all a sterling lover of the Indian people. Bombay will never see the like of him again.

CHAPTER XVIII.—THE HISTORY OF THE MINT AND COINAGE.

THOUGH the Mint is only of secondary importance relatively to the other great institutions of the fifties already described, some mention of it must be made in order to complete the syllabus of these institutions. The Mint as known in the fifties is the same building with the Doric colonnade as the one which meets the gaze of the passers-by in the Frere Road, north, on the harbour side. But this coining institution had no habitation when our far-sighted first maker of Bombay, Mr. Gerald Aungier, conceived and launched it in 1670. It was a primitive affair to coin the kind of rupees current in those days. The only other coin minted was that of copper known as the *paisa* or pice. It was located in a place now altogether unidentifiable, somewhere near the Town

Barracks. It is related by Mr. Edwardes that four specimens of the earliest rupee minted between 1665 and 1670 are deposited with the British Museum, which the curious Indian visiting that remarkable institute, a magnificent storehouse of all that is worth preservation of the ancient and modern world, may view. The location of the Mint later on for a hundred and fifty years is buried in obscurity and can only be revealed by some archæologist of the future who may be deputed by the Government of the day to ransack the ground underlying the Town Barracks and its surroundings. Meanwhile it may be more to the purpose to learn that eventually the present site was selected. But the ground (some 60,000 square yards) had first to be reclaimed in order to erect thereon a building which could be worthily called H. M.'s Mint. This was in 1823, and the building was completed in 1829 at a total cost of 36 lakhs, whereof the land cost 12½ lakhs, the building 16, and the machinery and other equipments 7½.

In the Fifties.

In the fifties the Mint occupied an extensive area, the larger part of which faced the west. All the ground which is now thrown in (at the southern end) the Frere Road, near the north-eastern extremity of the Town Hall steps, to the end of the Town Barracks in Bazargate Street, which is triangularly enclosed, and is now vested in the Improvement Trust, was part of the Mint area. Practically before 1866 there was no Frere Road. It was in that year that a road was cut through, as is to be seen to-day, up to the present Fort Market, and the prolongation of that road from there as far as the Carnac Bunder, where stands the goods terminus of the B. B. & C. I. Railway was ground reclaimed from the Mody Bay. What is called the Mint Road, from the Fort Market, in a westward direction, is also partly reclaimed ground, and partly the old narrow road adjoining what has already been described as the East Rampart Row, as far as the present new Post Office. Thus the southern part of the present Frere Road, from the Town Hall up to the Fort Market, in a line with the Bailard Pier Road was a complete *cul de sac*. The Mint was thus enclosed in the grounds known as the Castle. The site selected was the most eligible and appropriate. The projectors and builders of the Mint Building in 1824 knew what were the perils attendant on an attack from the sea by the piratical Seedies, Mahrattas and others who were even during the first quarter of the nineteenth century a dread. It was imperative that the Mint premises should lie under the shadow of the great Castle to be protected from all harm by the ponderous guns, if occasion needed.

The First Mint Master.

The first Mint Master imported from England, one Mr. Smith, must have been an exceedingly contented foreman-mechanic to come to serve here on a modest salary of £60 per annum. It may, however, be presumed that the work at the Mint in 1829 could not have been considerable. If, even in 1835, when the first Coinage Act was passed, and the rupee made legal tender, the amount coined did not exceed two crores, it must have been inconsiderable in the year the new Mint was first set going. When the Coinage Act was passed Bombay rupees, Madras rupees, Farukabad rupees and Sicca rupees were legal tender. The last was equivalent to a little more than the other descriptions of Rupees. A Bombay rupee was equal to 15/16 of the Sicca. It is a curious circumstance that, though the Governors of Bombay and Madras receive their monthly salary in rupees, they have been fixed by some antiqated enactment in Sicca rupees. Practically, therefore, these functionaries even to day teceieve something over and above 10,000 rupees. Similar is the case with the salary of the Governor-General which is also 20,000 Sicca rupees! The Sicca rupee, as a legal tender, was abolished by one of the Acts of 1836. The rupee till 1812, was known as Company's; but in that year it was by Act 13 called Government rupee. The silver imprinted in 1835 into coins of rupees, half rupees, etc., equalled 2·33 crore rupees. In 1850 the coinage amountedt o 2·61, but, as trade expanded, the coinage increased in volume. The value of silver coined in 1855 was 5·97 crores. When the American Civil War was in full swing (1861—63) India imported enormous quantities of bullion, specially in Bombay. It was the surplus profit of the immense shipments of cotton consigned to Liverpool which had to depend wholly on

Indian cotton during the war. The coinage rose from 4·67 crores in 1861-62 to 14·65 crores in 1865-66. The war ended in the spring of 1865 and when the crash of speculation in shares overtook Bombay, it began to recede. The Bombay Mint was exceedingly active and was not able to cope with the plethora of bullion tendered as the mail came, with the coinage as fast as the merchants wished, the machinery available not being equal to the task. Night was made joint labourer with the day. Rupees disappeared as soon as they came out of the Mint and it is a fact that they were scarcer at the end of 1864, when money was dear and the Bank of Bombay rate had gone up to 22 or 24 per cent.! The practice of the day was that private importers of the bullion tendered it to the Mint which passed a receipt for its value. This receipt was negotiable in the market as well as with the old exchange banks, besides the Bank of Bombay. The last holder of the receipt would present it after a fortnight or even more and get his rupees. It may be mentioned that a rupee contains ·165 grains of silver of standard fineness and 15 grains of alloy. Colonel Ballard was the Mint Master in those stirring times, the same able Royal Engineer who was afterwards the first Chairman of the Port Trust which in commemoration of his great service, named the pier at Mody Bay, the " Ballard Pier."

The Earliest Days of Coinage.

But let the writer hark back to the earliest days of Bombay, the days of the renowned Gerald Aungier and his successors. The values of the coins then were as follows :—

	s.	*d.*
A Rupee was equal to	2	6
A Seraphin equal to	1	8
A Persian Sahebi equal to	4	0
A Pagoda equal to.............	9	0

It should be remembered that the Pagoda was a Portuguese coin and the Sahebi belonged to the rule of the Moguls. There was a large number of these Persian rupees which remained in circulation well nigh up to the seventies, and there were rupees of the earliest days of the East India Company which were also stamped in Persian. These were to be seen discounted in the bazar in the native town by a large number of th petty shroffs, or properly speaking money exchangers. The rupees known to my boyhood were mostly the ones bearing the effigy of King William IV, stamped 1835, and that of Queen Victoria (without the crown) stamped 1840. The rupee with the crowned Queen was coined in 1862 for the first time, after India had in 1858 passed to the Crown. The old King William rupee, however, circulated till the eighties when it was finally withdrawn from circulatoin by a Government notification. When presented at the Currency Office or any of the Banks it was clipped and passed on to the Mint. In the fifties there were neither Pagodas nor Saraphins to be noticed. The last used to be called in Gujrathi by the name "asraphi." There was in copper coins, the pie (ardhi in Gujrathi), the paisa (3 pies) and the dhaboo or double pice equal to half an anna. The traders in the town, and even the old firms of English bankers and merchants used, at any rate till the seventies, to keep their accounts in rupees, quarters (powlas), docras (2 pies) and reis. The last may have been a coin during the occupation of the Portuguese but one had never seen it in the fifties. A hundred reis made a powla or four annas, and a hundred docras made a rupee (192 to 200 pies). Indian mental arithmetic, which is still in vogue with shopkeepers, traders and merchants in the town, and universally practised, treats of aliquot parts of currency of which the docra is still a dominant one. In reality the *docra* is a cent and would prove most efficient for accounts whenever the decimal coinage is universally established in India.

CHAPTER XIX.—MINOR PUBLIC EDIFICES AND PHILANTHROPIC INSTITUTIONS.

HAVING completed the "periplus," so to say, of the important public edifices within the Fort during the Arcadian period of the fifties of the nineteenth century, it may not be uninteresting to refer to minor buildings of social, religious or educational interest. Speaking first of the last, the Elphinstone Institution may be prominently mentioned. Originally established under the auspices of the Board of Education Society, it was, even in the fifties, popularly known as the "Society School." It was a commodious building, this Elphinstone Institution, and still stands to remind old Elphinstonians of *the* alma mater of their youth. It is no other than the existing one on the Esplanade Cross Road which is now the

Government Central Anglo-Vernacular School, a fine edifice next to where the Small Causes Court was situated till recently. It faces the east which was then a big *maidan* stretching far down to the precincts of the Fort, where stood the ramparts. It had no architectural pretensions at the period, nor has it any even to-day. But the locality where the Institution was built by the Education Society is in every way sanitary and admirably suited for its purpose. The east facing has a porch. Coming up the steps you pass a few feet along till is reached a grand staircase, broad and well lighted. It leads on the right to what was in the fifties an excellent hall which stood by itself in all its scholastic dignity and intellectual glory. Facing the hall in a northerly direction were class rooms, and also on its westerly frontage rooms for students of the college. The ground floor was divided into two big blocks or wings, one containing a series of class rooms opening into each other for the Gujrathi-speaking scholars, and the other for those speaking Marathi. There were spacious verandahs, well protected on each side of the blocks, and compounds beyond. The westerly one was a little narrower, but eminently adapted for a playground for flying kites or playing marbles and other games not demanding any wide space. In the easterly or north-easterly compound were a variety of out-houses. There were two entrances to the institution. The due northerly one with a gate was exceedingly convenient for those who came from Chandanwadi and the Kalbadevi side. The eastern one had two gates for those arriving from the Fort. The maidan opposite gave unlimited playground to the schoolboys early in the morning before school-time and at recess

The Bhistee Well.

Here and there at short distances were pucca-built wells, the gift of true philanthropists, all unknown to fame, who had endowed them for public use, want of potable drinking water being even then a dire necessity, specially in the summer season. There were also two or three wells dedicated to poor cattle. Here the *Bhistee* tribe could be seen during the livelong day filling their *pakhals* or leather bags, and laying them on the humble and patient bullock for watering and other purposes. A specially large one was known as the "Bhistee Well." The large tank known as Nacoda was not even constructed. The writer was an eye-witness to its digging some time in 1855 or 1856. In every way the site of the Elphinstone Institution was well adapted for its purpose. It is said that the ground landlord was Mr. Jugganath Sankershet, a keen educationist and a stalwart Indian member of the Education Society, which did admirable pioneer work for well nigh thirty years till the great Educational Charter of 1854 revolutionised all kinds of education in Bombay. This "Central" Institute, as it was sometimes called, not only accommodated the school but the College bearing the honoured name of Elphinstone. There were three class-rooms for the collegians, one of which was designated as the Normal Class, because scholars were trained to take duty afterwards as teachers in English, a rare professional class in those days and highly respected. One room was also allotted for imparting a knowledge of chemistry and connected with it was a miniature museum containing many botanical and geological specimens. This museum, in the fifties, was in the charge of the late Mr. Ardeshir Framji Moos, a distinguished scholar and teacher

Below the museum on the ground floor was the book depot which afterwards bloomed into a Government Central Book Depot. All text books, English and vernacular, were vended here for the convenience of the students and the schoolboys. The College was manned by three professors, one of whom was also the Principal both of School and College. In the fifties Mr. (afterwards Dr.) John Harkness of Aberdeen, was the Principal. Owing to the changes effected under Sir Charles Woods' Educational Despatch of 1854, the College was removed to a separate hired building on Babula Tank Road, exactly opposite the Grant Medical College. The bungalow which was occupied from 1856 to 1862 has been levelled to the ground, and as new modern buildings have been erected on the plot the exact locality cannot now be identified without the assistance of Laughton's Survey Map.

The Elphinstone School.

The Elphinstone Institution was then converted into Elphinstone School till the philanthropy of Sir Albert Sassoon gave it a magnificent architectural habitation, an ornament to our city, at the worth-west extremity of Cruickshank Road. The old building of the Education Society still serves the purpose of a school, nevertheless its pristine pride so well maintained for over half a century has long since gone. But it is yet deemed a hallowed building dedicated to the muse of education round which have centred many magnificent associations which are indelible. As we occasionally pass by this venerable edifice, old happy memories of our school days, our fun, our frolic, our innocent mischief, all come crowding in our mind and for the moment we feel an impulse to cross once more the gates and have a silent peep all round, like the "chief taking notes" to revive the days of old some sixty-five years back. May the edifice remain the intellectual shrine that it is for generations yet unborn.

Other Buildings.

Next to the Institution on its north-easterly side, facing the maidan, was a humble dispensary, with a few beds which served as a kind of hospital. It was a congerie of rooms on the ground floor where one Dr. Vitters dispensed medicines gratis to the poor and prescribed cures. The *hakim* in his day was well-known, and the dispensary was called the " Bombay Native Dispensary,"—a name by which it is still carried on in another and more populous, but less sanitary, part of the town. But its place of old knows it no more. The exigencies of the State had reared on its original ground a Sailors' Home till another newer home was built, opposite the Wellington fountain, in honour of the occasion of the visit of the late Duke of Edinburgh, the first scion of the royal house of the good Queen Victoria, who visited Bombay and travelled all over India in 1870. Thereafter, the building underwent some structural alterations, and was dedicated to the Bombay Volunteers. Beyond this in the east were a low range of "mochees" (shoemakers) shops, and a "pitha," or grog shop. Beyond these was the Free Church of Scotland which stood in a compound of its own with "heathen" surroundings on all sides. In all probability when this house of God was first built and consecrated, the locality was free from any kind of residential buildings, with the maidan opposite. But as population increased and trade expanded, business places shot up, the church was surrounded in the fifties by shops on both sides of it. As years rolled on, the quarter became both noisy and ill-suited for the purpose of the sacred edifice. Moreover, buildings of the State, on the maidan, like the Goculdas Tejpal Hose pital, began to rise. So at last the Church was sold, and from its proceeds a new one has been built in Waudby Road which is in every way more in harmony with the surroundings. The buildings which till late accommodated the Small Causes Court may also be briefly referred to in this place. Courts of justice, civil and criminal, in the city, superior and inferior, had had in the first halt of the nineteenth century no fitting and dignified habitations. We have already described the ups and downs and wanderings of the Supreme Court of Judicature for well nigh 150 years (till 1824) before it had a permanent edifice to conduct the administration of justice. Similarly with the Small Causes Court and the Police Courts. In the fifties, the former was located in a house adjoining the Elphinstone Institution on its north-west. But some time after, the work had so multiplied that it was essential to have another building next door to it. The late Mr. Manockji Cursetji was for long a judge of this Court and practically during the period we are now describing his name was intimately known to Marwari traders. Indeed, we may say that the Small Causes Court and Mr. Manockji were alternative terms. Judge Manockji's Court was the familiar way in which the Marwaris recognised the Small Causes Court. As scholars of the Elphinstone Institution, I and my classmates often used to enjoy their half-hour's afternoon recess in the court of this judge, who was a terror to all the usurious money-lenders who plied their suits there. We used to be greatly amused with the parley between judge and plaintiff. It was unique fun for us to pay frequent visits there.

A Revered Structure.

Framji Cowasji Institute is another building which to my boyish imagination carried great reverence, for the name of the founder of that Institute. He was a great philanthropist and venerated not only by members of his own community, but by those of the Hindu and Mahomedan. The big tank which has recently been reclaimed had stood there for upwards of three-quarters of a century. It was a tank where, they say, the dhobis used to wash dirty clothes. Some gave its origin from a dhobi who was supposed to be its original proprietor. The origin is involved in obscurity. But the *talao* or tank came to be the name of the surrounding locality, and to this day this part of the town, abutting on the north of the Marine Lines is called "Dhobi Talao." There was a big Persian wheel in the fifties and an inclined plane on which the poor bullocks were driven up and down as they still were till late at another well at the corner of the new College of Science. Water was drawn from this dhobi tank to sprinkle the roads in the locality and the Esplanade Road. In the adjoining vacant ground the Parsi philanthropist, who was a keen lover of education, built the Institute bearing his name. He endowed it partly for the purpose of a Native General Library and partly for accommodating a girls' school founded by old Elphinstonians under the name of the Student Girls' and Literary Society, which was greatly nursed in its heyday by the late Mr. Vishvanath Narayan Mandlik, and, later on, by that distinguished scholar and citizen, the late Mr. Kashinath Trimbak Telang, who eventually adorned the bench of our High Court from 1889 to 1893. Framji Cowasji was the descendant of the great family of the Banajis, one of the earliest settlers in Bombay, who carried on the business of brokers to English firms. The Banajis, the Wadias, the Setts and the Modis or Wachaghandis were the four important wealthy families who came to Bombay in the eighteenht century under the ægis of the East India Company, to pursue mercantile avocations.

The Banajis.

Cowasji Banaji was a great merchant and shipowner, as the Dadys were. He had five sons who were all distinguished, Rustomji established himself as far back as 1837 in Calcutta, and traded with his brother Dadabhoy. Both brothers were for a long time Consuls for Persia, Rustomji in Calcutta and Dadabhoy in Bombay. Framji was another brother, and so was Cursetji, who was more or less familiarly known as "Khatla Goga." Goga was a nick name of the Banajis. Cursetji was not so distinguished in the public life of Bombay as Framji. The former confined himself to commerce. The latter was both a man of commerce and a public citizen of renown, who in his day was a great pioneer of horticultural industry. He was the owner of the estate known as Pavai, near the village of Vehar, lately sold at an abnormal price. There he used to import and plant a variety of exotics. The Pavai estate was a kind of veritable botanical garden in his time; but alas, his commercial misfortunes overtook him and the estate fell into neglect. It is a part of this Pavai which in 1889 the Corporation bought at the instance of the then Municipal Commissioner, Mr. (afterwards Sir) Charles Ollivant, in order to have an auxiliary water reservoir to Vehar, there being an alarm of water famine, which however, never occurred. The Pavai reservoir was till very recently a white elephant and a monument to remind the present generation of the rate-paying public of the waste of their monies under ill-founded alarms or panics by the Municipal Executive. The Framji Cowasji Institute is the best and most useful permanent memorial Bombay possesses of a philanthropic citizen who flourished about sixty-two years ago. It may not be generally known that the late Sir P. M. Mehta was a Trustee of the Institute, and also its Chairman, and did during his enlightened chairmanship a great deal for the conservation and better welfare of the Institute. His last effort at improvement was directed to the reclaimed ground of the tank, a part of which is soon to be utilised for extending the premises of this most popular Institute.

The Robert Money School.

Speaking of educational edifices of the fifties one cannot refrain from referring to what till late was known as the Robert Money School, a handsome pile of buildings, elegant in its simplicity, which stood between the edge of the Girgaum Road on one side and the Kalbadevi Road on the other. It stood on the ground where is now erected a "glorified chawl" which has in reality destroyed the asthetic vista which the old Money School presented from the southern end of the Esplanade Road where stands in its solitary splendour the statue of Queen Victoria, endowed at a cost of 2½ lakhs by H. H. Khanderao, Maharaja of Baroda, the predecessor of the ill-fated Mulharrao, in 1870, along with that other gift, the Sailors' Home, in 1870, in honour of the visit of H. R. H. the Duke of Edinburgh. The statue of the Queen was unveiled by the late Lord Northbrook as Viceroy in 1874 midst stately pomp and dignity. The school was founded by Mr. Robert Money, who was a well-known Missionary teacher,

In Girgaum Back Road, which was more rural or suburban in the fifties than urban as it is at present, was situated Dr. Wilson's school. The house later on was owned or occupied by Mr. Bhaishanker Nanabhoy, solicitor. There was also in Agiary Street, in the flank of Kalbadevi Road, the General Assembly's Institution, where for many a year collegiate instruction was imparted by Scotch Missionaries. It is the same building which is now in the occupation of the Goculdas Tejpal Anglo-Vernacular School.

Private Seminaries.

Lastly, among the prominent educational institutions of the fifties mention must be made of two private seminaries in the Fort where English was taught to sons of wealthy Indians. These were the Boswell and Hinton, so named after the original founders and proprietors. The former school was located somewhere in Apollo Street. It was well frequented, and they say the late Sir Dinshaw Manockji Petit and his brother Nusserwanji were both educated there. Almost all the sons of rich Parsi and Hindu parents were instructed in good English and commercial knowledge in Boswell School. The late Mr. Vurjivandas Madhavdas and his brother Mr. Narotamdas also belonged to the same school. Boswell used to charge heavy fees. Who he was is unknown to this writer. Can it be that he was descended from the distinguished ancestor of that name who has made himself and Dr. Johnson so famous in English literature? Perhaps not, for some traditions say he was a retired army sergeant. Hinton was a better scholar, and his school was better attended than Boswell's. Eventually he was the only proprietor of a private English school in Bombay till the share speculation of 1864-65. Hinton, who, like others, was keenly in pursuit of riches, was greatly embarrassed and broke up the school, he becoming for a time a photographer. But it was a well-conducted school, and was located in a low house two or three doors northward from the town house of the Petits in Hornby Road.

CHAPTER XX.—OLD TIME HOTELS AND TAVERNS.

IN a survey of public institutions other than official, mention should be made of those local establishments which catered for creature comforts for the outdoor man, the fatigued traveller from the mofussil or from England and the Continent. In the fifties a good hotel of even modest dimensions, fairly equipped with tolerably good service, was a rarity. Practically hotel life was unknown, and ephemeral visitors by land or sea generally accommodated themselves under the hospitable roof of friends or acquaintances. Genuine British hospitality of the old-fashioned sort for which the stately and gorgeous species of the "Nabob' so vividly described by many an old and brilliant pen, had made themselves famous in the social annals of the servants of the Honourable the East India Company, had not yet died out. The guests whom those magnificent grandees honoured and treated under their hospitable roofs have left glowing reminiscences of their lavish aldermanic dinners, and of the profusion of those rich and mellowed foreign wines from their cellars with which they were regaled till the small hours of the morning, especially during a festive season like that of Christmas with its many jollities and revelries. Furlough and sick leave were rare because so difficult of accomplishment, with the tedious dull and monotonous voyage home occupying at least a hundred days by wooden ships. The stay at one time was longer in the country, and the longer the "Nabob" official or non-officiallived, the wider grew his fame for hospitality. Again, hotel life even in the old country, in the fifties was nothing comparable to the luxury and comfort of those palaces of to-day in Piccadilly or the Strand, in Northumberland Street or on the Embankment. So that it is a fact that in Bombay a decent hotel, as a hotel, was, conceived fifty or sixty years ago, was unknown, so the local historians say, till 1845. One christened "Hope Hall" and located at Mazagaon was then just emerging from its obscurity having been opened in 1837. The name still survives, but its pristine glory is faded and gone.

Parsi George and Portuguese George.

But about that period, it is related, there were several taverns of a character far from reputable. They would not be termed in those days any more than third-rate grogshops. Half-a-dozen of them were scattered in the locality of Sonapur, mostly frequented by soldiers and sailors and low-class clerks and others of the same kidney. Their names have been saved from entire oblivion, for the able compiler of the

" Bombay Gazetteer " has embalmed them in his pages. One was called " Parsi George " and the other " Portuguese George," the why and the wherefore of these two ambitious Georges is not told. It is, however, to be presumed that George was a generic and right royal name, the four Georges having so well followed each other during a greater part of the time that the East India Company held sovereign sway in the country. In all probability the owner was the same, but for convenience sake one restaurant or tavern was reserved for the jolly Parsi who would like to have bouts, specially in his favourite " Gulabee Mowra " (rosy Mowra spirit) in his own fashion; and the other for the Portuguese, that is the Goanese, who for over a century have spread themselves in a wide colony at Sonapur and the surrounding localities, notably what is facetiously called the " Dooker Gully," the lane for pigs to fatten on the offal provided by the residents. A third tavern had the funny name of "Paddy Goose," of which no local antiquarian has yet been able to give the origin. But more or less such names, it may be takenf or granted, were not the original which their proprietors gave but those conferred by some habitual frequenter, a soldier or a sailor, with a vein of vulgar humour. In all probability this tavern might have had a bit of turf at the back like a paddy where geese were allowed frequently to gobble before being sold. Pigs, turkeys and geese, were very largely raised in the Goanese locality in former years at Dhobi Talao which has been their favourite stronghold. There were two other taverns known as "Rustomji" and "Goadwad." In all probability they were christened after the names of their proprietors. We knew of one called the "Green Railing Tavern." A fine jolly place it was, where the tars and the blue-jackets made themselves exceedingly merry. Possibly vulgar buffoonery, drollery and railing were the chief attractions. It was situated in Parsi Bazar Street, next door to the family house of S. S. Bangalee.

Anyhow these taverns were the haunts of low-class folk and in many ways disreputable by reason of the vulgar venuses of the locality who were to be seen there angling. The barmaids did not come into vogue for another twenty years.

The Adelphi.

Thus Bombay was really innocent of a fairly decent hotel before 1845. The "Hope Hall" was respectable, and Mazagaon and Byculla were the fashionable suburbs. Visitors who could not be invited as guests by local magnates, would gladly resort to such a place to find such comforts as they could obtain. But the tolerable prosperity of the "Hope Hall" led in 1859 to the establishment of another known as the Adelphi, owned by a Parsi who came years afterwards, as he grew famous, to be known as *the* caterer *par excellence*. Both hotels were situated at Mazagaon and were well patronised. Hope Hall for long maintained its high respectability with aristocratic exclusiveness. It had an annexe to accommodate family people also which was known as the Hope Hall Family Hotel. That branch was most paying as married folk preferred themselves to be at a little distance from the bachelor quarters, and remain undisturbed. At the same time the proprietor rested on his oars, while Pallonji, with ample pluck, energy and hard work was able to rival his neighbour. He had a charming courtesy about him and was always intent on pleasing his visitors, rich or poor, with equal impartiality. He always kept an eye to the main chance in order to be a successful hotel proprietor. So his heart was in his work, and that work was how to please his customers and thereby attract more people.

"Old Pallonji."

Thus his perseverance, aided by the other excellent business virtues he possessed, especially courtesy and open-handedness, was able soon to surpass the Hope Hall. Civil and military officers began to swarm to his hotel, so much so that in a few years he removed to a more spacious premises in Clare Road, which was then a suburb and every way airy and open. "Pallonji" would get good hints for better management from some of his customers. These he invariably put into execution. So that "Pallonji" and later on "Old Pallonji" was a household word among the civil and military gentry and even among local citizens. A restaurant was added for the delectation of the latter. Thus he went on swimmingly and at no time better than during the argentine period of Bombay, the share mania, when so many hundreds used to come from far and near to be rich in a trice. Whether they fared well or ill Pallonji minted money and no mistake. And as he was a shrewd man of business he took special care of his investments which were more or less in land and property. One business qualification he had possessed in an eminent degree. Apart from his courtesy, affability, everything to all men and women, he learnt by practical experience that "terms positively cash" ought not to be as inflexible in hotel management as the laws of the Medes and Persians. A little judicious relaxation was essential There would be needy or indebted young army subalterns or fashionable young civilians. They would not have enough of the white or yellow metal jingling in their pockets. Could dear Pallonji oblige them and defer the discharge of his bills to a convenient period. Pallonji would obligingly acquiesce. So it came to pass the "tick" system was fairly in vogue. The impecunious, as he grew in service, might turn out to be a big man, a brigadier or a commander-in-chief, a judge or a member of Council. He would be a personage of position and influence and be of service for purposes of recommendation and so forth for increasing the greater prosperity of Pallonji's concern. In this way, it is said, he assisted many and they in turn were grateful to him. Pallonji was always ready with his purse for the needy and never dragged any one into court. He would wait for years and if even he despaired of payment he would forego his outstandings. He was the one famous hotel keeper in Bombay who made a name for the Adelphi.

The Origin of Watson's Hotel.

But the fifties soon receded into shade. The share speculation period brought large influx of foreigners in the city. There was the first Italian Ballet Company. There was the troupe Dave Carson, the great humorist, besides other theatrical companies. All wanted accommodation. So the demand for hotels sprang up and in the sixties there were half-a-dozen small hotels. But at the eventful hour old Mr. Watson, who had his shop at the south-west corner of Churchgate Street as a silk mercer, draper, hosier, etc., and had amassed a large fortune in his trade, and who was a man of great enterprise besides, conceived the happy idea of establishing an hotel of first-class reputation, on the model of the most well-equipped and well-managed caravanserais then springing up in the West End of London. The ramparts were pulled down. The vacant ground and a part of the maidan was plotted out by the State for purposes of residential and office quarters. The plots, scores in number, were put up for sale by public auction. These ranged from the corner where is now erected the College of Science to the verge of Hornby Road where stands now the Empire Buildings. The plots yielded a price which was then deemed "fabulous." Watson bade for the plot where the Esplanade Hotel now stands for Rs. 100 per square yard. Others fetched between Rs. 70 and Rs. 105. The Government of India, to whom the land belonged, netted half-a-crore as earnest money. Watson was his own architect and engineer. He devised his plan and carried it out with a patience, perseverance, and capital business sagacity which even in those days were the subject of admiration. Thus he was not only the proprietor but also the architect, engineer and builder of the hotel. It was completed in 1870 just about the time that the Duke of Edinburgh visited the city, and I vividly recollect how I had paid Rs. 20 for a ticket of admission to the newly built terrace at the top to view the magnificent fire-works, the first of their kind on an elaborate scale, on the Backbay opposite. Bombay owes a debt of gratitude to old Mr. Watson, for he was a pioneer of some of the best equipped modern hotels which have since been built and of which the Taj Mahal Palace Hotel, the enterprise of the late Mr. Tata, is the latest, the most fashionable and architectural, situated in the front of our picturesque harbour at the entrance of which will soon tower the magnificent marble arch to commemorate the landing of King George V, the first British sovereign, who along with his consort Queen Mary, came to proclaim his coronation as the King of England and Emperor of India.

CHAPTER XXI.—THE CLUBS. THE ICE HOUSE AND THE OBSERVATORY.

A LIFE-LONG resident of the Fort cannot refrain from referring to some other old public buildings of utility either for purposes of promoting science and education or the convenience and comfort of the inhabitants generally. As regards European Clubs I can say little of the Bombay and Byculla Clubs of the fifties. The latter had vicissitudes of its own for some years before it could afford a local habitation. It was somewhere after 1835 that that modest edifice began to rise above the ground in the very locality where it stands in its full blown completeness to-day. But it was more or less an arcadian establishment, quite in harmony with the social life of the

Anglo-Indians of the times, chiefly civil and military. To-day it has blossomed forth into a first class up-to-date residential club for the members of those services as well as for bachelors of the professional and mercantile classes and other non-official nondescripts. It is a convenient, comfortable and even luxurious oasis in the midst of what was once a popular aristocratic European quarter, but now an expansive glorified slum with big chawls and stables all around it. Since philistine industries began slowly to invade this once charming suburban area, the club seems to be quite a stranded place, far away from the centre of European society, so well colonised on Malabar Hill; especially since the day Sir Richard Temple deserted for good the Parel Government House and took up his quarters at Malabar Point, fringed with the shores of Back Bay and nestling in its own peculiar environments surrounded by Hindu villas and Hindu temples. The residential area of Byculla is more or less appropriated by middle class Europeans who mostly belong to the industrial and engineering fraternity. Again Byculla has been shorn of a great deal of its former glory, especially of the fifties and sixties, by reason of that younger institution, the Royal Bombay Yacht Club, which is now the premier social rendezvous of the European community, with its annexe of Club Chambers on the opposite side of the road. Thus, the Yacht Club, with its many superior amenities and attractions, has robbed the charm which once presumably belonged to its elder sister. However, Byculla Club is still proud and jealous of its ancient and time-honoured privilege of bidding farewell at the festive board to retiring Viceroys, Governors and distinguished members. This is as it should be. For it connects the old traditions with the new and thus keeps up its historical continuity which is so essential to vitality. The Club, sectional and sternly exclusive as it is, has a rich local history of its own, which in a sense is also public. And it is much to be wished that some venturesome member with literary accomplishments may indite its history and put together in a collected form the many post-prandial harrangues made thereat on the occasion of bidding farewell to distinguished guests. We couid then obtain many a sidelight on the actions of Governors and others whose administration or career had come under the searchlight of critical journalists of the type of a Buist, a Connon, a Maclean and a Knight.

The Old "Bombay Club."

In the Fort itself there was that historical Club founded by the members of the Indian Navy as far back as 1845. As suited them and their proud vessels it was within stone's throw of the dock and the harbour. It was situated in Rampart Row, west, which has sometimes been called Ropewalk. It was located in the premises which had been afterwards occupied for years by the P. & O. Company. This Club of course was confined to members of the Indian and Royal Navy. It, too, had its own rich naval traditions which seem to have been lost in oblivion, but one could wish that they were ransacked and collected in a readable form as they would constitute a distinctive and remarkable chapter in the making of Bombay for a century. In the fifties of the nineteenth century the "Bombay Club" as it was called, was a flourishing institution; and though strangers were confined to the tea-room, the one proud trophy the Club possessed was to be seen there. It was a bell which one of the warships of the Indian Navy had brought as a prize from the First Burmese War which was mostly a naval affair. The bell is still in existence, having been taken over as a valuable historical asset from the old Club by its successor. The present Bombay Club is in no sense a naval club. It is open to all European merchants, specially bankers, traders, mercantile assistants and brokers. But the glory which the Indian Navy shed on its own original institution is gone.

The Old Ice-House.

Coming to minor public edifices it may be worth while mentioning the old ice-house for many years past in disuse for the purpose originally built and now levelled to the ground. Long before 1845 it was realised that for the comforts of the citizens and for use in certain kinds of sickness, ice was an invaluable article. Indeed it was felt to be a first necessity in a tropical climate like Bombay with its annual holocaust of fevers. At last in 1845 public subscriptions were raised for the purpose of importing ice from America and storing it for use all through the summer in a suitable house specially constructed. It is related that the very first to introduce ice was the firm of Messrs. Jehangir N. Wadia and Co., as far back as 1835. From that time forward it was demonstrated practically that ice could be imported and even sold commercially. But in those comparatively sleepy times, with no steam communication, no inland telegraph system, let alone sea cables, with sailing vessels taking at least a hundred days on a voyage out from Southampton, and with the comparatively slow pace of commercial ventures and enterprises, it took another ten years to bring to a practical head the construction of the ice-house and the importation of ice from the United States. At a cost of Rs. 10,000, publicly subscribed, the building of the house was taken in hand on the plot of ground where it stood till late a structure so built as to prevent evaporation as much as possible, and accessible at the top by a circular iron staircase. It was a curiosity in those days and worth inspection till familiarity left it alone and in the fifties and sixties it was only frequented by the coolies employed to warehouse the ice and by the management. Messrs. Tudor and Company were the consignors in America, and every year two or more consignments used to arrive regularly. The very first to introduce ice and ice confectionery at festive entertainments was the first Sir Jamsetjee Jeejeebhoy. The ice was sold to the public at the fixed rate of 4 annas per pound. It was a comparative luxury for the well-to-do in those days, not an absolute necessity as has been the case since the seventies. In 1857 there was a regular famine of ice in Bombay to which the well-to-do had got accustomed. Again, dear freight, dear cost of landing and other matters made it prohibitory to import. There was a hue and cry and even a representation to Government to facilitate the importation. By 1860 the supply was fairly regular, there being a larger and larger consumption by people of moderate means, at the rate of 2 annas per pound. During the share speculation of 1864-65 ice became quite an ordinary article of consumption even by the poor. Another popularity in ice-selling was achieved by Messrs. Tudor and Company, by bringing a number of casks of luscious American apples along with the ice. The fruit came in a tolerably fair condition after a four months' voyage, about 30 to 35 per cent. in each cask being found uneatable. There was always a regular run for this refreshing American fruit. And no sooner was it advertised than it was sold. The supply would be exhausted within a week and the price being Rs. 2 per dozen for what would be called the "mandarin" apple and Re. 1-8-0 and 12 annas for the smaller varieties. But with the manufacture of local ice and the discontinuance of Tudor's ships in the latter end of the seventies, Bombay market was closed to the importation of the fruit, No one has since tasted such apples. though other varieties are procurable at different seasons of the year. With the construction of local ice factories the imported supply ceased. But it is a fact worthy of record and not generally known that it was as far back as 1863 that Messrs. Luke Thomas and Company agents of the P. and O. Company, at Aden, started an ice factory there in conjunction with their own machines for condensing salt into sweet fresh water. How strange that it was not until some twenty years later that progressive Bombay built its first ice factory! However, it sometimes happens in the evolution of cities that, in some respects, those considered backward have something to boast of as surpassing the most forward, the most enterprising and progressive. But the ice house had its day in Bombay. Its old place next to St. Andrew's Kirk in the Fort, opposite the Dock, was converted into an ordinary commercial warehouse till levelled to the ground later. As our Indians say, land and houses have their own destiny. At one time they are in the greatest quest and another time they lie in the greatest obscurity or go to rack and ruin. Look at the magnificent architectural remains of the Moguls. What fallen greatness may be read there! Veritably there is a sermon in stones which often tells most eloquently by their silence the vicissitudes of principalities, kingdoms and empires and their greatness, decline and fall!

The Colaba Observatory.

Another minor edifice of public utility may be mentioned here. In the fifties the Colaba Observatory was at least a quarter of a century old, and though the appliances and the apparatuses which were to be seen there then are either all cast away or partially in use while replaced by the most exact, the most sensitive, and the most skilfully constructed instruments which the modern science of astronomy and the rank and file of the great astronomers of the world have invented, it served very well the purpose for which it was built. They say it is really built on land reclaimed from the sea. It separates the harbour from the Back Bay. The Honourable the East India Company rendered homage to astronomical science by this erection of the Colaba Observatory. It aided science and it assisted commerce. For there was the lighthouse which served as a beacon to the sturdy mariners coming to Bombay from all quarters of the globe. Wrecks were common in the first eighty years of the nineteenth century and the Admiralty records might faithfully furnish the casualties of the wrecks of vessels approaching the harbour. The structure was built in 1826 and the first astronomer in charge of it was Mr. Curwen. But as the fates would have it, the original instruments imported were recorded to be full of flaws and could not work. In 1835, Mr. Orlebar, who was a Professor of Mathematics and Natural Philosophy in Elphinstone College, was appointed astronomer in succession to Mr. Curwen. Old Elphinstonians who learned their mathematics and physical science under him speak highly of his attainments. The Observatory for long, and specially during the period of my youthful recollection, was the object of curiosity as much as the Mint of local citizens as well as visitors from outside. Of course, those who have been in charge of it since the fifties have all done their work and kept themselves up to date as far as instruments of observation are concerned. And it may be truly said that no observatories in India is maintained in a higher state of efficiency and most modern equipments than those of Bombay and Madras. Mr. Pogson and his daughter were for long associated together in the Observatory at Madras and have left an excellent astronomical reputation behind them. In Bombay Mr. Chambers, after the distinguished Dr. Buist, was for many years a proficient star gazer and his successor, Dr. N. A. Moos, the first Indian appointed as Superintendent of the Colaba Observatory, was not a whit behind during his tenure of office in maintaining the first class reputation this useful institution has enjoyed for well nigh a century.

CHAPTER XXII.—PUBLIC EDIFICES. NO ARCHITECTURAL BEAUTY ABOUT THEM.

A STRANGER visiting Bombay will be irresistibly struck by the total absence of any kind of notable architecture in the places of religious worship of the principal communities. There is not one such edifice which can satisfy the artistic eye, though to-day we have over four hundred Hindu temples, shrines and fanes, dedicated to diverse gods and goddesses of the Hindu pantheon. Neither is there a single edifice of religious worship belonging to our great Mahomedan community on which the stranger, with the love of the beautiful, can feast his eyes to surfeit with its architectural merits. Among the leading fire temples of the Parsis there is no structure which we can point out and say " Behold and admire." Save the Cathedral with its comparative antiquity, there is none even among the old churches and chapels belonging to the Portuguese Roman Catholics which can boast of any architecture. As we have already observed even the Cathedral had an evolution of itself, having bloomed into the grey edifice which was so prominent in the fifties in the midst of the almost total absence of any building, save the Town Hall, with its rudimentary architecture. Even to-day, after the Government led the way in 1864, and especially after 1870, to the construction of public edifices possessing some architectural pretensions, Bombay cannot boast of a single edifice which could rejoice the heart of a Ruskin or Ferguson. The new structures—religious, educational and others which have sprung into existence after the sixties, are of no striking or original design. Almost all proclaim their poverty so far. What may be the reason? It is impossible to say. It lies in the obvious fact that it was no body's business to consult or engage European architects of fame and renown in the designing of the many structures that have been erected from time to time during the entire period, specially during the last half a century. No doubt the Government has employed architectual mediocrity for the purpose But we have had not the benefit of the. genius of such men as Wren or Gilbert Scott. Of the latter we have his own solitary specimen in the magnificent University Buildings and the ornamental Rajabai Clock Tower, attached to them. It seems deplorable that both in matters of sanitation and architecdeture Bombay has been exceedingly deficient. No master mind in Sanitation appears to have been engaged in the building up of the city. No wonder it has been so haphazardly built as to make it almost hopeless to rebuild it on the modern accepted principles of sanitation. So too with regard to architecture. There has been none known who could have been said to be saturated with the spirit which has inspired so many who reared the solemn and stately religious and other edifices in the West, specially those erected in mediæval times which are the admiration of an æsthetic world. Perhaps no religion in this respect has so vastly influenced architecture as that of the Vatican and, next to that, of the Moors and Saracens. The edifices scattered by the latter in the way of those gems of mosques to be witnessed in Spain and European Turkey and at Damascus a thousand years ago and more, are monuments of art and a tribute to the genius of the builders. Their successors did something to revive the art in the golden age of the Moghul in Northern and Central India, down as far as Aurangabad where there is the miniature Taj Mahal to the memory of the deceased daughter of the founder of that great city. Even Ahmedabad boasts of such Saracenic architecture which was the delight and unmixed admiration of Fergusson. But Bombay in the days of the Mogul was only a fishing village and just rising into importance. As we have observed before, the city is in reality an upstart, a parvenu, and cannot hold comparison beside the ancient Hindu shrines and temples in Northern and Southern India. Mathura in the North and Madura in the South, with Puri in the East and Somnath in the West; and also with the mosques, the mausoleums, and the royal palaces which the great descendants of Babar reared at Delhi, at Agra and other well-known places, which are still the admiration of strangers. Evidently in her evolutions since the days of the occupation of the Portuguese in the fifteenth and sixteenth centuries, she has hardly known how to impart to any of her religious edifices that stately dignity, that divine inspiration, that sublime altruism which a house dedicated to the Great Creator of the Universe suggests. There is none of the inspiration which maritime colonies like that of ancient Greece revealed wherever planted. Indeed, the very conception of the beautiful in art entertained and so extensively carried into execution by the Hellenic race seems to be woefully absent. Bombay has been intensely shopkeeping, and that is the reason why the temples, the mosques and other places of worship inspire neither reverence nor awe, let alone beauty and joy. In this respect her evolution is next to nothing, and one yearns to see a real genius rising in her midst who will impart the necessary impetus.

Church in the Fifties.

Meanwhile a survey may be taken of the principal places of religious worship in the fifties. The Cathedral, as stated, had a most humble beginning. It grew to its present stature from the modest room within the precincts of Bombay Castle which was christened the "Fort Chapel." As to the Roman Catholic Churches half-a-dozen of them had a respectable lineage. There was one known by the name of Esperance. It is related that it had been built in the sixteenth century during the Portuguese occupation and stood on the very site in the Marine Lines Esplanade where there stands a cross. Military exigencies demanded its removal and so it was demolished, the aforesaid cross being allowed to stand to mark the spot where this mediæval church was originally erected. The Government had to pay all the expenses of building a new one and the site chosen was in Kalbadevi which was then open to the sea. This was in 1760. It was consecrated as the Roman Catholic Cathedral. But as Bombay extended and expanded, the Cathedral, once open to the sea, found itself surrounded by roads and what the Christian would call heathen buildings, so much so that cheek by jowl there has subsequently been reared in its vicinity a Hindu temple dedicated to some divinity and in charge of a Maharaja. Some thirty or forty years ago the laymen of the temple used to crowd it and such was the deafening noise of the primitive drums and pipes, that the service in the Cathedral was often greatly disturbed. A civil suit had to be filed for the purpose of obtaining a perpetual injunction against the barbaric and deafening din of the music and of the clamours of the worshippers. To a visitor to the cathedral at least a hundred years old in Agiary

Street in Kalbadevi may appear strange how it came to be planted there. But, as just said, the builders of the day perhaps never thought that commercial and populous Bombay would so grow as to make it altogether an undesirable place, according to the Catholic notions of the principal place of God's worship. Happily a new and artistic cathedral has for some years past been built in a very eligible and lovely site in Wodehouse Road, with excellent surroundings, our well-known citizen, Mr. Chambers, being its architect. Another well-known church is that of N. S. de Gloria at Mazagaon. Indeed Mazagaon abounds in churches and chapels of which this one is the principal and the most popular. Worlee, Mahim and Bandora also abound in these. There are the usual Catholic decorations and certain internal structures which are purely Catholic; but the outer frontage has very little of architectural merit. Esperance Cathedral was described nearly a hundrd years ago by a traveller as the finest building in the island after the Town Hall. Perhaps the Church of Gloria was the next best. It was built by one Antonia Pàssoa who was "Lord of the Manor of Mazagaon" in 1548. The church underwent reconstruction some forty years ago. There was also the Church of San Miguel and many others scattered from Mazagaon to Mahim, but they are of no importance from the architectural point of view and have generally a sameness about them so peculiar to early Portuguese Churches. Two other old churches may be simply mentioned, the one at Cavel built in 1794 and the other known as Salvador built in 1596, that is at the very close of the reign of Queen Elizabeth. What a long tract of years to throw back to realise the occupation of Bombay by the one European nation which in the fifteenth and sixteenth centuries boasted of their great mercantile navy and explored the lands of the West and the East Indies alike! Lastly there is the church of Miguel in Upper Mahim built in 1540.

Hindu and Parsi Temples.

As to Hindu temples the one at Bhuleshwar is the earliest, and so, too, one at Naigaum. But the writer does not claim to have any intimate knowledge of their origin and history. Babulnath temple at Chowpati is another ancient place of worship. It was built in 1780, while the one at Bhuleshwar, with its congerie of smaller temples, shrines and fanes, is said to be about 200 years old. Thakoredwar was built in 1838 and the Jain temples in Pydhowni and Kalbadevi are a century old. But none of these temples have any striking architectural features about them. Neither have the

Parsi fire temples, the earliest of which was built by the well-known Dady Nusserwanji Dady of China trade fame and a great shipowner. It was built in 1783. The one known as Banaji's or Framji Cowasji's was first erected in 1843. But we must leave the Hindu and Parsi fire temples alone as there is nothing historical about them worth public notice ; neither is the big Jumma Musjid in Sheik Memon Street—an imposing sructure of stucco and plaster built in the orthodox Moslem style with its cupola sand minarets—in any way impressive or uncommon. It dates from 1775.

CHAPTER XXIII.—THE COTTON GREEN AND THE MARKETS.

THERE remains one secular or profane historical place yet to describe. It is what was once known for well-nigh two centuries as the Green or Cotton Green. The "Green" of Fryer's days had by the exigencies of the mercantile Bombay undergone a material reduction till what remained of it was the Maidan, as already circumstantially described, what it was in the fifties. In the same period the Green or Cotton Green was all the space now enclosed by the Elphinstone Circle. But before it was put to commercial use and next allowed to be a desert waste later on, it had a beauty and landscape of its own so vividly described by Grose in 1750. Thus over a hundred and sixty years ago it was a smiling plot with a beautiful garden pleasantly laid out and encircled by health-giving and shady trees, one of which a tamarind tree still stands, and with nice English houses, already referred to beyond the Circle. But commercialism as early as the opening of the nineteenth century had destroyed its beauty just as that of Byculla by the industrialism which has so ruthlessly invaded it since 1880. The trade in cotton just a century ago was being built up and as the cotton warehouses were very near, next to the opium godowns built under the direction of Mr. Henshaw, the dealers who had had to press the docras for shipment to Europe dumped the Green, despoiling its beauty and in the bargain making it an eyesore with all sorts of cotton seed, cotton leaves, old rope and other "cutchra." In 1813 the offices and the residents complained of the nuisance and memorialised the Government to keep the Green tidy. In the fifties as I saw it while daily resorting to the green plot for play and amusement, I found it entirely free from the nuisance, but I used to see scattered a good deal of opium dust on the south side, just about the canopied statue of Lord Cornwallis, which was well railed in and kept free from any sacrilege, so to say, of the vicinity. But there was to be seen during the season daily the *navganies* or big burly coolies, active at work dragging up the cotton docras to the Press, singing exactly as the labourers moving stones to the top of new buildings under construction sing even so to this day. This old screw, which was known as the Apollo Press, is now the Government of Bombay Central Printing Office. The Green of the fifties was really a place of recreation for the young, just as Elphinstone Circle gardens are at present. And the regimental band or the band of drums and fifes used to play every evening after sunset going up and down from the corner of Kemp's, which was the original Military Staff Building to the south end of what was till long the Medical Store, Office, at the east corner of Humam Street. where was located the office of the Town Major of the day. The Green remained till 1860 or 1861 when the plot was cleared and purchased by the Municipality. Afterwards, under the project of Mr. Charles Forjett, the Police Commissioner, the plots were sold to the public for the purposes of erecting the first group of really architectural office buildings in the form of a crescent, with a garden in the centre. The project had the cordial support first of Lord Elphinstone and then of Sir Bartle Frere during whose brilliant administration it was completed. That was the origin of what is now known as the Elphinstone Circle, once an aristocratic place but shorn of all its glory since the tall and handsome buildings reared their heads in Hornby Road and entirely eclipsed it.

Crawford Market.

Among minor institutions a reference needs to be made to the public markets of which Bombay boasted sixty years ago. It is an absolute fact to aver that there was no such thing as an up-to-date market in the seens we take it to-day. No one had any conception of such a struturea till the close of the sixties when the versatile Mr. Arthur Crawford conceived and carried out the idea he had entertained of a central market which would be the pride of the growing and prosperous city of Bombay and its Municipality. It was only when the great market bearing his name was completed and ready for occupation, that the masses at large realised in a concrete form the idea ot such a place of daily public utility. His resourceful talent alone gave body and form to the conception of a market as known in the more civilised and progressive cities of the West. The conception was his, and so, too, the design, and he spent money like water to rear an edifice worthy of the city. It was estimated to cost between four and six lakhs, but actually cost evleven lakhs and more,—an expenditure considered at the time as a piece of unparalleled municipal extravagance, which could not be condoned and which wrought eventually the downfall of the first ædile, who must still be recognised the *facile princeps* of all Commissioners who have held the reins of the Municipality. But the extravagant cost is altogether another story. It has long long since been acknowledged that Arthur Crawford was as bold in his conception of the market as he was far-sighted in his vision as to the future requirements of the city. The vision was that of a practical statesman, But one has only to recall the condition of what by the merest apology were called markets in the fifties. Practically the markets, public, semi-public or private which existed at the time, of course scattered all over the then town, were either shanties or congeries of mean lowly huts or sheds, exceedingly insanitary, and every way unworthy of Bombay. To visitors coming to the city for the first time and viewing other public edifices, such as were then to be witnessed, it was a matter of astonishment that we had not a single place where a lady or gentleman could resort to with comfort and convenience for the purpose of making purchases of daily food, specially meat, vegetables and fruit. All the apologies which went by the appellation of "markets" were of an extremely primitive kind and might have served the needs of the population of the fifteenth and sixteenth centuries but not that of the nineteenth. The only market approaching to the rudimentary conception of a market of the mid-Victorian age was the one in the Fort which will be presently described.

The Earliest Record.

The earliest record, however, of a market in the Fort was that of the one erected in 1696, the exact identity of its *locale* being unknown. It was allowed to be used free of any charge. Some seventy-five years later two more respectable sheds were built where meat was vended, as also fruits and vegetables. It was a Government institution. A caretaker under the high-sounding appellation of constable was appointed, he being allowed just four annas of the Honourable East India Company's current coin for his trouble per diem! A little later, somewhere in the town a private market, known as Mahomed, was said to be in existence serving somewhat the needs of the population there.

It was between 1809 and 1819 that that great Governor, Jonathan Duncan, caused to be built a market in the Fort which was deemed tolerably decent. Its locality was known as the Governor's old horse stable. The reader can form his own conception of this market when a condemned horse stable was converted into it. Well, it was, however, something better than the shanties of a more ancient period. It was to this sublime height that Jonathan Duncan's Government could soar a hundred years ago to provide an old stable for the purposes of a market to meet the needs of the important population of the Fort, including the Governor and his staff, the King's judges, the Admiral and his suite and so on! The original Erskine Road market was built in 1837 and they were wise enough to appoint a Clerk of the Markets. Squatters were not allowed.

Private Markets.

Then there were some markets in Abdul Rehman and adjoining streets. The one in the former may perhaps be traced to the street still going by the name of "Bhajipala" that is vegetables. Private markets in Dhobi Talao and elsewhere were also to be noticed. The "Cheera Bazar" still holds fast to its original locality in Girgaum Road. In Null Bazar, too, a private market was seen. Besides there were small private shops here and there in the town which served the needs of the poorest. In 1847 an enclosure was built next to the east ramparts just about the place where the tram lines pass by the Fort Mahajanwady in Mint Road. That was purely for Hindus who were vegetarians. There was a slaughter house at Bori Bunder and another a little further on, the sites of which are unidentifiable. Practically, then, in the fifties, the only "respectable" market for meat, vegetables, flowers, fish, etc., was the one situated a few hundred yards from the Mint. Its exact locality may be fixed on the Mint Road, where the tram lines pass by just near or about the present Fort Market. It was approached from the west by two lanes called the Agiary and "Homla Dingee," both in the old Mody Street. It was also approached from the north corner of the Town Barracks. Perhaps, if we say that it was about a few yards in a southerly direction opposite the "Sanj Vartaman Press," it would better recall the locality to the denizens of the fifties in the Fort. It was an enclosed space with three double sheds. As you entered the gate from the north you saw the fisherwomen vending a variety of fishes for which Bombay still bears a good reputation. The back shed was located for the dirty dressed butchers, of course, all Mahomedans. With a walking space of about 10 feet between there was the second shed dedicated to the vendors of all sorts of vegetables on one side and dry condiments, like chillies, onions, and so forth on the other. The third shed was generally cleaner and more sanitary, seeing that flower and fruit vendors were all accommodated there and there was a special space allotted to the "murgiwallas" or vendors in fowls and ducks.

The Fun of the Market.

The fun of the market was to be seen when it was most crowded, say, between 8 and 10 in the morning. The evening purchasers were fewer. The market was closed on its south in the direction of the Mint, the boundary of which extended far into what is now the Frere Road skirting the southern extremity of the barracks which are now railed off. Beyond it was a *cul de sac*, and there was no through passage at the end of what is called the Barrack Lane whence there is egress and ingress now. A beef market in a northerly direction, adjoining the Fort Market, served those who indulged in that flesh. The market fully supplied the needs of the Fort and Colaba and was held of sufficient importance in the fifties to accommodate a superintendent on a modest salary. It was his duty regularly to inspect the markets daily early in the morning and in the afternoon, to see that the stalls, specially the meat and fish ones, were properly washed and cleaned and kept "sanitary" as the word was conceived sixty years ago in Bombay. Perhaps, save this market, the rest, either semi-public or private, were dirty and hardly deserved the name. To-day they would be called "disgraceful" in the most emphatic sense. It was to wipe off that disgrace that Arthur Crawford, with his customary farsightedness, conceived the idea of a central market, of an up-to-date character, and æsthetically constructed, and eventually materialised it into the structure which has been so long associated with his name. It was he again who wiped off another " disgrace " from the town, the bloody, reeking, stinking, abominable slaughter-houses at Bori Bunder, the very sight of which used to give a shock. They were a standing reproach to growing Bombay and the present generation should be grateful to that first Municipal Commissioner for having, after insuperable efforts, made the final arrangement, changing the locality of the slaughter-houses to Bandora in 1866-7 and erecting houses of a character which were neither insanitary nor an eyesore. But how many are indeed the handiwork of Mr. Arthur Crawford for which Bombay is exceedingly grateful to him. Indeed it can never be forgotten that he was the founder of the new Bombay which sprang into existence after the sixties with its many wide roads, new thoroughfares and other improvements which are our admiration even to-day. The wisdom and choice of Sir Bartle Frere were amply justified.

Chapter XXIV.—THEATRES. ACTORS, AMATEUR AND PROFESSIONAL.

If Urbs Primus in Indis, even to-day after a century of British civilisation, is woefully deficient in literature, art and music, the reader may well imagine the cimmerian condition which presented itself in this respect half-a-century ago. There may have been here and there genuine devotees of the Muses and the Graces; but whatever their own individual accomplishments, their influence, jointly or severally, on the money-making denizens was next to nothing. Amateurs may have at rare intervals improvised a kind of stage where the spirit of the British drama was faintly sought to be reflected. But it was only for the time. How may it be possible to conceive of anything approaching a steady and regular cultivation of the drama in the benighted Bombay of the fifties, when one sighs in the year of grace 1919 for even a single theatre where one may pass a couple of hours in the intellectual recreations of a really good play by consummate and practised actors of fair renown. You sigh in vain for such a play and such actors. Bombay is not only a beggar in the dramatic art, but a bankrupt to maintain even a single really good company for four weeks. They are all a brotherhood of shop-keepers, glorified or debased. Till recently we had mere apologies for theatres by way of huge ill-constructed sheds of corrugated iron and glaring paint, with curtains and dropscenes as execrable as the outside of the ugly structures. Again, these were more or less concentrated in Grant or Falkland Road, amidst surroundings which had better remain undescribed. The first really good theatre with anything akin to a modern house of drama was built by an enthusiastic amateur just thirty-five years ago, in an eligible place at the north-east corner of Waudby Road, thanks chiefly to the encouragement of Sir Richard Temple who was then Governor of Bombay. The Gaiety was the first theatre of any civilised pretensions. Major Cowper, the real *entrepreneur*, was active in bringing out a company who on the whole did well and put on the boards many plays of the time popular in England. Between 1880 and 1900 there was a gap till the opening of the twentieth century witnessed, rising in our midst in Ravelin Street, the Excelsior, a really good theatre with some architectural pretensions and an auditorium with some amenities. The sister building next door, in the Hornby Road, is the Empire, but it is not so lovely as the Excelsior. The Royal Opera House on Hughes

Road is a fine theatre but its doors are hardly open for more than four months in the year. Thus, though we have three fairly good theatres in eligible localities, central, comfortable and every way convenient to pass a couple of hours at the end of a weary busy day, it must be observed that there has not yet arrived any dramatic company over which a critical audience, appreciating true drama, can go into raptures. It is to be presumed Bombay may have to wait till perhaps the Greek Kalends. It must, however, be stated here that the original Bandmann Company and, later, Mrs. Brown Porter, gave excellent Shaksperian performances.

Egyptian Darkness in the fifties.

But meanwhile it is meet to refer to the Egyptian darkness of the fifties and relate what were the places of amenities then. Our ancient chroniclers of Bombay of the time relate that there was a theatre in the Fort, near the old Bombay Green, built by public subscriptions as far back as 1770. What a vista of time over which to stretch our imagination in order to get a conception of it! What did it look like internally and externally, the chroniclers do not relate. All that is known is that the building was vested in trustees. But that it stood even till 1818, albeit in a dilapidated condition, is sufficient testimony of its worth. It was the only play-house of the period and in all probability served its purpose. Half-a-century of struggling life is enough. The tumble-down premises were repaired in 1819, for which a fund of Rs. 17,000 was raised. But the expenses, of erection eventually mounted to Rs. 23,000,—a considerable sum in those days when "cash" was scarce and the old Company in Leadenhall Street used to lament the great drain of silver.

Evidently the purchasing power of the rupee was great as the merchants of the day always thought of their rupee being worth 22 to 24 shillings! Exchange was, of course, considered a jolly good one. The great private bankers, Messrs. Forbes and Company, with Charles Forbes at the head, were contributors to a great portion of those 23,000 rupees, which amount was, of course, guaranteed by the Government. It is to be presumed that those State bankers who advanced equally for theatres as for wars with the piratical Marathas and others must have taken precious care that the silver coins were all reaped in good and sound money, and not in the debased currency which till late was computed at 16 pence!

Then comes a period of lull, as in the interval the playhouse had come to grief, and a debt had been incurred which had eventually to be defrayed by the guarantors, the deficit being Rs. 14,000. Another well-known theatre in the early period of the nineteenth century was the Artillery theatre situated in distant Matunga where high dramatic jinks were held amidst all the suburban picturesqueness of that spot, now made so hideous by industrialism on the one hand and the operations of the precious Bombay Improvement Trust on the other, chiefly, in erecting glorified chawls to here, there and everywhere. It is recorded that in 1820 all Bombay Society, including the Governor, flocked there to witness a performance called "Miss in her Teens and the Padlock." Even suppers and balls were given in a large house, in the vicinity of the theatre, which was afterwards bought by the late Sir Dinshaw M. Petit.

The Old Play House in Grant Road.

The year 1842 was historical in the annals of Bombay drama and melodrama. The great Sunkersett, or to call him by his full name, Jagannath Sunkersett, whose stately Maratha effigy in marble graces the north-eastern vestibule of the Town Hall, offered a piece of his own land in Grant Road on which to build a new theatre house worthy of the early Victorian age. But the offer required all the solemnity and formality of public meeting for consideration and acceptance. Ye gods, what a mighty effort it must have been to ensconce the dramatic Muse in the then suburb of Grant Road mostly dedicated to the scions of the rich families of Sir Roger de Faria, a friend of Sir Jamsetji Jijibhoy, and the De Gas—Portuguese families, alas, blotted out by the aftermath of 1865-66. But the meeting disapproved of the original locality! It seems, however, that

Jagannath Sunkersett eventually did build a theatre house on another locality in Grant Road, which bore the name of Grant Road Theatre, and eminently served the purpose till the mushroom corrugated shed theatres sprang up after 1870 in another part of the town to amuse and entertain the low classes of the population surrounding them and to become first rate " places of advertisement " for the dusky *vulgar Venuses* abounding in the vicinity. But as the Fates would have it Grant Road Theatre, after a prosperous existence of well-nigh fifty years became converted into a bakery, the owner being one Mr. Freeborn, a retired superintendent of the Government Savings Bank! But during its most flourishing period, say from 1863 to 1880, it gave hospitality to a large number of its " paying guests " including a first rate Italian Opera Company during those halcyon days when gold and silver flew in every man's lap like so many rosebuds. The company was imported by a first class syndicate of Europeans, connoisseurs in drama and music, Professor Sinclair, of the Elphinstone College, being one of the members. But the company was not to the taste of the puritan literateur and Professor of Materia Medica,—Sir George Birdwood. He condemned the troupe as being composed of belles who were "fair, fat and forty."

Dave Carson.

But it was that humourist, Dave Carson, who really made the Grant Road Theatre famous among the play-going folk of Bombay and for years together attracted thousands to the house with gratification to them and great pecuniary benefit to himself, and his versatile company. Dave Carson himself was a facetious actor, of ready wit and humour and knew how to catch his audience, specially with local topics of interest and many a topical song. He was Protean in many respects and was never more happy than when he donned the garb of the Parsi masher of the period and made love to "Rati Madam." The house used to go into roars of laughter at both his sallies of wit and his songs. He was a gifted actor and on the boards of the Grant Road theatre played many parts which those who heard him could even recall to-day with the greatest pleasure. But the skit with which Dave Carson's name will long be remembered is his caricature of the Bengalee Baboo in the famous song of the same name. Even to-day the Indian bands known as *Nan Khatai* play this tune. The "Bengalee Baboo" is an inevitable item in the repertories of this fraternity of musicians (?) who play jumbled music from cornets which won't blow and clarionets that squeak at Hindu weddings or at the doors of the Parsis on their New Year's

Day. I cannot recall the whole song, but here is the first stanza as far as I can recollect :—

I very good Bengalee Baboo
In Calcutta I long time stop ;
Ramchand Tunda Ghosh my name,
Radha Bazar I keep my shop.
Very good Hindu, smoke my *hooka*,
Eat my *dal bhat* every day ;
Night come I make plenty *pooja*
Here is the *nautchwalla* tom tom play.
Kooch parwa nahi good time coming
Babu never make *islave* (slave).

Madame Carlotta Tasca.

Later, say in the seventies, the company which was most popular and consisted of really good actors was that known by the name of Madame Carlotta Tasca. It was a strong company of whom one named Elcia May was the best actress, with more histrionic talents than I have known in later times. There was also an actor by the name of Fairclough whose dramatic talents were certainly admirable. He played a variety of parts such as those of Hamlet, Othello, Macbeth and others, almost to perfection such as one sees on the stage in London. Elcia May played the female parts of Ophelia, Desdemona, Portia and so on. No company, not even Herr Bandmann's, who came some few years afterwards, gave so many dramatic lifelike representations of Shakespeare's plays as this one, the chief of whom was Carlotta Tasca. Fairclough also gave a magnificent dramatic reading in the Town Hall which was greatly applauded and appreciated. He electrified the *elite* of Bombay with his readings of passages from Shakespeare's Henry V and Tennyson's "Charge of the Light Brigade." Edgar Allen Poe's "Raven" was also admirably executed.

Grant Road Theatre in the sixties was extremely popular and houses were crowded to see a variety of artistes.

One of these was a company of dwarfs headed by the world-renowned General Tom Thumb. They were most refined and civilised and were great popular favourites who used to appear in rich dresses and gowns worn before royalties in Europe, including the Emperor Louis Napoleon. General Tom Thumb was the leader and took Bombay almost by storm. But the glory of the Grant Road Theatre departed, and none of the older generation has known of subsequent dramatic companies having ever reached the quality of those already described. Bombay has fallen on evil days, as we said at the outset in reference to literature, arts and music. Among her millionaires there is not one who could be pointed out as a lover of real art and a patron of the best drama. So far Bombay is dead and can never deserve to be called the first city in India. A word, in conclusion, must be said in praise of an enterprising amateur company of young Parsis who in the sixties started a dramatic company called "The Elphinstone Dramatic Club." They were mostly students of Elphinstone College, the most accomplished among whom was the late Mr. Hirjee A. Khambata. He was known as a first-rate English scholar and gifted with a histrionic talent rarely to be seen since his days. The Society was an amateur one, but it did its best to enliven Bombay and give excellent dramatic representations from Shakespeare. The brothers Khandalawala as well as Mr. Pestonji Nusservanji Wadia and the two brothers Dr. Dhanjisha and Mr. Nusservanji Parakh were also well appreciated. Eventually the late Mr. Cooverji S. Nazir became the proprietor and for a long time carried on his company with credit and to the gratification of the play-going public. There were also some Gujrathi dramatic clubs engineered by Parsi gentlemen of no little histrionic talent oneof whom was known as "Dady Christ," the last name being given, because at one time he had avowed Christianity as his religion till brought back to the old path of his Zoroastrian ancestors. All these have been gathered to the majority, including Mr. K. N. Kabraji who, in the seventies, placed the Gujrathi drama on a sound footing by writing plays from ancient Persian history, the very first of which created a great furore, namely, "Bazon and Menijeh." Mr. Hirji Khambatta died about seven years ago and was for long a contributor to the English columns of the "Hindi Punch" under the pseudonym of the *Corporator Faineant.* His memory deserves to be enshrined by all lovers of art and humour, of drama and satire. Of the earliest founders of the Gujrathi drama there survived till late one Mr. Edulji J. Khory, who, after having been a barrister in Rangoon, had retired to London. He was a playwright of no mean ability and power and closely associated with Mr. Kabraji. He mȧde his debut as the author of a facetious and humorous play called " Hajambad and Thuggnaj."

CHAPTER XXV.—EARLIEST LITERARY AND BENEVOLENT SOCIETIES.

IN the long roll of public offices and institutions the Pinjrapole, the Sassoon Mechanics, Institute, and Sir Jamsetji Jeejeebhoy School of Arts and the Bombay Branch of the Royal Asiatic Society need an honourable mention. They are all old institutions, each of great public utility in its own zone and sphere of influence. They have played their part with credit and honour in the past and are bound by their very constitution to be of ampler scope and utility in the future. Three of them at least are now almost a century old and have thus become highly respected for their age, apart from the service they have rendered to the public, specially during their respective early career. When we throw back the shroud of a hundred years and come to relate their humble origin, and when we bear in mind what the early beginnings of Bombay were a century ago, beginnings many of which have already been narrated, we cannot but express our deep gratitude to their respective founders. Not only are we bound to express our gratitude to them. We must recognise the philanthropy and liberality of those original founders, their foresight, and their regard for the welfare of the generations that were to be born after them. And yet how in the bustle and turmoil of our own days, days of high pressure wrought by advancing civilisation, and days when the work of twelve hours has come to be crowded in six, many of us, if not all, are apt to forget the beginnings of such and other kindred institutions. The very sterility of public activity in those days, more or less Arcadian in their simplicity, which some might be tempted to call the days of Sleepy Hollow, necessitated, it would seem, that vent must be found for the display not only of pure benevolence but for intellectual activity. It is not difficult to imagine the dull and weary monotony of those who flourished in Bombay a century ago. Life without some kind of mental recreation must have been positively dull. We, who have our daily newspapers, furnishing us with the news of the entire globe of a day previous, who live and move in telegraphs, telephones and æroplanes who travel in luxurious railway carriages at the rate of thirty and forty miles an hour, who voyage to and fro, not only to London, but Yokohama in the East and San Francisco in the West, in less than thirty days; we who get a regular weekly mail from foreign parts and enjoy the luxury of seven deliveries of inland post, who can get books and periodicals of our choice week after week and can obtain other intellectual food from half-a-dozen well-established firms of booksellers, have only to recall the days of 1815 to realise the efforts of the contemporaries of that period to obtain all that we get to-day so easily, so freely, like clock-work. Imagine how Sir James Mackintosh and Mountstuart Elphinstone must have sorely felt the want of that intellectual pabulum without which it is impossible to live,—mental recreation of the purest kind, and to commune with the best thoughts of Europe and the West in arts and literature, and elevate all that is noble and altruistic in our common humanity. It is only when we come to reflect on the disabilities of those days, disabilities of which we have absolutely no experience that we can understand why the small band of intellectuals panted and why they set about founding literary, scientific, geographical and other societies to improve themselves and to add to the sum of their knowledge. The necessity which the European fraction of the population then felt could not, of course, be realised by their Indian contemporaries for obvious reasons.

Educational Darkness.

As far as education was concerned there was darkness or at the best visible darkness. The great Hindu community, no doubt were content with the Sanscrit or Marathi or Gujrathi literature. The great Mahomedan community confined their education to the Koran, which to them was the Encyclopædia of all knowledge, being a divine book. The Parsis were a shade better, but their early association with the English factory agents and "writers" made them acquire a smattering of the English with great facility. But there was nothing beyond.

Thus it was that the early period of the nineteenth century in Bombay witnessed the foundation of literary societies for special branches which eventually merged into one comprehensive Society which is now known as the Bombay Branch of the Royal Asiatic Society. But in the early years there was a literary society, a medical society, and a society for mechanical science literature. Then the great Indian Navy, so memorable in the annals of the East India Company, established a Geographical Society which did solid pioneer work. Apart from these societies there was a philanthropic movement which eventually culminated in the founding of what is known as the Pinjrapole, an hospital for the sick and infirm animals, specially cows, bullocks, horses, sheep and so on. Mercy to these animals who so well serve our humanity, was a deep religious sentiment which has never so well materialised in the world as it has in

India. When such materialisation took place must be left to learned Hindu savants of the pre-historic and historic Sanscrit literature. The great Buddha taught the sentiment of mercy to lower animals, and the great Asoka and his successors cultivated it with a piety and fervour of which there are many evidences. History and archæology as interpreted by our latest savants tell us, that among other benevolent institutions maintained and supported by the Asoka dynasty and its successors, such as dharmashalas and hospitals, was the erection of houses for the protection of domestic animals, weak and infirm.

Hindu Benevolence.

From those days downwards we find scores of instances of the benevolence of the Hindus who have founded hospitals for dumb animals, generally known as Pinjrapoles. Some eighty years ago and more there were prowling about the streets of Bombay stray dogs which sometimes caught hydrophobia. The Government issued orders for either shooting or catching these dogs. It is on record that there was once a regular riot on account of the dogs, in which one Mr. Pestonji Dadabhoy Wadia, an influential Parsi merchant, greatly interested himself to abate this nuisance. The community was greatly exercised and felt itself hurt. But protest meetings were rare and memorialising was only in extreme cases. So the well-balanced minds of those days took up a constructive policy which was really a happy *via media* to avert further bad blood between the authorities on the one side and the peaceful citizens on the other. It was resolved to have a home where ownerless dogs, cows, bullocks, horses and other animals could be confined so as to do no harm. A wealthy Shravak Bania merchant, named Motichand Amichand, donated a lakh of rupees in 1834 to build a Pinjrapole. To this Mr. Jagannath Sunkersett and the first Sir Jamsetji Jeejibhoy contributed handsome sums. A trust deed was drawn up and the management of the funds and the animal asylum was vested in Trustees. And such has been the sentiment of prevention of cruelty to animals, specially domesticated, that rich and poor have since that time gone on enriching the fund till it is stated that the principal has now reached 12 lakhs and the income derived from various profitable investments brings as much as 1½ lakhs per annum. Motichand was a name to be conjured with. He built a temple in the Fort which is still known by his name; also a most spacious chawl for Shravaks of moderate means to live and carry on their trade.

The Bombay Geographical Society.

This Society was first established in 1831 till it was eventually merged in the Royal Asiatic Society somewhere about 1864. It was founded by officers of the Indian Navy, whose explorations of the Arabian and Red Seas and of the Bay of Bengal are too well-known to need any mention here. There is a record of them in the library of the Royal Asiatic Society which is a monument of the navigation researches of those gallant men.

The Mechanics' Institute.

Next there was a medical and literary society founded in 1781. Again an Agricultural and Horticultural Society was established in 1830. Another was called the Literary and Scientific Society and founded in 1848. Then there was the Mechanics' Institute founded in 1841 by the foremen mechanics of the Mint and the Dockyard to keep themselves abreast of the literature on their special profession and also to give public lectures on scientific subjects of great practical interest. It flourished admirably in the fifties and many were the interesting lectures delivered in the Town Hall on behalf of this most useful institution. The writer well recalls some of the lectures he attended, specially those of the late Mr. Berkley, the eminent engineer of the G. I. P. Railway whose name is intimately associated with the formidable work of tunnelling the two Ghauts. The locale of this institution originally was in one of the rooms of the Dock block where the clock tower is situated. The increasing attendance of members and the extension of the library necessitated its removal elsewhere and a home for itself. Thanks to the generosity of the Government a plot for it was found on the ground where the Sassoon Machanics'

Institute has stood since 1867. Sir Albert Sassoon had previously given Rs. 60,000 for the building. Various other donations were given for additions to its library and for new furniture adapted to the new and handsome building which was opened by Sir Bartle Frere in 1867. It is a pleasure to see the Institute flourishing and continuing to attract public interest by means of a regular series of lectures annually during the cold season. It may be worth noticing here that the first President of the Society was Sir Erskine Perry who was ever ready to encourage and support any public institution, European or Indian, having for its object the dissemination of literature and science. Even to-day Sir Erskine is much remembered for his judicial lore and sterling independence on the Bench, as for his whole-hearted co-operation in all educational movements of his day.

The School of Art.

A few words may be said in reference to the School of Art which bears the honoured name of Sir Jamsetji Jeejeebhoy, the founder and benefactor. After the great exhibition of 1851 in London at the Crystal Palace there was a wide movement for the establishment of Schools of Art in the United Kingdom. The contagion spread to Bombay which was then beginning to show the first satisfactory progress in education. In 1853 Sir Jamsetji donated a lakh of rupees for a school of drawing. A committee was appointed by Government and Sir William Yardley, King's Judge of the Supreme Court of Judicanure, was the first President. At first there were two professors, Messrs. Paton and Terry. The former retired soon and the latter became the head of the school. It was at first located in the Elphinstone Institution, on the Esplanade

Cross Road, but was afterwards accommodated in 1859 in the premises of the Elphinstone College, on the Babula Tank Road. It was here that the writer first began his elementary lessons in drawing. Mr. Terry was a capital teacher for beginners and remained at the head of the School of Art even after a local habitation was found for it in the present premises. It may not be generally known that Mr. Terry was a first-rate humourist and cartoonist. He found some vent for the display of his talents in this direction in 1864-5 when " Punch in India " was started, which unfortunately had a brief existence of only two years. It did not receive that support which it deserved. The paper died and we have not heard that any other illustrated paper has been since published in any part of India save the facetious " Looker on " in Calcutta, since 1919. Of course, we have our old and valued friend the " Hindi Punch," but it is an Anglo-Vernacular "Punch," not purely English, though conducted with considerable ability which is a credit to its proprietor and editor. One fact needs to be recalled to memory in reference to a cartoon of "Punch in India" which at the time made a great sensation. Sir John Lawrence was the Viceroy. Afghanistan, whose Amir was then Shere Ali, was simmering in civil war. There were the frontier chauvinists of those days. Sir John's policy, a right and wise one for that era, was not to interfere in the internal *khatpat* of the Amir's dominions, until India's own borders were threatened. We were still consolidating our British Indian Empire and the State had inadequate funds to carry on the ordinary duties of the administration, besides finding the wherewithal for the construction of railways. The policy of non-interference was deliberately adopted by Sir John with the cordial support of the

Home Government, though in the India Council there was the stalwart Sir Henry Rawlinson who was identified with the "Forward Policy" of the Anglo-Indian military service, and its organs of public opinion. The policy of non-interference was severely criticised by these, but Sir John Lawrence, the most distinguished and trusted Frontier officer of pre-Mutiny days, was not to be moved from his firm policy. "Punch in India" echoed the policy in a cartoon called "Masterly Inactivity." Yet another cartoon was in reference to a domestic quarrel between Sir William Mansfield (afterwards the first Lord Sandhurst) and his military household secretary, Captain Jervis. Sir William was a stern disciplinarian and a regular martinet as to keeping of finance, being himself no mean man of economics and currency. The squabble rose to such a pitch that Captain Jervis was placed before a military court for the offence of keeping irregular accounts, in the matter of cheese and bacon, jams and jellies, wines and spirits of the household. Both were wrong. Both committed serious errors of judgment. Of course poor Captain Jervis had to be cashiered and great sympathy was displayed in his favour by his brother officers. At the same time Sir William was inexorable. "Punch in India" had an excellent cartoon on the subject with the following jingling doggrel which for a time was lustily recited everywhere.

"Sir William Mansfield, K.S.I., Knight of jam and potted pie."

CHAPTER XXVI.—SIR JAMES MACINTOSH AND THE FOUNDATION OF THE ROYAL ASIATIC SOCIETY.

THE only scientific and literary institution of distinction and established reputation of which the first city in India can boast is the Bombay Branch of the Royal Asiatic Society. True it is that there are other societies of a sort, devoted to literature and arts which are occasionally heard of, but they are almost of a negligible character. We should be bowed with shame when we are unable to point out to a stranger, imbued with the love of literature, in its most comprehensive sense, any but this solitary institution, the only one of which it can be averred with truth that it has grown with the growth and expansion of Bombay and prospered with her prosperity. When the capital of the two sister presidencies can make a tolerably fair display of literary institutions, Bombay has none but this. It is a singular fact that Bombay which plumes herself on its progressive career all throughout these one hundred and fifty years, should be so miserably poor, almost a bankrupt, in her literary institutions. One reason of this poverty may be ascribed to her commercial spirit. Her citizens are undoubtedly absorbed year in and year out in the pursuit of riches, almost ignoring the fact that the treasures of arts and literature are infinitely of greater value than the millions in gold, silver and jewellery they have amassed. Gold and silver have their ultimate use; not in the enjoyment of their possession as hoards, but in their free and discriminate use, one of which is the founding of great libraries, museums and other temples of learning where the richest thoughts of the world may be serenely enjoyed. The worship of the Golden

Calf may be a form of pastime but what can surpass the contemplation of the inestimable and imperishable gifts of intellect endowed by Nature! But it is of no use further moralising on the intellectual poverty of Bombay. There is no doubt that the Colossus of Mammon is at one gate, and there is a Lazarus of Arts, Science and Literature at the other. It is much to be wished that this reproach proud Bombay, the first city of the Empire, will soon wipe off, and so exert herself as to point in years to come with pride to many literary and other institutions which her cultured and wealthy citizens may provide.

Origin of the Bombay Branch of the Royal Asiatic Society.

Turning to the Bombay Branch of the Royal Asiactic Society and its literary and other activities during the fifties and sixties of the past century, we may take a brief survey of its origin and growth. As the Rev. Dr. Scott rightly observed in his learned speech on the occasion of the centenary of this institution fifteen years ago, the rise and growth may be conveniently divided into three stages, each stage comprising the proceedings of a generation. Prior to its solid foundation by that distinguished scholar, statesman and philosopher, Sir James Mackintosh, in 1805, there was a literary and medical society, chiefly consisting of lawyers and medical men who, in order to enliven the dull monotony of those archaic days at the close of the eighteenth century, seriously felt the want of an intellectual club where they might interchange the current thoughts of the West and add to their own mines of knowledge. When Sir James arrived in Bombay at the opening of the nineteenth century, to assume the Recordership of Bombay, which was then equivalent to the Chief Justiceship, he was disappointed to find the absence of any kind of society where literary activities of himself and others might find free play and where intellectual amenities might be freely exchanged. So, after a brief survey of the situation and the récognition of the crying need of a really good literary institute, he took the initiative towards providing that need.

Sir James Mackintosh.

It should be observed that Sir James arrived in Bombay with a European reputation. In England he and his college friend, Mr. Hall, were known as the Castor and Pollux of the Northern Isles, a genuine compliment to Caledonia stern and wild, which is not only the mother of poets but the parent also of great metaphysicians and philosophers. At other times they were known as the Scotch Plato and Heredotus. At any rate that was the reputation in which they were held by their contemporaries a century ago and more. Sir James was accredited with a "Baconian mind." And he came to Bombay as a valiant but honourable combatant, who had had his historical fight with the great Burke, orator and political philosopher of imperishable fame. He was also recognised as one of the most philosophic lawyers and profound thinkers that England had known. This was the distinguished personage who, soon after his arrival in 1803, laboured most whole-heartedly, strenuously and sagaciously, to found a literary society like that of the Asiatic Society of Bengal, founded by another renowned literary man and linguist, Sir William Jones, 20 years before. So a first meeting was called on 26th November 1804, whereat 17 persons were present including two globe-trotters. The name chosen was the "Literary Society of Bombay." It was agreed that a meeting of the Society should be held in the last Monday of every month. The object was to "investigate and bring together what could be discovered of the East so as to form a contribution to the thoughts and learning of the West." Thus, Sir James a century ago nobly worked, with the eye of the accomplished scholar and the far-sightedness of the statesman, to bring the so-called "unchanging East" nearer to the West by means of that common bond of human heritage,—man's intellect. And who can gainsay the fact of the immeasurable effect which literary societies of the dignity and reputation of the Royal Asiatic Society have wrought on the mind both of Europe and Asia; in how many directions is there a pleasurable rapprochement between them for the world's greater good and the closer union of humanity irrespective of race and creed. But to proceed.

The literary society founded by Sir James Mackintosh with 17 accomplished men, but whose number immediately rose to 30, had not only an intellectual cast. It had also its social aspect. In the absence of clubs the small society of men from Europe panted to meet together socially where there might be as much the feast of reason as the flow of soul. Of course, the founder of the Society was its first President.

Sir Charles Forbes.

And who could better look after the modest finances of that institution than that great banker, and the first leading non-official of the European community in Bombay, Sir Charles Forbes, a name still to be conjured with for all that is useful and noble, for all that contributes to the wealth and prosperity of a rising city, for all that is best in a wealthy and cultivated European whose love for his Indian brothers in the commercial life of Bombay was deep and abiding. Bombay, especially her Indian citizens of those days, admirably expressed their gratitude for the many signal services that the merchant rendered by raising the magnificent statue in his honour on his retirement, an admirable work of art of the sculptor and an adornment of the Society of which he was the first Treasurer. Where are the Forbeses of to-day?

This then was the Literary Society of which Mountstuart Elphinstone and Sir John Malcolm were also presidents a little later. But it may be interesting to enquire who were the globe-trotters. The earliest journals tell us that they were Lord Valentia and his friend Mr. H. Sault. In February 1805 the choice library of a gentleman retiring was offered for sale. So on the 25th of that month steps were taken to buy the books, which was to be the first effort for the nucleus of a library which was destined to grow ever more,—a library which, after a century and over counts upon its shelves as many as a lakh of the best books, the best thoughts of the world's most intellectual men, books classic and books rare, books of reference and books of long forgotten history, besides many manuscripts. I can well recall the peculiar scintilla of intellectual inspiration I felt when for the first time in 1858 I entered the hallowed precincts of that great storehouse of thought. It was akin to what I felt twice again when visiting the great library in the British Museum in 1897, and also when visiting that sacred and venerable edifice in Westminster, the Abbey. A peculiar but pleasurable sensation came over me. To the youthful mind of the writer the Library looked like a great Temple of Learning in reality, a Valahalla where lay buried the great thoughts of great men of all the centuries! Never has his love and enthusiasm for that Library, so sacred to the memory of Sir James Mackintosh, waned. Verily, as the Revd. Dr. Scott justly observed in his centenary speech—a speech worthy of the occasion, dignified and lofty, delivered with all the eloquence of which he was such a master, and with all that verve and nerve of the English which was at his command—Sir James was a great scholar imbued with great practical ideas. Indeed I may say that he was a fine type of the utilitarian philosopher. It will be interesting and instructive to give one instance only of those practical ideas in connection with the Literary Society which was soon after to blossom into the Royal Asiatic Society.

A Herculean Task.

Three practical proposals were agreed to. (1) To take into hand the preparation of a statistical account of the town and island and of its economic products and the condition of the people; (2) the preparation of a comparative vocabulary of the different languages, dialects, and forms spoken in India; and (3) the translation of Oriental classics into English. What a herculean, but all-absorbing, task for an infant literary society to take under the inspiration of one who himself was a giant in intellect. When we bear in mind what meagre resources were available a century ago for an economic survey, what little progress was made by Oriental pundits of the East and savants of the West in philology and what a fund of oriental classic lore was needed, besides scholarly study of the Indian languages, to carry out the proposals, the actual difficulty of the gigantic task may be easily imagined. But we might take it that the proposals were to be the great potential features in times to come of the infant institution rather than a realisation of them even within a quarter of a century. Sir James had taken full mental notes of the Egyptian darkness of the land in Western education and what tracts of time might intervene before those ideals, practical as they were, could be materialised. He knew that the torch of Western knowledge had been hardly kindled. The East India Company, even at the opening of the nineteenth century, was almost wholly absorbed either in territorial acquisitions, forced or unforced, or acquiring trade monopolies to secure fat dividends for its proprietary at home. At the date of the arrival of Sir James Mackintosh it was well-known that the Company had entirely ignored its first duty of imparting even the rudiments of English to the people under its sway. The better mind of the few English of high intellectual attainments deplored this culpable negligence and strove its best, through friends in England, to insist upon something being done towards that education when the next charter (1813) came to be renewed.

A Practical Philosopher.

And it is a fact on the records of the Parliamentary Committee of that year that it strongly urged on the Court of Directors to allocate just £10,000 on education in the territories belonging to the Company. Sir James was a far-sighted practical philosopher and his proposals were fully endorsed in order to stimulate his successors in the Presidential chair of the Society to work day and night for their slow but steady realisation. The journals of the Society for over three-quarters of a century and more inform us what a mass of valuable papers were read from time to time, which all aimed at achieving more and more the fundamental objects. The history of these is indeed most fascinating and one of the most remarkable efforts of earnest men with a love of literature to lift the purdah, so to say, of Indian and oriental classics, and make it familiar to the scholars of the West. As to Indian literature itself it was there, hoary with age in a variety of forms in a variety of places all over the country. But the learning had been greatly neglected, chiefly owing to the waves of foreign conquests which began with the descent of the Scythian and Parthian monarchs in the first century of Christ, to those of Mahomed, he of the dozen invasions in the rich soil of Gujrat and Kathiawar, and who carried away the gates of the great sanctuary of Somnath. There was a revival of learning during the reign of Akbar but its flame burnt only for a short time and it was impossible to rekindle it under the rule of that stern follower of Puritanic Islam, Aurangzeb, who was the ruthless iconoclast of all Hindu religious edifices and shrines, as much as the Imperial vandal of Berlin, who wrought in the great European war (1914-1918) destruction to ancient and venerable monuments and priceless works of religious and other arts in Belgium and Northern France where the Allied forces eventually triumphed, hurling back the tide of his unrighteous invasion.

But to return to Sir James Mackintosh. For seven years and more he silently but strenuously worked hard to place the Society on a solid and permanent footing. He retired in 1811, but had the satisfaction of knowing that he had reared a monument of his own which was more durable than brass or the kingly pyramids of Egypt, as Horace would sing.

Chapter XXVII.—HISTORICAL RESEARCH.

TO Sandy Seventy picking up random shells on his native strand has been a pleasurable pastime. Not only the selection of the shells but their collection and classification has been a recreation in order to build up a miniature museum of local recollections of half a century and more. Their true significance must be interpreted by someone imbued with the genuine historic spirit and the gift of a pen rivalling that of Gibbon or Macaulay. A gazetteer, however elaborately prepared, is too bald for such a purpose. At the best its writer is merely a busy book-worm who ferrets out a bit of food here and there, to fatten his ponderous compendium. The compendium itself by its very nature and task imposes a restriction and a limitation which forbid anything like the collection of personal recollections which a single individual could furnish. Thus a gazetteer, however useful in a way, is after all but a brief, dry, and unenlivening record of the life and life career of a local institution or public edifice, of its true origin, of the many conditions and circumstances under which it came into existence, the men of quality, influence and position who were its sponsors, and the influence which such was destined to exercise on future generations. Personal recollections by a variety of individuals who may have flourished in a given tract of time, on a diversity of men and things,—these alone contribute to the making of a great city like Bombay. To carry out the ideal in its ample entirety is indeed the labour not of one but many lives. Our colleges and universities are launching on the ocean of a busy world and an active life thousands of fairly equipped graduates. If only a fraction of such would devote their time and attention to historical research the history of the past two centuries of Bombay could be excellently revised and presented to popular view with a fullness far surpassing many other fruitless efforts in other fields. Like Isiah, whose hallowed lips were inspired with the spirituality of his time and age, we must have local Isiahs in history to accomplish what is needed. Even now there is ample pabulum by way of official records and papers, lectures, proceedings of many a learned society and institution, of books by divers authors whose very existence has passed away from men's memory, to be diligently investigated only by a dozen workers, methodically and simultaneously working towards the identical goal to accomplish the great work.

The Temple of Learning Closed.

But, as already observed, at any rate in Bombay, the Temple of Learning seems to be as good as closed. We look vainly for those High Priests who could popularise that sacred shrine, and bring within its solemn precincts a noble band of earnest worshippers, devoted to its service. We do not see any ot the signs so agreeably visible elsewhere, as for instance in Madras and Calcutta, of men's minds widening under the daily process of the sun. The axis round which knowledge should revolve seems to be at a standstill here. It is a most petrifying feature in the active busy life of Bombay. All the activity seems to effervesce either on the bourse or the bank, the factory or the docks, or in the variety of gymkhanas so well dotted over the most eligible part of the city Well may a literary Eddie Ochiltree, taking notes like a chiel, enquire where is the seat of the Temple of Knowledge where one can roam and muse, where one can quarry into the rich treasures of the past and enlighten and enliven the benighted and the prosaic whose daily life consists of drudgery in pursuit of wealth.

Vanished Landmarks.

From the shells already picked up it must have been clear to those who have examined them with the eyes of history and curiosity combined, who and what were the men and things that were in the making of Bombay half a century and more,—men and things dead and gone, but on which the present greatness of Bombay actually rests. In order to realise the true proportion of the great material progress Bombay has made since the fifties, it is necessary to take a brief survey of what one sees around him. It can be best realised by those who were blossoming into life at the date that Bombay was rising from its early obscurity to take her proud stand as the second city of the great British Empire. Let one of such stand on the summit of the Ridge and realise the view presented to him with the one he actually saw, say in 1850 or 1855. What chains of memories! What oases of recollections! What mighty mazes, though not without a plan! What a colossus of active life and work on land and sea! Take the Fort itself, the busiest of the many busy beehives of beautiful Bombay. Save the steeple of the hoary Cathedral, what presented itself to his gaze far and wide, stretching from Wellington Fountain to St. Xavier's College south and north? And what panorama is presented to him east and west to-day from Mody Bay harbour and the Mint to the distant Back Bay glimmering in the golden sunshine of the setting sun under the black shadow of the palmy Malabar Hill. How many steeples and minarets, turrets and towers he can gaze upon to-day within the boundaries of the great Fort? How many are the tall buildings in

Hornby Road, rising like so many Chinese Walls shutting out the grateful breeze to the northern Fort? How largely is the number of residential quarters crowded and congested richly to deserve the name of slums which the fatted calf of the Improvement Trust is too indolent yet to recognise and improve? Where is the old Apollo Buuder and where can he identify the watermark which divided the sea in that locality from the mainland? Where was the saluting battery? Where was the Post Office? Where the Bank of Bombay? Where the Secretariat? Where are the open maidans to which thousands resorted for recreation and amusement of an afternoon? Where are the ramparts and the *glacis*, and the inner forts, and where the moats and ditches, the Bazargate and the Churchgate? All are effaced. Almost every old landmark in the Fort of 1850 and 1855 has vanished from view. A few alone remain. These have already been described. It remains only to recall the personalities who moved on the stage of Bombay and who were chiefly instrumental in contributing to her present greatness. And it may also be of some use to refer to the condition of the people at the time, social, intellectual, political and economical. In short we shall try to paint the thoughts that throng the present with the colours of the period between 1850 and 1860.

CHAPTER XXVIII.—HAPHAZARD BUILDING OF BOMBAY. FLUCTUATION OF POPULATION. (1661-1801).

AT the present hour when the divers communities of Bombay, be they those residing in salubrious localities in their luxurious villas or those living in glorified flats on "economic" rents, or the thousands who manage to burrow themselves in what are called "one room tenements," insufficiently lighted and ventilated, or not lighted and ventilated at all, are invited to the novel Town Planning Exhibition in their great Town Hall, and listen awhile morning and evening to the discourses of a learned and practical expert on town planning. it may not be inopportune to say something touching this subject and house building as it was a hundred or even fifty and sixty years ago. Our expert town planning professor, Mr. Geddes, has only to play the bookworm, in the first instance, in the historic hall of the Royal Asiatic Society, take down from the ancient shelves equally ancient records, official and non-official, touching population and the progress of house building in the city, say from the days of Garcia de Orta to those of Jonathan Duncan, and from the days of that great Governor to those of Sir Bartle Frere, an equally brilliant and distinguished satrap, to discover for himself whether at any time there was even the rudimentary semblance of building the town and island of Bombay on some kind of plan. And when he has fully gorged himself with this uninviting pabulum, he might, in the second instance, proceed to visit not only the broad streets and thoroughfares but the lanes and the bylanes from Colaba to Mahim, at all points of the compass, to realise for himself the maze or complicated network of human hives in which the mass of Bombay humanity has been accustomed to live during half a century past, if not a century. But he must go about on his rambles with his eyes open, and accompanied by an intelligent guide, an indigenous architect, by preference, an architect who has known old and new Bombay alike, in order to be thoroughly able to take into his capacious mind the evolution of the divers quarters he may visit and equally of housebuilding in the city, from the primitive hut of the fisherman and the coolie in the distant Mahim village or the equally distant Colaba Koliwada, to the one floor villas, the two storied buildings of the early thirties and fifties, to the modern tall chawls for the factory operatives and the glorified chawls for the man of modest means eking out a bare living with a wife and two children. Without in any way generalising on this complicated subject, he would be able to find out for himself how Bombay has been built without any plan at all, and that in a most haphazard manner defying all rules of light and air.

The advent of Professor Geddes is cordially welcomed by " Sandy Seventy " however much the officials may look askance at his mission and his outspoken views. The bureaucracy of official architects and engineers are no better than their brothers of the civil administration. All the same his lectures are sure to be listened to with attention by our unofficial sanitarians who wish to see Bombay regenerated, and the scores of insanitary slums replaced by dwellings fit for poor humanity without any of the fads of the so-called Improvement Trust, which needs itself to be improved off the face of Bombay if any real solid advance is to be made in town planning in the best acceptation of the term.

A Bird's Eye View.

Meanwhile it may be instructive to have a bird's eye survey of the population and the condition of houses in the town. It is related by our earliest chroniclers that as far back as 1661 the town and island of Bombay numbered just 10,000 souls. But by 1675, the number according to that faithful traveller, Fryer, was just six times as many, consisting of a handful of pure Portuguese blood, Topases or Indo-Portuguese, of native Christians, kunbis or agriculturists and the depressed class of dheds There was also a sprinkling of Mahomedans at Mahim, that place being the strong-hold of the Islamites from the very first occupation of the town, in the thirteenth century. There were a few of the Prabhu colony, that sect being the literates of the day. In those very early days, it is not known whether any Parsi colony lived in Bombay.

But the Gazetteer records that one Dorabji Nanabhoy resided and transacted business with the indigenous population on behalf of the Portuguese, having been a resident from 1640 downwards. This solitary specimen of enterprising Parsi humanity deserves to live down in Parsi history, seeing what a factotum he was of the Portuguese occupiers of Bombay prior to its passing to the British. But strange to say by 1715, according to another census chronicler, Reverend Richard Cobbe, the population had dwindled down to 16,000, or a little more than the population of 1661. The causes have been attributed to divers events of that period. Piracy on the Bombay coast, both by the Angrias and the Moplas, was rife. This had the effect of fluttering the dovecots of many humble residents, agriculturists as well as traders. Where life and property were unsafe it was inadvisable to stay. That has been the law of life. And in obedience to that law a considerable migration took place inland, thus denuding Bombay. Next the pestilential marshes for which Bombay had earned an uneviable name and fame from the days of Garcia de Orta and before him, were another contributing cause to the *hejira* of the population elsewhere. Lastly, there was the trade rivalry. Bombay must have been in a parlous condition in 1715, when the first Hanoverian sovereign was on the throne of England, to have led to such a flight of the population. But there was another wave, this time of a flowing and not ebbing character. And it is chronicled that in 1744 the population rose to 70,000. Here we have the opposite conditions to account for the rise. Peace, which came with the contending faction of the trading companies, was prevalent, the cement having been brought by the fall of Bassein. There was a drain from the mainland back to Bombay which was slowly developing as a trade centre, though her potential greatness was still in embryo. Banias, Bhatias, Shenvi Brahmins and Parsis, all peaceful and trading men, flocked here. As yet the colony of the, last named was sparse. But it is recorded that another Parsi by name Rustomji Dorabji was resident, and such was his power of organisation and such his prowess that he held the proud official position of the great Patel of Bombay, a kind of urban prefect. Cowasji Patel Street, still keeps his memory green as cherished by his immediate descendants.

The First of the Wadias.

Then there came also on the scene in the wake of the shipbuilding yard at Apollo Bunder, already described, Lowji Nusserwanji Wadia, the first of a long line of illustrious naval architects who spread their fame to distant England where the Admiralty fully appreciated their worth. Lastly to finish, the eighteenth century population of Bombay, it may be observed that in 1780, there was a famine of food grains. The authorities were necessarily led into ascertaining the population in order to discover whether the grain imported sufficed to feed the residents. The Committee appointed for the purpose roughly estimated it at one lakh. Forbes confirmed it in 1784, saying the tide of the people from the mainland was still moving on faster to the shores of Bombay with its Pax Brittanica and expanding trade. Thus, between 1661, when the population numbered 10,000 and 1800 when it was one lakh, the flow was with one arrest, continuous and satisfactory.

CHAPTER XXIX.—A COSMOPOLITAN POPULATION AND OLD TIME HOUSES.

THE opening of the nineteenth century thus found Bombay with a population of a hundred thousand while a hundred years later it swelled to ten times that number. But it may be interesting to mark the intervening epochs which showed a striking growth. It so happened, however, that by 1806 a kind of rough census estimated it at two lakhs. How far it was even approximately correct is now of no special interest. But there is no doubt of the fact that, owing to a severe famine in 1802 a part of the famishing population from the mainland gravitated to the capital city,—a phenomenon not uncommon, seeing that during three severest famines of our own day thousands flocked as refugees to get food from the districts stricken with famine. In 1876, 1896 and in 1899, Bombay knows to its cost how the famine-stricken crowded into the city and invaded all sorts of vacant places and even footpaths for shelter and food. It is on record that famine fever then greatly raged; we mean in 1876. Dr. Vandyke Carter, an able bacteriologist, when bacteriology was still in its infancy, discovered what has been known as the spirillum fever microbe in many of the starving. There were many victims to that famine disease which undoubtedly aggravated the total mortality of that year. So too in 1896, and 1899. But the famine stricken were greatly afraid of the plague. However, the influx in 1806 was large enough and rightly or wrongly estimated at two lakhs. Of these two hundred thousand, it was related by a Mrs. Graham in 1809, that the Parsis numbered 6,000 to 8,000, which is a remarkable immigration from their orthodox strongholds of Surat, Navsari, Billimora and Gandevi. The Jews, then also swelling like the Parsis, were reckoned at about 3,000 to 4,000. The bulk of the population consisted of Indian Chritians, decendants of the original Portuguese, and Hindus of all castes.

A Truly Cosmopoliton Population.

In 1812, Captain Hall of the Royal Navy, according to the Gazetteer, observed as follows: "Bombay being the only perfectly secure spot in that quarter of India, had drawn to it in the course of years many of the native inhabitants together with much of the wealth of the adjacent countries. Each year brought more wealthy settlers and every sea breeze wafted into the crowded harbour of Bombay ships of every port from China to Peru." He, however, is more modest and therefore more reliable in the estimate he formed of the population which was 160,000.

But it is reasonable to suppose, even from the analogy ot to-day, that during a brief period of great commercial activity or some physical cause or another, the population swelled and reached two lakhs. Do we not see every year how when trade is active in the busy season people from the south and north, especially the Pathans, the Afghans and others, throng to our markets. Then look at the number of Arab and Somali and other Mahomedan mariners, crews of buglows from Muscat, Makalla, Aden, Basra and Zanzibar who are to be seen in large numbers at our docks and more distant bunders. Is it not literally true that in modern Bombay we witness a truly cosmopolitan population in which every nationality is represented, not only from China but from Japan on the east, and from Brazil, Mexico, California and San Fransisco on the West? So that the gallant Captain of the Royal Navy of 1812 anchoring in Bombay was indeed a most faithful chronicler of the population of that year. In 1813 there was a census of the popultion residing within the walls of the Fort. It numbered 10,801. Of these, according to the official record, 250 were English, 5,464 Parsis, 4,061 Hindus, 775 Moors, 146 Portuguese and 105 Armenians. This is a most interesting census of the Fort. It is evident that the trading Parsis well established were the strongest in number. Their enterprise in China and elsewhere attracted them to near the harbour. And, having regard to the fact that the principal traders were also brokers to the great European banking houses and firms of the day, the numerical superiority of the Parsis in the Fort is quite intelligible. There were the great China merchants, the Banajis, the Dadys, the Readymoneys and so forth. Then, as the Parsis were also contractors for the Commissariat and other army stores, like the Vachagandhis and the Shroffs (the forbears of Manockji Cursetji) they congregated in the Fort and the wealthier lived very near the European merchants' offices, the Government offices, the Customs House and the Town Barracks.

Old Time Houses.

The town houses of those century-old traders still stand, especially the house of the Dadys, at the south end of Cowasji Patel Street, just opposite the Hongkong Bank. That house to-day is well-nigh 150 years old and is worth being inspected by our distinguished town planner, Mr. Geddes, only to learn how substantially houses were built in those days and what the architects of the times, mostly Parsis, did by way of structural arrangements for light and air. A spacious *chowk* in the middle of the rich Parsi houses was a *sine qua non* and next a well and water tank to provide themselves with a fair supply of water during the periodic water famine of the annual summer. These wells served not only for ordinary purposes but for religious ones also. Hence it is that in the Fort almost every well-to-do Parsi house had a well. But in those days the finical sanitarian, and the empiric bacteriologist were not born. And there were no Cadells and Turners *et hoc genus* to air their unverified stories of malaria bearing insects to vex the soul of the orthodox, male and female. A true and authentic history of wells in Bombay would indeed be a great eye-opener, and well may a commission be appointed to impartially investigate how for it is expedient to close all wells and verify the unsubstantiated expedients of the executive officers, armed with a municipal bludgeon. Despite the closing of hundreds of wells during the last few years, malaria is adrift as ever, which clearly indicates the empiricism of the bacteriologists as to malaria wells.

Of course, the Hindus, generally a poor population, spread outside the Fort walls. There were some rich Banias living in the Fort, descendants of whom may yet be seen in the Rupji Manordas Street and the Bazargate Street. The ancestors of the late Messrs, Vurjivandas and Narotomdas lived in the former locality.

Beautiful and Wonderful.

It is estimated that, commencing from the Bazargate and going northwards to Parel, there was a population of 140,000. After 1814, when the security of life, at the close almost of the Peninsular War was great, the influx of traders like the Memons, the Cutchees the Khojas, and so on, was steady. They came to settle down in Bombay as traders and year by year swelled the population. And here we may for the present close the chapters, once more giving the graphic description of Bombay as it struck that very observant Captain Hall who was besides a faithful chronicler, " We can see nothing in China or Java or the Phillipine Islands or along the Malaya Peninsula or even in the interior parts of India, no singlecaste or dress or custom or form of superstition nor anything else belonging peculiarly to Eastern manners which we may not witness in Bombay in as genuine and apparently unsophisticated condition as on the spot to which it properly belongs. In 20 minutes' walk through the bazar of Bombay my ears have been struck by the sound of every language that I have heard in any other part of the world, uttered not in corners and by chance, as it were, but in a tone and manner which implied that the speakers felt quite at home." What a faithful picture and what would Captain Hall say were he to-day to revisit the scenes of his close observations of 1812-15! Verily, Bombay is not only beautiful but wonderful.

CHAPTER XXX—CENSUS—TAKING DURING THE FIRST HALF OF THE NINETEENTH CENTURY. HABITATIONS OF SPECIFIC COMMUNITIES.

THE next stage to be noticed in the enumeration of the population is that during the twenties of the 19th century, Census-taking was then a very primitive affair with none of the organisation we are now accustomed to. Neither was it possible with the most imperfect official machine to take it on a single day. Census schedules were yet undreamt of and census-marking and blocking an unknown art. It was the old, old way of counting heads at leisure by houses. So that it is a fact that it took in 1826 fully four months for a fresh enumeration after the one of 1815, say from August to November. The results were leisurely prepared with the tortoise-like pace of those arcadian days. So that it was as late as 1839 that Major Jervis, a most prominent name, associated with assiduity and education, gave a resume of it in 1839-40 in a paper read before the Bombay Geographical Society. The total then was one lakh fifty-two thousand, including a population in the harbour of 20,000 and of the military cantonments of 10,000. The Parsis had swelled to 6,000 in the Fort and 4,400 outside the Fort. The Hindus totalled 82,000 and Mussalmans 26,000. Of the English there were about 900 and the Portuguese 8,000. But four years later Mr. Lagrange estimated the number at two lakhs and twenty-nine thousand while in 1836, it increased by about 7,000 more. In 1846, Bombay—, thanks to a more orderly administration and a peaceful expansion of trade, boasted of five lakhs and a half. Thus by the middle of the nineteenth century Bombay had nearly quintupled her population. She was also able to make distinct progress in her trade and commerce, ot which a great deal later on. Suffice it to say that the first statutory Census was taken soon after 1863 when an Act was passed. But even at that period such was the conservatism or nervousness of the grand lords in Leadenhall Street in London, the august Board of the East Indian Company, that they vehemently opposed the Census Act! But they had an enlightened and tenacious ruler of Bombay in the person of Sir Bartle Frere, who, as the Satrap on the spot, knew infinitely better why a Census was wanted than the antiquated fossils of London. Sir Bartle was an enlightened Tartar and was therefore able to carry the day with him. Now, it happened that, owing to the American Civil War, there had begun the tide of immigration from the interior for the purposes of trading in cotton which by 1863 had already reached unprecedented exports. Next, the wild financial speculation which followed in its train brought a much larger number of people from the mofussil, all intent on amassing fortunes beyond the dreams of avarice. They said, " Luxmi the Goddess was dancing " in the city; so they must at once reap a rich harvest of gold. "Make hay while the sun shines" is a universalproverb, and the wisdom of the sages of old was justified in the population which gravitated to Bombay. Money was simply thrown into the lap. They had to gather it and quickly hie away to their native home, thanks to the great Golden Calf whom all then worshipped in the person of Premchand Roychand.

A Population of nearly a Million.

Dr. Leith was appointed the Census Officer and his enumeration gave a population of 864,000 souls. It was no doubt a little inaccurate, but all the same the influx into the city from outside could not have been even less than two lakhs of souls during the height of the speculation mania. It may be useful to remember that the shipping had greatly increased. Argosies after argosies entered and departed. King Cotton was supreme and the conveyance of the raw staple to Liverpool made a great demand on the shipowners of England; while, thanks to the same sovereign lord imports of enormous quantities of bullion had to come as the net profits of the great cotton merchants, besides heavy imports of Lancashire goods and other English commodities. That shipping made the harbour, the middle ground, live with skippers and the gallant crew,—"those hearts of oak," whose successors during the recent four year's blockade of the North Sea were so triumphant, keeping at bay the Huns who would have Europe kneeling at their feet. So that it is not at all surprising that there were as many as 32,000 seamen afloat in Mody Bay.

There were at the time 25,994 houses. The town which then largely comprised the Market, Doongri, Dhobi Talao and Girgaum was thickly crowded, though the three and four storied tall houses of our day were to be seen here and there only and counted on one's fingers. The official chronicler has observed that in those dense quarters there lived from 3,71 to 9.42 families in the two storied buildings. While the number of persons ranged in each house from 39 to 83.

A Contrast with To-day.

What a contrast the residential quarters of the fifties are with those of to-day. In the first place, it should be remembered that the tight little island being extremely limited in area, it was not then more than 16 square miles, the people had either to spread themselves laterally or vertically Except in the Fort, which was, as now, the centre of all banking and mercantile. business, the Market, Bhuleshwar and Mandvi, which were also the hives of a large inland trade, houses in these localities were not tall, going generally to a ground floor and two stories. No doubt in each section there were houses of three stories, but only a few. Elsewhere the population generally spread out laterally. There was more elbow room in the fifties for such spread than with the existing increased area of over 22 miles, being principally reclaimed ground. Fewer Europeans, than at the commencement of the century, had lived in the Fort. The principal merchants and their assistants lived at Byculla, Mazagaon and Sewri, which were absolutely suburban and presented none of the hideous sights of an interminable range of tall chawls of an insanitary character.

These outlying suburbs were all verdant and there were detached villas where the elite of the European community resided. The Governor and his Councillors and the Judges more or less lived in the vicinity of the Government House at Parel. Here and there you may still see vestiges of the old class of villas which that community occupied. These would give a fair idea of the locality and their accommodation. But most of the villas are gone. Between industrialism and jerry structure the suburbs have been swept away, the rural population has been driven northwards, first from Dadar, later on from Mahim and lastly from Bandora. Matunga was a marshy field where only rice cultivation was practised.

The Various Communities.

It was not till 1861, generally after 1864, that Malabar Hill began to be well populated. The remaining population in the Fort, specially the north, was occupied by Parsi merchants and traders, the Kapole Banias, men of the rank and wealth of Mangaldas Nathoobhoy and Vurjivandas Madhovdas, lived here and there in central town houses which still stand. Next were the wealthy Bhatias who resided in Bazargate Street and in old Mody Street, lying parallel to the east, in the direction of Mody Bay. Goculdas Tejpal, Goculdas Liladhar Pasta, Khatao Makanji, Jivraj Baloo, Jairam Sewji and such occupied the Bazargate Street, from the north end as far as the Parsi Agiary Street, south. In Holee Chukla also the population was Bhattia. This extended as far as Parsi Bazar Street, near the end of Gola Lane. Generically it was known as "Bhattia Wad." The "Bhattia Bag" in Fort Street, now renovated and rechristened "Victoria Place" was so called because all along its south the Bhattia population greatly preponderated when the "bag" so called was first built in the later part of the sixties. A few rich Arabs, Moguls and Borahs lived in old Mody Street, somewhere from the locality where an old Musjid stands at the corner of "Chana Street." The Arabs had a "Kava Khana" there. They were mostly horse dealers, but of a highly respectable and wealthy class. It was on this account that the Chana Street is more commonly known as "Kava Khana" lane. Among the Borahs, Mr. Tayabji, the father of the late Mr. Badrudin and his brothers, lived in old Mody Street. And another respectable Borah, then trading with China, was Mr. Ebrahim Nooroodin who had his business place in Bazargate Street, facing west, at the south corner of "Chana Street." A microscopic colony of Bagdad Jews, of whom, of course, the late Mr. David Sassoon was the most prominent, lived in Military Square and its vicinity in the Southern Fort. Thus, while the Southern Fort was mostly occupied by the English firms of whom the Forbes, the Remingtons, the Grahams, the Greys, the Peel Cassels, and others were most conspicuous, the Northern Fort, from Churchgate Street and Town Hall was almost wholly occupied by Parsis and rich Banias and Bhatias. As to the houses they were seldom over two stories but the one peculiarity was that each and all had high plinths, not less than 3 or 4 feet high, and each house had its verandah or otla, while the interior had their open places for light and ventilation called "chowks." So the town-planners and the builders of those days, though unscientific, knew better how to have light and air than your modern Improvement Trust.

Chapter XXXI.—THE EPOCH-MAKING FIFTIES. GREAT EVENTS AND INSTITUTIONS.

THE fifties in Bombay may be said to have been memorable in more ways than one. Not only was the population increasing but trade with foreign countries was expanding, the two great trunk railways were beginning to push forward, while overcoming great physical difficulties by land and sea, the first financial institutions under far-sighted men of business were being established, even the first cotton factory was well founded, while all around there were encouraging symptoms of her growing greatness and importance. Recalling the many stirring events of that eventful decade, the writer cannot help observing that to his boyish intelligence the city seemed to be aglow with busy life. There was about her nothing of the Sleepy Hollow of many an old and conservative Indian town. There was none of the Eastern torpor, none of the Eastern leisurely, nay dilatory, way of going about, none of that decrepitude which was fast stealing over the trades, industries and enterprise elsewhere. Thana, Calian, Surat, Broach, —all seemed to be so many shadows of medieval greatness, mere echoes of a decade of centuries buried in oblivion. Bombay was brisk and bright. Life was active. Life was earnest. The Fort was even in those days a huge beehive. And so was the heart of the town, notably the Market, Moombadevi, Bhuleshwar and Girgaum.

Locally the commencement of the decade (1850-60) must have been full of the highest significance to the ruling elders and the elderly Indian population. There was to be noticed that novel system of locomotion,—a steam engine in front puffing and emitting a suffocating smoke, and a few carriages being dragged along in its train on iron rails. It was the wonder of the world of Bombay. I can recall to my mind even today the scene which was vividly impressed on my memory as I stood midst an admiringcrowd, a few yards from the old level crossing at Byculla (just near the southern spur of the Nesbit Road overbridge) as the first train was opened for passenger traffic to a short distance. The railway was a new impression and a new dispensation, the unlimited potentiality of which for universal beneficence was, of course, unthinkable to my boyish imagination. Only there was a very pleasant feeling akin to a sensation that on that eventful opening day something Titanic was seen passing over a crowded part of Bombay.

The First Baloonist.

But if our first tiny railway train gave us so many pleasurable memories, not yet effaced, what is to be said about another memorable event far surpassing the railway which crossed the mind of the boy of 8. It was a transcendent scene enacted at Byculla by a Mr. Kyte, the first balloonist! Flight in the air! What may be that fairylike ball which could enable one to soar empyrean height, cleave the liquid air till in a few minutes' time it sped upward and upward on its ethereal course, showing only as a speck as it soared higher! Wonderful! The boyish astonishment surpassed the wonder with which the first railway train was viewed. When was the baloon seen? Why, somewhere from the place where now stand the stately Victoria and Albert Museum and the smiling and all-encircling Victoria Gardens. It was then a vacant suburban site allotted to the grass dealers of Bombay to stack their hay. There were little hillocks of grass, packed and piled close to each other for well nigh half a mile, just as one sees to-day in the burning sun of May thousands of cotton bales stacked on the Colaba Green. All Bombay and its wife in their hundreds and thousands had turned out from all points of the compass to view this new fairylike thing. The owners of the haystacks must have reaped a rich harvest of rupees for admitting private families to stand or sit at the top, wait for two or three hours to enjoy the scene all around and specially to view the baloon in the near distance on the ground moving to and fro as the aeronaut was inflating it with gas. To our boyish sight this process of inflation was an unextinguishable delight. As it moved to and fro, while yet captive, every five minutes, there would be a buzz and hum from hundreds of lips, "See, see, how it rocks and plays." "Ah, now it is distending." "See, see how it is bulging and puffing." And so on, *ad infinitum*, till the string was cut and Mr. Kyte flew into the air midst the hurrahs and huzzas of thousands of throats of the amazed and delighted spectators. Mr. Kyte was to be seen waving his white handerkchief as they lustily cheered him. The ascent was in the afternoon. There were three or four more ascents as the first was not successful owing to high winds, and they say the baloon landed somewhere on the opposite coast of Thana or Uran. However, the sight of the first baloon which ever ascended the azure sky of Bombay is still vivid in my memory. It was the wonder of wonders and the talk of every unit for many a day. Some versifier of the day commemorated in rhyme the praise of the valiant Kyte who soared like the eagle upwards to reach the heavens!

As to the unmistakable expansion of foreign trade a separate chaptér is devoted in the sequel. But meanwhile it may be observed here that Lord Elphinstone was the Governor of Bombay for fully seven years of the fifties. And in replying to the valedictory address presented to him by the Chamber of Commerce on the eve of the relinquishment of his high office he bore ample testimony to the growth of the Bombay foreign trade and paid his tribute of admiration to that body for its commercial sagacity and mercantile enterprise.

Economic Developments.

But the fifties witnessed two other great economic developments. Or rather, to be more accurate, two other foundations were laid in that decade for the greater financial facilities which the increasing commerce of Bombay imperiously demanded and for the institution of a new industry which since then has grown to such enormous proportions culminating in the gratifying prosperity of the city and the Presidency. No doubt, the Bank of Bombay about which more later on, was established in 1841. More or less it fairly served the financial needs of Bombay mercantile men. But it was clearly discerned that a single monetary institution could not adequately meet the growing requirements. There were also private bankers like the Forbes and the Remingtons. Still the need was great, so that in the early fifties the enterprise of some Parsi gentlemen, notably the Camas, with the co-operation of Mr. Cowasji Nanabhoy Davar, started what was long known as the Chartered Mercantile Bank of India, London and China, which, as the reconstructed Mercantile Bank is still flourishing among us, after having weathered more than one severe crisis in its onward destiny. The Oriental Bank, once a "pillar of gold," and the "Commercial Bank," both "chartered" in the legal sense of the term, followed. The uprising of these banking institutions,—they were mostly "Swadeshi,"

—based on sound banking principles, under the most trained, experienced and careful European management, was a sure sign of the steady expansion of Bombay's inland and foreign trade. And the first promoters and directors of all the banks were the great pioneers of those which a few years later sprang up like mushroom awhile and flourished during the golden days of the speculation of 1863-64.

As to the first cotton mill it has already been previously observed that it owed its origin to the talent, energy and enterprise of Mr. Cowasji Nanabhoy Davar, who may well be called the Tata of the fifties. It is a curious coincidence that a small cotton mill was established about the same time (1854-55) in Broach by a Lancashire man named Landon, the same which came to be later known as the Broach Cotton Spinning and Weaving Company under the management of Messrs. Greaves Cotton and Co. There survived till recently a Parsi octogenarian, Fardunji Munsif, in Broach who was the first carder of that factory.

A Great Civic Public Work.

Lastly, a great civic public work was also accomplished about the close of the fifties. The Vehar water-works projected in 1851-52, became an accomplished fact and the first waters of a few thousand gallons were introduced into the city in 1858-59, though the first sod of the works was turned as early as January 1856, by India's last Governor-General and the first Viceroy and Governor-General, Lord Canning. But the history of the supply of pure potable water in the fifties deserves to be separately narrated. So far, however, the reader will have noticed from the foregoing events recorded that the fifties of the nineteenth century was a memorable period in the annuals of our city. It was epoch-making in many respects. The early beginnings of new Bombay, the highway of Asia, must be reckoned from that era.

CHAPTER XXXII.—GREAT FIRE OF 1803 WATER FAMINE AND EXTENSIVE CONSTRUCTION OF WELLS AND TANKS. HEAVY CHOLERA MORTALITY OWING TO FOUL WATER.

IT has been previously observed that one of the greatest sanitary evils from which the Town and Island of Bombay lamentably suffered was the insufficiency of the supply of potable water during the annual summer season. In the fifties the citizens of the day, along with the Government, were keenly alive to the imperative necessity of removing that evil, having regard to the grievous fact that the impurity of drinkable water was the prime cause of the terrible annual mortality of over two thousand people on an average, from cholera, and of as many as over 4,000 during the years of epidemic of that fell disease. It is now sixty years since the Vehar water was introduced into Bombay, while two other supply lakes have been supplemented at a cost of over two crores rupees. But the cry of the insufficiency of water is still loudly heard in the hall of the Corporation while it is notorious the prolonged wai of the poorest of the masses for water whenever unhappily breakdowns occur in the mains. At such times it becomes most difficult and distressing for these waifs and strays of humanity to obtain the first necessity of life at the nearest public tap from their dwelling places. It may, therefore, be realised how the inhabitants of the town must have suffered each summer from the famine of water all throughout the first two centuries say, from the date of the acquisition of Bombay by the British. No doubt, till the beginning of the nineteenth century, the population of the island was even less than a lakh of souls and, therefore, the scarcity could not have been so deeply felt as it was after 1800. Many indeed are the stray notes of observant citizens and travellers which tell us of this woeful inadequacy of water. It is quite conceivable therefore how the city fared when such a calamity as a fire took place in those days of primitive appliances and backward civilisation. In one of the earliest chapters of these recollections, it has been recorded how a great fire overtook the Fort on the 17th February, 1803, and ravaged almost the entire north-eastern part as far as the Bazargate Street. Jonathan Duncan was the Governor of Bombay and resided not very far from the scene of that calamitous occurrence. The Old Secretariat was the gubernatorial residence at the time, and we can imagine with what feelings of dismay and regret that great and distinguished Governor must have watched the ravages of that fire while helpless to do any material service for its extinction, the want of water being so great.

The Great Fire of 1803.

Nothing awoke him so much as the plight of the afflicted citizens of that year to the paramount necessity of doing something solid and practical for a reasonable and continuous supply of water all throughout the season, which should be adequate not only to meet the necessities of domestic life, but to protect life and property themselves from the conflagration of the type of 1803. It may not be uninteresting here to quote the words of Jonathan Duncan himself as to that fire, in order that the present citizens of Bombay may truly appreciate the feelings and sentiments of their predecessors at the beginning of the nineteenth century and the chronic ills from which they suffered. We of to-day, who are on the whole so well served with water, despite the spasmodic wails of the poorest and the fierce jeremiads of the press and the Corporation, may thank ourselves that the catastrophe was the real beginning of the remedies which were finally resolved upon but which like everything official in India took another half a century to be fairly realised. It is indeed remarkable to reflect upon the tortoise pace at which so many important affairs and things have progressed. It would beat in reality even a colossal tortoise of the Celestial Government at Pekin. But here are the words of Jonathan Duncan in the Despatch which he addressed to his august masters, the Honourable the Court of Directors of the East India Company, in London :—

"So great and violent was the conflagration that at sunset the destruction of every house in the Fort was apprehended. The flames directed their course in a south-easterly direction from that part of the bazar opposite to the Cumberland Ravelin quite down to the King's Barracks. During the whole of the day every effort was used to oppose its progress, but the fierceness of the fire driven rapidly on by the wind baffled all attempts; nor did in visibly abate till nearly a third part of the town within the walls had been consumed."

The official chronicler ot old Bombay records that 471 houses, 6 "places of worship," and 5 barracks were destroyed. Such was the terrible catastrophe and though others of a similar character had from time to time taken place, notably the one of 1837, Bombay during the last half a century has never known of a conflagration of the character just described. The inadequacy of the water-supply in the town at the commencement of the nineteenth century may therefore be well imagined.

A Happy Contrast.

What a happy contrast is the condition of supply at the beginning of the twentieth century and the equipment and preparations of meeting the occurrence of even the largest fire. But as they say from evil cometh good and the first step was taken by Jonathan Duncan to remedy the evil before the last embers of that appalling occurrence had died out. Events, however, as already observed, moved slowly. The start was made. Hope sprung in the breast of the population of the day, but as Lord Bacon has observed hope makes a good breakfast though not always a good dinner. But the hope that something effectual was to be soon taken on hand satisfied a population which was patient and contented to an exemplary degree in striking contrast with the impatience and discontentment of the men of to-day.

The Water Famine of 1824.

If the great fire of 1803 was an evil that led to the beginning of good it was not till 1825 that a fresh stimulus had become necessary. The interval was occupied in prolonged consideration of the ways and means of obtaining the necessary water supply and of the sources from which it should be obtained. Official correspondence had to go backward and forward, red-tape and circumlocution were necessarily at their acme in those arcadian days of leisure, days when what could be accomplished today was postponed till to-morrow. Delay was inevitable on another account also. There were no telegraphs. Steam navigation was unknown, if even dreamt of. Despatches overland or *via* the Cape were the only means of communication so that at the best they had no more than three occasions in a twelve month to correspond with the

Honourable Court. Thus time sped on and another physical calamity again overtook Bombay in 1824. This time it was a water famine, the rainfall registered by the end of August having been no more than 25 inches. At the date Bombay was again fortunate in having at the helm of its administration another great statesman of renown, no other than Mountstuart Elphinstone. When we of to-day bear in mind that even with a population of a million souls with three great supply lakes delivering over 40 million gallons of water per day, we cry aloud for water and when, within our memory, the rainfall was twice less than 40 inches we should try to realise the state of the city with a population only one-fifth and with a short rainfall so unprecedented as 25 inches. Is it not possible to imagine the sufferings of those thirsty souls in that water famine year of 1824 and sympathise with their great hardships, inconveniences and privations! Elphinstone, after the manner of his great predecessor Duncan, appointed a Committee without loss of time to consider the grievous situation. It was resolved at once to repair a large number of wells and tanks which were then an absolute necessity in the city, never mind whether or not those wells and tanks contained the anopheles of the new fangled bacteriologists and the modern malaria-mongers. Indeed, during the first half of the nineteenth century, and even before, it would have been hopelessly impossible for any persons, high or low, to live without his water-supply being drawn from his own private well or from the public wells and tanks constructed by men of all castes and creeds with the true spirit of philanthropy. The malarial campaignist of to-day seems to be utterly oblivious of the past history of those tanks and wells. Had these sciolists been half so well acquainted with that history as with their own pretentious empiricism, they would see how great is the necessity even to-day of preserving the 3 or 4 thousand wells, tanks and reservoirs which abound in the city, never mind the anopheles. Malaria is a preventible disease, but what have they to say to the absolute famine of water ? Can they lay their hand on their heart, can they lay the flattering unction to their soul, and dare declare that rather the existing wells, tanks and reservoirs shouldbe closed than that people in times of water famine or emergency should get their supplies from those auxiliary sources provided by the foresight, humanity and the benevolence of a bygone people who had felt and suffered all the perils arising from the want of water. It was Mountstuart Elphinstone who not only directed old wells and tanks to be repaired and cleaned but to sink new wells, *cutcha* and *pucca*, of all varieties here, there and everywhere. Again, at no mean expense to the State he ordered the erection of many wells and tanks, in localities where there was the greatest want of water or to be improved and enlarged

The Tank at Dhobi Talao.

Thus it was that the confabulations, correspondence and Committees on water-supply which began with Jonathan Duncan and continued through the administration of Mountstuart Elphinstone at the pace of the snail, were not brought to a practical beginning till the construction of the Vehar reservoir was ordered to be taken on hand in 1850. Meanwhile the supply of water by means not only of old tanks and wells, but by the construction of new ones, went on apace. Reference may be made here to the tank still known to us as Framji Cowasji at Dhobi Talao. It was built in 1831. In 1849 the tank known as Babula was constructed and even so late as 1855 there was found a great necessity to have a large tank on the Esplanade known as the Nakhoda. "Sandy Seventy" as a schoolboy ot the Elphinstone Institution in that year has a vivid recollection of the excavations which had then just begun. The earth dug up was heaped in mounds all round and he and his other schoolmates used to go to the top to have some fun or play or even a little tobaggonning when the mounds were not very high. He also recollects two other large wells being *pucca* built at the north-west corner of the Cruikshank road which still exist. So also he had seen *cutcha* wells being dug up about the approach of every summer season in the southern Maidan which is now occupied by the Oval. They were opened every year about March and closed again as soon as the monsoon came. This practice continued till the introduction of the waters of the Vehar into the city became general in the early sixties. One has only to leisurely go round the town to-day and find out for himself the history of many of the tanks from Bhuleshwar to Parel and from Parel to Mahim. Indeed even in the Fort two wells were so well-known as to be a household word in every family. These were the wells known as Ganbava and Ramlal. The former was situated at the eastern end of the street bearing that name where the Borah Bazar street crosses it, both in a southerly and northerly direction. It was a famous well and the writer had seen with his own eyes how in the fifties men, women and children crowded at the well from morn to eve. How wrangles used to take place and how, as the summer season advanced, they went there as early as 1 o'clock in the raw morning to fill their chatties wits water. This well has now been filled up. The Ramlal well was situated in what was also a part of the southern maidan. It was a large affair and such was said to be the efficacy of the spring water to be drawn from it that crowds from the Fort resorted to it. It was built by a rich Marwaree of that name. It still exists there, but almost wholly filled in with only a two-feet opening at the top, just near the judges' entrance gate of the High Court, facing the Oval. Again, underneath the rampart walls, specially in what is now known as the Hornby Road, as well as in Fort Street and the Mint Road, wells had been constructed which even in the fifties were deemed to be "ancient." These wells also were crowded from early morning till night all throughout the summer season. But the names of the benevolent builders of these wells have now lapsed into oblivion unless the Municipal Corporation has a record of them.

CHAPTER XXXIII.—PHILANTHROPY FOR THE SUPPLY OF WATER, CHRONIC INADEQUACY, CONSTRUCTION OF THE VEHAR LAKE.

REFERENCE has more than once been made in previous chapters to that great name in Bombay philanthropy, viz., Framji Cowasji. He was not only a genuine philanthropist but a leader of men and high enterprise. Many were his benevolent activities which have been time out of number referred to by his contemporaries and which have been recognised by the present generation. Among those activities may be mentioned one or two in regard to the water-supply of Bombay during his own lifetime. It was he who first conceived the very practical idea of diverting water from a distant source to where it was most needed. In 1837, it is recorded, that he obtained the freehold lease of what is known as the Pawai Estate. This estate covered a very large area of fertile ground with an ample supply of water. Mr. Framji here carried on a large number of experiments in agriculture and horticulture. He was enabled to gratify this favourite pursuit of his because of the abundant supply of water there and in its vicinity. That vicinity, as we all know, was later on fully surveyed with the view of securing for the city a large reservoir. Vehar, which is only next to Pawai, was considered a great catchment area for the water flowing from the surrounding hills. Now it happened that a large tank was built some years ago before by another benevolent Parsi gentleman known as Mr. Cowasji Patel. It was constructed on a very central site in the town, the same where it so long stood till wholly filled in the other day. It was next door to the great charitable institution known as Madhav Bag founded by Messrs. Vurjivandas and Narottamdas, two dutiful and honoured sons of Madhavdas, who was a leader of the Kapole community in his own days. Cowasji Patel Tank Road, which should not be confounded with Cowasji Patel Street in the Fort, derives its name from this tank. In 1846 this tank which was so largely resorted to by the inhabitants of the locality in which it was situated, was found short of its normal quantity of water, and it is related that Framji Cowasji conceived the happy idea of supplying the deficiency by causing water to be conveyed there from the oart known as Mugbhat. He caused three wells to be sunk in that oart and water was supplied to the tank thence by means of steam machinery which cost about Rs. 30,000. Again, from Cowasji Patel Tank he introduced by means of an aqueduct water in two other tanks at Duncan

Road popularly known as "Do Tanki." But he had also undertaken to keep these two tanks supplied with water on certain conditions he made with the Government of the day in reference to the rents and revenues of his Pawai Estate. These facts tell us how a philanthropist of the type of Framji Cowasji removed the hardships of the chronic deficiency of water in a crowded part of the town of Bombay. It was the same spirit of benevolence which led a number of well-to-do and wealthy persons to dig wells and tanks all over the city here, there and everywhere for the free use of the people. In reference to the "Do Tanki" (Two Tanks) it may be here mentioned that it was the gift of a Mahomedan gentleman, one Suslaji Subanji, who constructed them in 1826. Mastan Tank, Nawab's Tank, Sankli Tank and so on, names still extant, at once inform us how charitable Hindus and Mahomedans of the first half of the nineteenth century vied with each other to supply this great necessary of life to the masses in the town by the construction of large tanks. The Municipal Executive of our day seem to give the go-by to the history of wells and tanks and brush aside all reasonable suggestions to keep open a large number of these, which even to-day supply potable water to the poor instead of indiscriminately causing them to be filled in under the pretext of their breeding anopheles a big bugbear.

First Attempt At a Reservoir.

But let us now come to the first practical attempt at constructing a large reservoir where water may be collected and eventually supplied by means of gravitation to the city. Colonel Crawford submitted to the Government or the Municipal authorities of the day three projects. The first was for intercepting the water (as related by Mr. Michael in his history of the Bombay Municipal Corporation) "of the stream which formerly took its rise near the village of Vehar, at a point not far from Koorla. Here the water was to be pumped up and brought under pressure into Bombay by iron pipes. The dam was not to be built to retain any large quantity of water, but merely to give sufficient depth to pump from. This supply every year could last so long only as the stream continued to flow or from the setting in of the monsoon up to about December. For the supply of the town during the other months a series of reservoirs were to be formed along the course of the stream above the dam, and as the stream dried up, the water in these reservoirs was to be let down to the lowest one where the pumps were to be placed."

"An alternative scheme suggested by him was to drain the Kurla valley by a system of underground channels to the point where the water was to be pumped up."

"His second project was to erect an engine at a favourable point on a hill in the village of Vehar near Kurla (12th milestone from Bombay) and to convey water to Bombay by pipes. This project was estimated to cost £52,063."

Other projects followed. One from Colonel De Lisle and another from Mr. Conybeare who was engineer to the Board of Conservancy in 1851. Both were disapproved of by the Government. At last in 1855, Mr. Conybeare submitted another alternative report which was finally adopted and it was on the basis of that report that the present Vehar Lake was constructed.

The First Water Supply From Vehar.

Many were the vicissitudes that occurred before the completion of the works, but, after all, the people of Bombay were gratified when they first got their water at their own doors from Vehar in 1864; though the water was actually introduced into the city in 1859. The distribution service in the town was not completed till 4 or 5 years after. There was universal joy on the occasion and everybody hopefully looked forward to an era of a constant and adequate supply and to the diminution of cholera. But it must be observed here that in the fifties the scarcity of water was a crying evil and the writer himself can bear his personal testimony to the scenes he viewed with his own eyes which happened in the Fort where he lived all throughout this period during summer. It should be remembered that such scenes were not only common to the Fort. They were experienced outside the Fort by many an old resident still living, septuagenarians, octogenarians and nonogenarians. But what are we to say to almost identical scenes which meet us even to-day, fully half a century after the introduction of Vehar water and nearly a quarter of a century after that of Tansa ? In the fifties the population was no more than between five and six lakhs. At the date of the introduction of Vehar water in the early sixties the population had swelled to eight lakhs and over, principally owing to the large influx of traders in cotton during the course of the American Civil War and to the fever of speculation which raged so furiously during the two years ending 31st March, 1865. The population to-day estimated at twelve lakhs, practically 50 per cent. more than what it was in 1864. But the quantity of water supplied has been immensely increased, say more than double, by the auxiliary Tulsi and the great Tansa. Under the circumstances, is it not reasonable to enquire why in the face of such statistical facts the poorest masses should, on the breakdown of our supplv for even six hours and more, present scenes at the public taps and elsewhere not unlike those of the days when the water deficiency was chronic? More. We have two balancing reservoirs, one at Bhandarwada and one at Malabar Hill. It seems there is a large daily draw off by the 90 cotton factories now in our midst, besides flour and other minor establishments. Again, there is a huge floating population at the docks and in the harbour. Look at the number of steam vessels and native craft annually arriving and departing from our shores. Lastly, there is the enormous consumption of water by those modern glorified caravanserais euphemistically called hotels. Just consider the influx of passengers from all the four quarters of the globe between October and March. We may add to our list the two big railways with their termini and the quantity of water which their workshops and locomotives consume from day to-day. These causes may be reasonably pleaded against the parrot-cry of those who are perpetually raising their lamentations on the inadequacy of the water-supply in and out of the Corporation.

But having said so much, there is yet a residue in the matter of our water-supply which is not yet satisfactorily explained by our Municipal Executive. Our successive water engineers have been perfectly at sea when questioned on this one residuum of fact. Is it a wonder if there is the same cry of insufficiency of water to-day with a population of 12 lakhs as when 50 years ago there was with a population of eight lakhs and when neither Vehar nor Tulsi nor Tansa Lake waters were available ? This is a puzzle, and Bombay would gladly give a prize of ten thousand pounds to any expert who could propound the real solution of this great hydraulic problem.

CHAPTER XXXVI.—SEWERS AND DRAINS.

AFTER a reference to the state of the population and water-supply in the city in 1850-60, it will be in the fitness of things that the condition of drainage should be described. Half a century ago and more the town was unsewered. Drainage in the modern acceptation of the term, that is to say, as understood by our latter day *hakims* of sanitation, was unknown. There were storm water drains as far as Girgaum and Grant Road. The then suburban sections of the city were innocent of even these primitive sanitary contrivances. These drains were in the middle of roads, streets and lanes and were so constructed as to allow of ventilation by means of perforated square stone covers on the surface of the road. Types of these primitive contrivances may still be seen in parts of the Northern Fort and in the town. The practice was to clean these by uncovering the perforated stone and by ladling out the dirty waters mixed with sullage in a horrible state of decomposition. The black foul semi liquid stuff was first thrown out on both sides of a street or road in a heap and after a day or two carted away. The work was generallly done by the lowest class of people commonly known as "parvaris" a class still flourishing in the city. The cleansing out operation was performed twice a year in the principal thoroughfares and srteets and once in the lanes. The decomposed gases emitted from the perforated covers saturated the atmosphere with foul exhalations and were not a mean contributory cause of fevers which in those days were not so minutely classified as they have been for some years past. Typhoid and remittant fever may have been known to the dŏctors of the period, but the masses only knew them by the generic name of fever all the divers kinds presently nomenclatured.

Open Sewers.

Beyond the storm water sewers there were open sewers, a foot or so wide. They were like so many trenches which went in front of dwelling houses chiefly in the crowded localities outside the Fort. The whole of Dhobitalao, Chandanwadi, Girgaum proper, Mandvi, Khara Kuva and so on had these elongated cesspools. The only difference between the covered sewers and these cesspools was that the latter had the advantage of sunlight and open air. So far these cesspools were not so deadly in their effect on the health of the residents in the localities mentioned as the other. The foulest matter used to be discharged at certain points on the eastern and western foreshores, which were connected by some old obsolete kinds of drains built as far back as 1824. Some of the channels may still be discovered when dug out.

There is not the slightest doubt that the extremely rudimentary system of sewers, for there was no drainage, was the principal cause of engendering fevers. If the insufficient and impure supply of water annually claimed a large holocaust causing deaths from cholera from 2,000 to 4,000 and more this condition of the sewers and the cesspools sowed the germs of fever. Add to this the low vitality of the mass who lived in their *kotris*, as insanitary as those to be witnessed in scores of slums to-day, together with their overcrowding and it will be intelligible why Bombay in the fifties and the early sixties was so unhealthy. The report of that able sanitary officer, Dr. Leith, and a little later on of Dr. Haines, an equally able sanitarian, whom I still recall as my Professor of Chemistry and Botany in Elphinstone College (1858-59) show what the unhealthy condition was. Perhaps the following quotation from Dr. Haines' report would not be uninstructive for comparing notes with the condition of health still prevalent in what is magniloquently called "Beautiful Bombay—" or the "Bombay of Palms and Palaces." Yet, the *purdah* only of the beauty of the outer part of the city needs to be uplifted to enable the impartial sanitarian of to-day to see what points of sameness were to be found in the beginning of the sixties when Dr. Haines made his report. He observed that the average of male mortality between 1853 and 1861 was 125 to 100 females. In those days the first great tide of labour immigration in the city had not set in till after 1858 or thereabouts when the pioneers of public works by private enterprise came on the scene. The Elphinstone Land Company, established by the great firm of Messrs. Nicol and Company, had just started works of reclamation of the eastern foreshore. And later on, in 1863, was the second great tide caused by similar reclamation of Backbay under the direction of another equally distinguished firm, that of Messrs. Ritchie Stuart and Company. The brothers Fleming were conspicuous in the first and Messrs. Tracey and Michael Scott in the second enterprise. But to proceed with Dr. Haines' report: "It is sufficiently obvious from the figures that the state of public health in this town is in the highest degree unsatisfactory." He pointed out the causes which contributed to that insanitary condition. Those which fatally contributed to the result were "squalid filth within doors and without, deficient arrangements for scavenging and imperfect drainage." As to the low state of vitality of the masses, Dr. Haines said: It was "caused by the difficulty of procuring sufficient and wholesome food and especially by their breathing for ten or twelve hours out of the twenty-four the stifling atmosphere of their narrow and crowded chambers loaded with animal exhalations." What a dismal, sickening picture that was of the life of the masses in those days! Are they any better off to-day? That is a problem which may well engage the attention of our sanitarians. Overcrowding is as intense in 1919 as it was in 1860 and 1863.

Insanitary Chawls of to-day.

Then as to the insanitary *kotris*. How are the labouring masses better situated! Are those insanitary chawls to be found by the hundreds in the slums in any way better than the more lowly ones of fifty and sixty years ago? Just reflect on this important aspect of the question from another point. In those days municipal conservancy was of a rudimentary character; there was no organised Municipality and no Health

Officer with a well-paid staff of deputies and a host of outdoor inspectors. There was an impure and indequate water-supply : there was only an apology for any kind of drains, scientific or unscientific, ancient or modern. They had hardly even two lakhs per annum to spend on the whole conservancy of the town numbering between five lakhs to eight lakhs at the date of Dr. Haines' report, where we now spend the liberal sum of 25 lakhs as our gross expenditure on sanitation and conservancy. But what is the result ? Can it be honestly averred that sanitarily Bombay is better to-day ? We have now a water-supply of fairly pure, water which brings in a fat revenue of over 15 lakhs. Our water works have cost over three and a half crores. We have what is euphemistically called a "scientific system of drainage," huge underground ovoid sewers which generate the most poisonous gases; and we have many new-fangled sanitary institutions of the day, besides big hospitals and a dozen municipal dispensaries. Is overcrowding less or more? And if the state of things described by Dr. Haines nearly 60 years ago is still existent, perhaps, with a shade of amelioration here and there, can we lay the flattering unction to our conscience and unhesitatingly declare that the Bombay of 1919 is sanitarily better off than that of 1850-60? And how much of insanitation is owing to our scientific drains? But thereby hangs a dismal, nay gruesome, tale which must be related.

CHAPTER XXXV.—MR. CONYBEARE'S GRUESOME PICTURE OF DRAINS—DR. BLANEY—THE DRAINAGE COMMISSION.

SOMETHING fuller and more authoritative in matters of conservancy in the city during the fifties needs to be related. For instance, in 1852, Mr. Conybeare, Superintedent of repairs to the Municipality of the day, had submitted a report to the Board of Conservancy in the matter of the so-called drains then existing which it is useful to recall here. "Open drains," he said, "or rather receptacles for filth abound to the native town to an extent, I believe, to be unparalleled elsewhere. Secondly, that in most divisions of native towns our population is overcrowded beyond all English precedents. And for these two reasons I think we may confidently expect that in Bombay the drainage of undrained streets will be attended by so much larger reduction in the death-rate than has been found to result from similar improvement in England." But it took another quarter of a century and more to make a start, and that not without the machinery of a drainage commission as a preliminary. Later on, a reference to that Commission will be made. But meanwhile another extract may be quoted from Mr. Conybeare's report to inform the sanitary student of the day of the description the drains. "The open drains, or rather uncovered receptacles of filth, that I have alluded to, are the open side gutters by which nearly every street in the native town is polluted. These do not deserve the name of drains.... These side gutters can therefore only be considered in the light of continuous open cesspools extending along both sides the whole length of nearly every street of the native town and rendered (irrespective of their of their greater extent) more objectionable than ordinary cesspools by the circumstance of their being in actual contact with and soaking into the foundations of the whole street frontage of each house." Here is a graphic but faithful description of the rudimentary drains or cesspools which existed in the town nearly three-quarters of a century ago. The writer can add his own testimony to the above statement of facts. How dangerous were these cesspools to public health, and yet how they were tolerated even in the fifties no man can tell. Perhaps a guess may be allowed in one direction, namely, that sanitary science was elementary at that period for practical purposes even in England and on the Continent. Thus all was darkness in Bombay and one generation after another lived in a happy-go-lucky style oblivious of the heavy bill of annual mortality and altogether ignorant of what the local sanitary authority continuously reported to his Government. Said Mr. Conybeare: "The evils arising from cesspools or open receptacles of filth of even ordinary extent and position is thus stated inthe first report of Her Majesty's Commissioners for enquiry into the state of large town and districts." "The medical witnesses have brought before us facts in support of their strongly urged and unanimous opinion that no population can be healthy *which lived amidst cesspools or upon a soil permeated by decomposing animal or vegetable refuse giving off impurities to the air in their houses and in the streets.*" Many instances occur where the walls of the adjoining houses are constantly wet with fœtid fluid which frequently affects the atmosphere of the rooms so as to render it impossible to keep food for one single night without its being tainted."

But judging from events it seemed as if Mr. Conybeare, the sanitarian in advance of his times in Bombay city, had cried in the wilderness and the narrative he related in his report further emphasises the fact.

Police More Important Than Drains !!!

For, at a meeting of their Worships, the ancient Bench of Justices, the wise men composing it resolved that a policeman was of greater necessity to prevent a murder here and there than any consideration of sanitation! So in conformity with this wonderful civic logic, they resolved to spend Rs. 20,000 in strengthening the police, but refused to spend the same sum on the improvement of public health! They entirely forgot what overcrowding and the miasmatic cesspools did by way of killing innocent people in a year. The policeman, so bitterly argued Mr. Conybeare, at the best would be useful in saving 3 per cent. of murders, but the Rs. 20,000 on sanitation would save 30 per cent. of lives lost by preventible causes, specially by reason of poisonous drains! But the cimmerian darkness on sanitation prevalent in the fifties has not entirely been dissipated even in the year of grace 1919. For the person walking in the many congested streets of the town to-day, with eyes open and his olfactory nerves attuned to a lively sensibility, might tell us that the ignorance still prevailing is astounding, despite the leaflets and the limelights, besides the lecturers and the sisters of mercy, which the indefatigable Dr. Turner had been so assiduous in thrusting on them with all the reasoned enthusiasm of the benevolent samaritan. Such is the knowledge of rudimentary sanitation among the masses to-day. This unit is oblivious and heedless of aught else save how daily to fill his belly and that of his children. The stern necessity of maintenance or nourishment overrides the trumpet call of the sanitarian. Education alone is the solvent.

Dr. Blaney.

There was that good citizen of renown and medicine, Dr. Blaney. An Irishman by birth, he set foot on the soil of Bombay in 1845, when Sandy Seventy was in his swaddling clothes. He made the city his domicile to carry on his profession. But after a few years' experience, with eyes and ears open, he soon came to the conclusion that the two dire necessities of the growing and changing Bombay were a pure supply of water and a clean town, free from poisonous and insidious gases. And as he watched, like the onlooker from a near distance, what was going on and what the witches at Bombay Castle were about, he determined to be himself a sanitary reformer. As his practice grew he discovered how al kinds of poisonous fevers claimed a larger and larger number of victims. So he began hammering away on the subject with observation and experience, first in the newspapers and later on from his proper place at the Bench of Justices and its successor, the Bombay Municipal Corporation. The proceedings of the Legislative Council in 1865, when Mr. Walter Cassels, a great name in the mercantile community, thundered away on the insanitary condition of Bombay, on the introduction by him of the first Bombay Municipal Bill, were a great stimulus to the public spirit and activity of that good doctor. Conservancy for years together was the principal theme of his song in the Corporation. Time rolled on its onward course. Municipal Commissioners in turn deplored the undrained condition of the town and the annual holocausts from fever. So too did the Health Officers in their turn, till one day at last public opinion forced the hands of the Government to give practical effect to the cries of the enlightened citizens for a perfect, well-considered and well-digested scheme of drainage. So in the October of 1877 the Government by a Resolution appointed a Committee to investigate the whole problem as to how the drainage of the city could be best carried out and at what expense.

A Lamentable Mistake.

The scope of the reference was wide and embraced many an enquiry into divers directions. The Committee consisted of Dr. Hunter, First Physician of Sir J. J. Hospital as President, Mr. Wilson Bell, Engineer of the G. I. P. Railway Company, Mr. Walton, Municipal Engineer, Mr. Pedder, once Municipal Commissioner, Mr. Ormiston of the Port Trust, Mr. Arthur Crawford, Dr. Cook, and Captain Maryatt, then Deputy Consulting Engineer for Railways Ample evidence of all kinds ot experts was taken and owing to the peremptory instructions of Sir Richard Temple, who, for reward of his labours as the Imperial Famine Commissioner of 1876-77 was appointed Governor of Bombay, the report was hastened on and submitted to Government by 22nd January 1878. The beauty of this ill-digested and hastily considered report was that its main recommendation to construct ovoid underground drains was against the weight of the majority of expert evidence. Dr. Blaney was no mean witness and he opined that such drains were utterly unsuited to a tropical city and would be the largest generators of poisonous gases converting the city into a "huge mephitic temple." That prophecy has been most lamentably realised for years past and a crore of rupees and more has been wasted. Another 2 crores will now be needed to convert the "mephitic temple" into a perfect Hygeia.

CHAPTER XXXVI.—PRIMITIVE LIGHTING IN THE FIFTIES.

LIGHTING and police have long since been recognised as the two eyes of a great city. So much so that it is a common phrase on the lip of the man in the street, that a shining light in a street is worth two policemen. The service which public lighting renders to a community is deemed so invaluable for purposes of protection of life and property that throughout the civilised world lighting is deemed a *sine qua non* of modern civilisation. It is impos sible for us, who inherit the civilisation of centuries from historic times, to conceive how the ancients, whether in India, Persia, Arabia and Asia Minor or in Egypt or in Greece or Rome managed without street lights. Lamps or lights there may have been in dwelling houses in cities as in rural areas. But there is no record of lighting public roads and streets. So that it is possible to conceive the cimmerian darkness which must have clothed cities from times immemorial to within three or four centuries ago. He would make a name for himself who could enter on this virgin field of research as to lighting from historic times to date. Ours is an age prolific in a variety of researches. Why then should not a research in this direction be undertaken by some one competent for the task?

Rudimentary Lighting.

Leaving this subject alone, it may be worth knowing how Bombay fared in reference to public lighting during the fifties? Thereby hangs a tale which is as instructive as that of water-supply and drainage. The city had a kind of rudimentary lighting on some of the public roads. At long distances on the Esplanade Road were to be seen after dusk oil buttees with dirty oil and flickering wicks which gave an exceedingly dim light. Were one to compare its power with that of the gas and electric lamps of the day it would be no exaggeration to say that the street buttees of the fifties were like so many farthing rush lights. Still that was even a good beginning when the fact is recalled that prior to 1842 the city remained in a condition of blissful darkness after eventide. The first few oil lamps on posts came to be used after 1842, thanks to the wonderful civic energy displayed by the Worshipful Bench of Justices of the times. The matter was mooted as far back as 1832. But it took ten long years to introduce this "great" reform! Nevertheless, the citizens of 1842 may thank their stars that the delay was not so provoking or protracted as that which first gave her an adequate supply of pure water after fully fifty years of circumlocution and red tape. Verily in all respects Bombay, was an Arcadia, or a Sleepy Hollow if you please during well nigh the first two centuries after her acquisition by the British. Her progress in all vital directions was at the pace of the snail, though we are bound to say that she has made up and more than made up five hundredfold, for her past Arcadian simplicity of civilisation between 1850 and now. She has really grown and expanded since the railway era with all the speed of the fastest express.

20 Years' Progress.

And here we might just give a glimpse, and a glimpse only, of what had taken place since 1832 when the matter of public street lighting was seriously mooted by the Bench of Justices. That historical entity of the times met in the first place to find out authoritatively whether they were empowered at all to undertake the lighting. The legal adviser having set at rest all qualms of civic conscience, so sensitive of law and order, on the point, the worshipful masters of the city might resolved to enquire as to the localities or areas where lights should be and what the cost of lamps, posts and oil buttees would be. They went to sleep thereafter, taking perhaps their forty winks, before again rising themselves to a fever of activity. A few lamps, number unknown, were placed in position in 1843. And it seems that ten years later their number did not exceed 50 ! ! ! But the want of the eternal pence was the greatest drawback to carry out any number of improvements suggested to the Justices. And with that economic conscience which is still to be seen so keenly rampant in their successors of to-day in civic affairs, the Justices would only light the lamps from dusk to midnight and none during the moonlight hours. And what may be the annual cost of each such lamp? Just Rs. 17.

Chronic House-breaking.

It may at this stage be useful to recall the dismal fact that both lighting and police had been forced on the Justices by reason of the chronic condition of housebreaking and theft prevailing in the town after dark. The least crowded were most liable. So also the maidans. It has been authentically related that gangs of thieves used to go about armed, causing great terror to the law-abiding citizens. Life and property were considerably unsafe. And many were the complaints of the leading citizens to those in authority to do something effective to allay that terror. Murders were not infrequent, and it was hardly the case that more than 20 to 25 per cent. of the stolen property was recovered by the sparse police of those days. Sandy Seventy well remembers some thrilling stories of the raids of those armed crews of thieves at Girgaum which was more or less a suburb. It was one of the strongholds of these men owing to many exposed parts and fields and oarts. There was a country-house where his father used to resort and twice in one memorable year the gharry conveying him and his parents to the Fort was pursued by these rascals. As the Angrias were the pirates on the high seas so this fraternity on land, these highway robbers, were carrying on their nightly raids with impunity. Each house with a verandah in the Fort, in Khetwady, Chandanwady and Girgaum had a lantern with a lamp hung. The doors and windows of the ground floor of the houses were fast locked and bolted after dark and the well-to-do kept Ramosis of the old village watchmen type to guard their premises at night. These robbers greatly frightened women and children. Persons driving in carriages used to keep fast-going horses so that the armed robbers, with naked swords in their hands, should not overtake them. But more of this when the police of the period comes to be described.

The First Gas Lamps.

Sufficient to say that buttee lamps, which increased year after year, in numbers were universally deemed inefficient to light the town So that in 1859 the Justices resolved to introduce gas. Some correspondence ensued as to the financing of lighting by gas when finally introduced. The Government suggested that the Justices should raise a special loan. But eventually it was deemed best that an English Company should be invited to take up the work. And some enterprising citizens of the day, including the firm of Messrs. Nicol and Company, arranged for the successful floating of what is now the Bombay Gas Company. It was in 1865 that Bombay was first lit with gas, that is to say, the principal public streets. The first year had only 220 gas lamps. Great as was the satisfaction of the citizens when Vehar water was first introduced into the city a little earlier, there was greater satisfaction when gas light was introduced. And so remarkably did the people appreciate it that some rich citizens offered the Municipality, then just established, to present those huge five and three light lamps with fine posts at the junction of the great roads in the city. Mr. Arthur Crawford was greatly instrumental in thus promoting this branch of civic utility, and it is well known that some worthy wag of the time nick-named those triangular lights as "Crawford's fireflies," from the fact that the lamps when lighted looked from a distance like so many fireflies hanging in the air!

Chapter XXXVII.—The Evolution of the Police.

THE writer of these lines frankly confesses his ignorance of the existence of any elaborate and comprehensive history of the Police from historic times. Should such a history exist it would prove not only a most interesting and instructive narrative but an invaluable *vade mecum* for all the great States of the world, East and West. More. From the point of the political philosopher, it would make a fascinating chapter of human evolution. Modern civilisation traces our complex society to the humble primitive village. And it is to be presumed that the history of the village from historic times would give us the genesis of the police, beginning with the village watchman. He may be taken as the embryo, the protoplasmic entity, whence has blossomed the full-blown policeman, not forgetting the modern spy, so disagreeably in vogue on the surface of the globe, and nowhere a more disagreeable intruder and unwelcome guest than in this police-riddled and police-ridden country. In the pastoral age the shepherd must have been the chief person who kept watch and guard over his sheep lest his neighbour should spirit away his lamb or ewe. And in the agricultural condition which followed it, the cultivator in the field whence later on sprung the village watchman.

The watch, it may be imagined, was communal in its character till the development of the rural area into the urban brought with it the first faint glimmerings of keeping watch and guard over individual property. The guard over life must have come many a generation later on, as the village headman, in process of time became the patriarch, and afterwards the chief tribesman, to be eventually transfigured into the king. The patriarch or the headman of the tribe or the king would have not only property to watch, but his personality to protect. Family feuds, leading to bloodshed, would necessitate superior class of watchmen, the *dwarpal* of ancient India, that is say, the keeper of the gate. But as township developed and population grew, and the idea of military fortifications began to dawn, to prevent a next door chief from making a raid on his neighbour, the superior naboths eyeing with jealousy the adjoining vineyards, the gates of the town would have then sentinels and watchmen. And if the town was surrounded with hills, those hills themselves would be the natural towers or turrets for its guarding. Later on beacon fires must have come into use by these watchmen to give signal to other friendly hills. That was the ancient telegraphic or signalling system of which Aeschylus in his

"Agamemnon" and "Persians" has given us such a graphic description, till we come to the days of border chivalry in feudal and mediaeval ages and the Fiery Cross and beacon lights of Walter Scott. It would, however, be roaming into entirely a philosophic or evolutionary region to talk about the primitive system of watch which in our days has developed into the police, albeit the word is a derivation from the Greek *polis*.

The Chowkidar.

In the village communities of India the watchman or "Chowkidar" was an important entity, and our belief is that were modern civilisation to decline and sink back into the pristine condition it was thousands of years ago, this entity would be bound to exist. The chowkidar is immortal. The complexity, however, of modern society, has brought into play the policeman as we know him to-day. Even this modern *avatar* does not carry his pedigree beyond a hundred years or more. The idea of a regular legion of watchmen to safeguard life and property is the product of our modern society of at the utmost fifteen decades. It is only in a civilised country, where wealth accumulates and where property springs up, and where, above all, the division of labour in its manifold aspects is well understood, that the ideal policeman can be manufactured and made to flourish. And our Indian policeman of the day is simply a miniature mockery of the great Bobby of London, the theme of world-wide admiration.

The earliest settlers of British in Bombay no doubt brought with them from the old country their ideas of the policeman. That first and far-sighted maker of Bombay, Gerald Aungier, is said to have intuitively discovered in the Bhandari of Mahim and Mazagaon the men well fitted to keep watch and ward. The tapper of the toddy tree, perched on one of its topmost branches may be taken as a good specimen of keen-eyed observer, looking afar like the sailor of an English ship, who could keep his watch all round at a great distance. It may be that the Bhandari was there as such during the Portuguese occupation of Bombay, having regard to the fact that the immediate predecessors of the British in the town and island had their fortifications at Sion, Worlee, Sewree, Mahim, Bassein and so on They may have been soldiers undoubtedly, but in all probability the Bhandaris were also enlisted as a kind of auxiliary so that it is intelligible to understand Gerald Aungier organising them into a regular militia for keeping watch at certain places in the town. But night patrols were not instituted till 1694. It has been already observed more than once that lawlessness and brigandage were most rampant in the seventeenth and eighteenth centuries. The Portuguese occupation of Bombay was frequently interrupted by the Angria and Moplah pirates and their counterparts on land. They were a terror to the town. And it is an historical fact how about the close of the seventeenth century the Seedees had invaded the Fort and how the conspicuous gallantry of Cowasji Patel had freed that locality from those lawless marauders. That gallantry was generously rewarded by the East India Company by way of inam lands to him and his successors, and it is well known that till the middle of the nineteenth century the members of the Patel family enjoyed those lands till the vicissitudes of fortune obliged them to part with a considerable amount. Highway robbery and brigandage continued rife spasmodically for well nigh a hundred and forty years with varying fortune.

The First Regular Police.

But so long as the gang of thieves and robbers infested the town coming down or swooping like the Assyrian, they were a great terror to the populace, specially to those living in less crowded parts of the town. It is said that Girgaum was their great objective and partly the Esplanade. They would retire to the sequestered suburban localities of Sion, Mahim and Worlee, and as there was no organised force to pursue them day after day till arrested, they came down whenever it suited their purpose and robbed and murdered people with impunity. It was this chronic condition of the unsafety of life and property that led to the disbandment of the Bhandari militia and their conversion in 1771 to a regular police. The strength, as recorded by our official chronicler, was 45 officers and 400 men. A few years later there was an addition in order that the watch may be continuous by day and night. The chief was designated Lieutenant of Police, and the first holder of the office was one Mr. James Tod. It is not exactly known where his headquarters were; but it may be presumed by analogy that it was in the Fort like all other important offices of the administration. It would be interesting to learn whether the street called Tod, in the Fort, running at right angles from Hornby Road, near Alice Buildings, was named after that officer. It should be remembered, as stated in one of the earliest chapters, that the greater part of the Fort was occupied by a number of civil officers, as it was mostly unbuilt and open altogether to the fresh westerly breezes. The Gunbow Street, which runs parallel in a northerly direction to Tod Street with Cowasji Patel Street between the two, was equally unbuilt in the west, and there for a time our early civil court was accommodated in the large oart, afterwards known as Mopla's pole. There is the tablet which marks the place where the court sat. Similarly, it is to be presumed, the lane leading from Tod Street, north, to a short distance was called Barber Lane, generally attributed to a surgeon of that name. In all probability the surgeon and the Lieutenant of the Police were given accommodation for their office as well as residence in that locality.

CHAPTER XXXVIII.—THE POLICEMAN OF THE FIFTIES. AND FAMOUS POLICE COMMISSIONER.

IF the fifties of the nineteenth century in Bombay were an epoch-making period in the history of the City of Bombay in many respects, as already narrated, they were not less so in the matter of police. But before describing some of the outstanding features during that decade which stands out as a great landmark, a few minor incidents in the evolution of the police prior to it may be briefly recorded here. One broad fact should be remembered, that from the date of the original formation of the police, its cost was defrayed by the city whose administration was entrusted to the Bench of Justices. But, while the cost of the city police elsewhere, as years rolled on, was defrayed in every other part of the country by the Government,

Bombay was, curiously enough, most exceptionally treated. The cost continued to be charged to the Municipality which, however, vainly attempted time out of number to have it transferred to the shoulders of the provincial authorities but without avail. It was only the persistent efforts and the courageous public spirit of Sir Pherozeshah M. Mehta which, after a protracted struggle of 50 years, led during the generous administration of Lord Lamington, to the police charges being wholly defrayed by the Bombay Government under certain well-guarded limitations and conditions.

A "Deputy of Police."

Though the designation of the Lieutenant of Police given by the local authorities in 1779 was not sanctioned by the Court of Directors in London, a year later they grudgingly sanctioned the magnificent sum of rupees three thousand per annum for a "Deputy of Police." Wonderful Court of Directors were they, capable of ringing the refrain of Tweedledum and Tweedledee, and worthy of some Gilbertian pen of that day! Was it not a memorable event for that august authority only to substitude the word "Deputy" for "Lieutenant"? But the poor paid Deputy on Rs. 250 per month was scarcely able to cope with the robberies and other more serious crimes prevalent then, having regard to the microscopic body of the police he was in charge of. Some regulations urgently needed were passed in 1779. These, however, would seem not to have had the slightest effect in reducing crime. For it has been related that the Grand Jury was constrained in 1787 to make an emphatic protest against the inefficiency of the police in repressing crime. The Grand Jury, it may be observed, was the authority who had to find what was called a "true bill" of indictment against the accused committed by the Magistrate to the quarterly Sessions. These functionaries had, therefore, the necessary data before them to make the strong protest they did. They returned once more to their charge in 1793 which led to the passing of a Police Act in that year. As a corollary, it is to be presumed, of that enactment, the designation of the Deputy Commissioner came to be altered to Superintendent. It was no doubt a more imposing title indicating the importance of the authority. And this title, it may be here observed, continued till Sir Frank Souter had it changed into the "Commissioner" in the seventies, after the Second Municipal Act or, as it is more generally known, the Municipal Reform Bill, was passed. That gallant Bahadur, who had earned a reputation for pursuing and arresting the rebel Tantia Topee, was ambitious of a first class designation for a first class police in a city which had already assumed the self-constituted but not unjustifiable title of the First City in India. But the more immediate effect of the Police Act of 1793 was the great improvement effected in the scheme of patrolling the City by day and night.

It seemed, however, that the tribe of hardened robbers, in spite of all police vigilance and reforms, carried on their nefarious trade merrily, snapping their fingers at the full blown superintendent and laughing him and his posse of sepoys to scorn. At last the Government was constrained to appoint a strong Committee to investigate the matter and report what drastic methods should be adopted for the suppression so greatly vexed and of crime which frightened the peaceful population. And once more in 1809 Sir James Mackintosh addressed the Grand Jury on the inefficiency of the Police. More, the Police Magistrate himself was inveighed against for the unlawful practice of sentencing criminals in his police office which was deemed irregular. The same distinguished Judge or Recorder as he was then called promulgated his ordinance in 1802. In the teeth of all that was done gangs of well armed robbers infested the city. Affairs continued in this parlous state till 1839 when the Worshipful Bench so badly wanting in the eternal pence for many a civic reform augmented the Police force at a cost of Rs. 10,000 per year, a considerable sum indeed for those days of inelastic Municipal revenue.

Things jogged on. The sea pirates and their masterful counterparts on land were unabated in their awful depredations. At last the Bombay Chamber of Commerce came to the rescue of the city. In those days it was not only a power for good and potential influence in matters of commerce only. It took the keenest interest in civic affairs other than commercial. The Chamber, in response to an earnest appeal by the Indian citizens, addressed a long letter to the Government bringing to its notice the condition of affairs and the urgent expediency of saving mercantile goods traffic especially, from molestation. The following extract from its Report of the meeting of the Chamber of Commerce, held on 28th September 1853, will inform the reader of the deplorable state of things in the city.

"Your Committee had its attention directed in June last to the alarming prevalence of robberies in the Fort, native town and Colaba and to the inefficieny of the Police force for the prevention and detection of these depredations, an inefficiency the more remarkable as the robberies referred to frequently occurred as well as by day as by night. The property abstracted, comprised cotton bales and other bulky packages, the removal and after concealment of which in crowded localities must have been a matter of extreme difficulty under an active or trustworthy system of Police. On enquiry it appeared that robber gangs, systematically organized for the purpose of plunder, infested the island and harbour, and the dread of their vengeance coupled with an utter want of confidence in the Police force, completley paralysed that system of the native trading community who were the chief sufferers and prevented aggrieved parties from lodging complaint with the magistrates or adopting any united efforts to bring so serious an evil before the notice of the authorities."

Mr. (afterwards Sir Henry) Anderson, who was the Chief Secretary, readily and most courteously responded to the appeal of the Committee, and with great alacrity and promptitude undertook to abate the evil. Said the Chamber: "The result has been in the opinion of your Committee to check in a great degree those disorders, and to allay the active alarm which the native trading community entertained on this subject." In their next year's report the Chamber gratefully acknowledged the efforts which the Government of the distinguished Lord Elphinstone had made to check the robberies. "Your Committee has the pleasure to confirm and continue the favourable testimony of its predecessors to the salutary effects of the reorganisation, and the real ability with which the operations of the force, preventive and detective, have been directed and superintended by Mr. Forjett, the officer specially selected for the arduous and delicate duty of introducing the much needed reform."

Idol of the Public.

Act 13 of 1856 which was passed had had the most beneficial effects. Apart from the inefficiency of the Police, the Committee of Inquiry insttuted about the time by the Government brought to light the rampant corruption which prevailed in the force, European and Indian. It was fortunate indeed that Lord Elphinstone was able to engage in this arduous and responsible post of the Superintendent of Police an officer of the calibre, detective talent and unceasing energy of Mr. Charles Forjett. With the police reformed under his able and active guidance and control it soon became a fine force, real guardians of the life and property of the citizens. The model force was highly praised. Mr. Forjett's ubiquity, suppleness, liguistic lore and all other high qualifications made him the idol of the public. He was every inch appreciated as the Superintendent of Police. His name was a household word in the community. It was on the lips of the oldest person in the city and the youngest, after his daring discovery of the dangerous plot concocted by a subedar of the late Marine Battalion and a private of the 10th Native Infantry, with half a dozen others, to raise a mutiny in the city on the Dhun-teras Day preceding the Dewali of the dark days of 1857 and pillage the town. The story of that magnificent detective ability is too well known to need any further mention here.

The writer often saw this "beau ideal" of a Police Commissioner, a sun-dried man, of middle height, firmly seated in his saddle, generally in top-boots, going his round of the town. He also saw him on important public occasions when immense crowds gathered in the streets, especially on the auspicious day of the Queen's Proclamation of 1858, soon after sunset when the town was illuminated and all Bombay and its wife had turned out in the streets. Never have the contemporaries of that period, still surviving, known another Police Commissioner of Mr. Forjett's fearless courage, unique detective faculty, wealth of resources, great tact and diverse linguistic lore, although many able Commissioners have since adorned the Chiefship of the Bombay Police, from Sir Frank Souter down to the able and capable Mr. Edwardes. He was the Bayard of the Bombay Police, unsurpassed and still unapproached. He retired in 1863, though not so full of honours as Bombay had wished, seeing the number of invaluable services he had rendered. Surely he was the Saviour of Bombay in 1857.

In conclusion, a few words must be said about the general impression the Police of the fifties made on the mind of the writer prior to its radical renovation by Mr. Forjett. The force was even then inadequate for the needs of the city then fast growing in population and also in trade. The men on patrol were planted far and wide so that it was always complained of that if any extraordinary events took place one could not find a policeman within half a mile, let alone a stone's throw, of the disturbance. The constabulary was ill-clad and ill-equipped albeit that the uniform was the same, the yellow pugree and the black coat which earned from some wit the soubriquet of the "Yellow sealed bottle." But worse was that not even five persons in the force knew how to read and write. Their pay was Rs. 6 which, perhaps, was not inadequate considering that the cost of living then was cheap enough, while the ordinary day labourer earned two annas per day. Indeed the police was not so much in evidence as it is to-day. They looked, when on duty like men who had just come from the land of Rip Van Winkle. There was not a whit of difference between them and the common coolie from whose class they were recruited. They moved about leisurely a stolid unintelligent, unresourceful body of men. The police in those days were in charge of the fire extinguishing service. Even here they had never been known to display any great presence of mind or the special aptitude needed for that kind of work. Indeed it impressed one as if they belonged to the Arcadian age of Bombay of the seventeenth and eighteenth centuries. The European element in the force was very limited, while there were no mounted troops. They did not come into existence till 1893. Neither was there any armed police. Altogether the policeman of the fifties was a sorry specimen everyway of a watchman for a fast growing city like Bombay.

CHAPTER XXXIX.—THE EARLY EUROPEAN MERCHANTS OF BOMBAY.

HAVING briefly glanced at the condition of the city during the fifties in respect of population, health, water-supply, conservancy, lighting and police, it will be in the fitness of things to take a fairly broad survey of the trade conditions generally of that eventful decade. In the first instance, it is essential to recall the fact of the very imperfect system of registration of the foreign trade at Bombay port. Considering that, even in Great Britain, the value of an accurate registration of imports and exports was only beginning to be realised, it need not surprise us that tha customs authorities at all the principal Indian ports, Bombay included, had only a most rudimentary organisation for the purpose. No doubt the Government had some time before created the post of what was known as "The Reporter General of External Commerce." He could not have been a person regularly trained for the purpose, seeing that the Bombay Chamber of Commerce, itself a young, though active and vigorous, institution of about fourteen years' standing, had been wrangling somewhere between 1848 and 1850 with the local Government about a burden which was attempted to be toisted on that juvenile organisation of Bombay trade at that date. Rudimentary as the system of registration was, the Chamber was asked to contribute a hundred rupees per month towards the printing of the returns which that body wished to be furnished with. It contended that it was the duty of the State to keep itself well informed for its own revenue and statistical purposes, and, therefore, whatever the expense ought to be borne by it. It was no part of the Chamber's functions to take upon itself such a duty, and if it demanded a regular monthly return of imports and exports, it was simply to help the State in stimulating the trade of the port the potentialities of which were so great and manifest. None could say that the contention of the Bombay Chamber was ill-grounded. But one has to remember that in those days the East India Company was exceedingly tight as to its purse. It was extravagant to a fault in certain directions, while cheese-paring in other ways. One has to go through the ponderous tomes of the Parliamentary enquiry instituted every 21 years, on the renewal of its charter, to be quite posted in reference to their modes of expenditure. The cross-examination by independent members of some of the "bigwigs" of the Court of Directors, will be found refreshing and instructive even at this date. The enquiries of 1831 and of 1853 are both exceedingly informing.

Jealousy of the Company.

No wonder then that the Company which strained at gnats and swallowed camels should have been so mean as to attempt to place the burden of the cost of the registration of the seaborne trade of this port on the Chamber. But, perhaps, there was another reason which can be surmised; the general attitude of the Company towards the "interlopers," that is, persons other than those serving under a covenant with the Company who were allowed by the Charter Act of 1833 to have free and unrestricted trade in India, was one of great suspicion. The Company looked with a jealous eye on these "interlopers" who had, after half a century's continued agitation, been able to succeed in achieving their object. Even to the British traders of the forties of the last century, India was still a land of the Pagoda tree. The tree had only to be shaken to collect any number of silver pagodas in the lap. The pagoda, as the reader may be aware, was the coin of the realm current during the prosperous era of Portuguese trade. The Company's servants looked askance at the new class of traders, so enterprising and so keen, but so different in political and economic beliefs from them. Whereas the Company was a great monopolist and protectionist, the Interlopers were mostly of free trade persuasion. It was entirely owing to the freedom allowed under the Charter Act of 1833 to all British traders to carry on their trade unfettered in this country that it became practical for the English merchants in Bombay in the latter part of the thirties to establish what has been since known as the Bombay Chamber of Commerce. This was in 1836.

But the first founders, of whom more in the sequel, were shrewd and canny. Their wisdom and mercantile sagacity are much to be admired. Their golden motto was to move slowly. There were scores of mercantile and marine matters which their short experience informed needed reform. But they at once understood the expediency of going forward step by step. So the matter of registration of trade returns was not taken in hand for nearly ten years after the Chamber was established. We could well understand how the authorities of the East India Company must have tried their best that the "interlopers" should know as little of the movements of the trade as possible, being themselves such close monopolists of Indian commerce for over a century. But none can stay the march of events and the Company soon found out that the men of the Bombay Chamber of Commerce had come to stay. And staid they have. The Chamber has grown with the growth of years and strengthened itself with the strength acquired by its unique influence and position.

So it happened that the problem of the registration of the trade was eventually solved by the Reporter-General giving up the original proposal to charge the Chamber rupees one hundred per month and allow that body through its Secretary or other officer deputed to inspect at the Custom House the daily or weekly registrations. That was the primitive way in which those stalwart but enterprising men of commerce began to feel their way and understood the dynamics of the seaborne trade—how cotton and other produce came to Bombay, how and where it was shipped, and so on. But the most useful and arduous pioneer work which the early men of the Chamber did demands one or two chapters by themselves. It was they who really laid broad and deep the foundations of Bombay's commercial greatness, and thus the men of commerce of to-day, be they Indian or European, owe them a deep debt of gratitude, and the Government of Bombay itself must feel grateful to them for the invaluable services they rendered, which while, benefitting them, also contributed largely to expand the revenues of Bombay.

CHAPTER XL.—THE MEN WHO MADE COMMERCIAL BOMBAY.

THERE is no public institution in Bombay which can lay claim to a long career of eighty-four years as the Bombay Chamber of Commerce, save the Bombay Branch of the Royal Asiatic Society. The latter was founded, as already observed in a previous chapter, by the distinguished jurist and eminent political philosopher, Sir James Mackintosh, in 1805. Fifteen years ago its centenary was fittingly celebrated under the presidency of the Rev. Dr. Scott, a countryman of Sir James and a learned scholar whose popularity as a Professor of Wilson College has been so well-known. The Bombay Chamber of Commerce, on the other hand, was established in September 1836, but it is worthy of record that its founders also were mostly

Scotchmen—Mr. Skinner, of the then firm of Messrs. Skinner & Co., who long since have earned a reputation for commercial enterprise in what may be called the East Indies. They had branches in Calcutta and elsewhere in this country and also in China, which still exists under the more widely known title of Jardine, Skinner & Co. In this firm may be well discerned the typical enterprise of longheaded and hard-headed Scotchmen. In China and in other parts of the civilised world where they have large dealings, the name of the firm is a household word. If they have amassed great wealth and earned an enviable reputation for stern commercial integrity, it is owing no doubt to the eminent qualities the sons of Caledonia possess, wherever they plant or colonise themselves. In India and China, the Scotch no doubt were the pioneers not only of trade. They were pioneers of education also. It is with the name of a Scotchman, no other than the renowned and brilliant Mountstuart Elphinstone, that the first collegiate institution established in this great city is associated. The earliest professors were chiefly Scotchmen. Our Grand Old Man had had his academic career under them. And his Professor of Mathematics, a science in which Mr. Dadabhoy was so proficient, was Mr. Paton, a Scotchman. The Elphinstone Institution had for its Principal Dr. John Harkness, who was a born Scotsman with all his broad native accents and mannerisms. As Professor of Logic and Moral Philosophy in the fifties, the writer can recall how fond the worthy Principal was of his great countryman and metaphysician, Sir William Hamilton. Not a lecture was delivered but there was some reference or another to that eminent authority. He was followed by Sir Alexander Grant, by far the most learned Principal and Professor of European reputation, Elphinstone

College had the good fortune to have between 1860 and 1866. He, too, was a Scotchman of the Scot, with an historical lineage, and who had by his translation of the ethics of Aristotle earned a distinct European reputation. The writer learnt all about Greek history and Greek democracy under him; also his Bacon. And many have been the Scotchmen who have been the educators of Indian youths in this and other Presidencies. But more of them when the chapter on early education in Bombay in the fifties is reached. Not only Bombay but all India is proud of its Scottish merchants who were the pioneers of Commerce.

Messrs. Skinner & Co.,

Messrs. Skinner & Co. then founded the Chamber of Commerce under the auspices of a good and well-known Governor, whose name is prominently associated with the Medical College in our midst, Sir Robert Grant. Bombay also boasts of a well-known public thoroughfare which bears his name. It was then slowly emerging from its obscurity into commercial importance, thanks to its unsurpassed geographical position in Asia. Who could have dreamt, however, even in the days of Pliny that this Heptensia of ours was to be the greatest gateway of trade between Europe and the East. And yet Bombay was even in 1836 a comparatively obscure port, albeit that the canny Scottish traders had espied its incalculable value for purposes of commerce and the potential greatness of which it was capable later on. Thus. then, on the 22nd day of September, 1836, when the Chamber was founded, it boasted of the following firms as members. Their names are worthy of record as the merchants who had the farsightedness to assess Bombay at its true value and the commercial eminence to which it was destined to rise. That eminence has long since been attained, but it remains to be seen whether that other fishing village on the banks of the Indus is going in the near future to deprive it of that eminence. If none else, that ardent lover of Karachi, and its most able and indefatigable merchant, so long Chairman of the Chamber there, Mr. Montagu Webb, will obtain for it. But he will have to wait till the Euphrates Valley Railway project, once more revived, is an accomplished fact and Europe joins hands with Asia at this rising port. But meanwhile we have to see to the members of the first Chamber of 1836. They were eleven all told.

Skinner & Co ,
Nicol & Co.,
Duncan, Gill & Co.,
Leckie & Co.,
Gisborne, Menzines & Co.,
Ritchie Stuart & Co.,
Mac Vicker, Bure & Co.,

McGregor, Browning & Co.,
Dixon Carter & Co.,
Gillanders, Ewart & Co., and
Firth & Co.

And here we may tarry for a few minutes to gaze at the long interval of 80 years to recount the "roll of honour" of these valiant captains of trade to whom Bombay is so vastly indebted. Some names since changed may be identified, but alas, how many find their place no more in the Yearly Calendar of the Chamber. The Skinners long since retired from this city to take up a wider field of commerce at Calcutta and China. In this instance happily, they survive and are still flourishing at Shanghai where they have become the great pioneers of the cotton industry and railways. Bombay wishes them every prosperity and centuries of a flourishing commercial career. Nicol & Co., however, or as they were lately styled, William Nicol & Co., are gone. And it is sad to relate their place knows them no more either here or in Glasgow. And yet it is necessary to remind Bombay merchants that, if to-day they are proud of their docks, their basins and their bunders, it is owing to the original enterprise of that firm, of whom the brothers John and James Fleming were leading partners. It was they who first launched the enterprise then known as the Elphinstone Land and Press Company, each individual shareholder of which was a most substantial merchant or landed proprietor. It was a Scotch Governor, Lord Elphinstone, who offered the concession to reclaim the basin at Carnac Bunder and further north, and it was a Scotch firm, again, which boldly entered on that high enterprise, the fruition of which was the first Prince's Dock (1880) and the sister docks since built.

The end of Nicol & Co.

The Nicols must be deemed the makers of the colossal Bombay trade which we witness to-day. But it would be too long to narrate the instructive, but highly interesting, history of Messrs. Nicol and Co., which, owing to the financial embarrassments wrought by the mad speculations of 1864-65 was partially crippled—an embarrassment from which it was never able to recover but succumbed when that mighty crash of the Glasgow Bank overtook the United Kingdom in the memorable year 1878. An equally enterprising contemporary firm was that of Messrs. Ritchie, Stuart and Co. They, too, launched another colossal scheme of public works, the well-known Back Bay Reclamation Co. A sound and substantial concern, it was practically wrecked by the failure of the Asiatic Bank, which had nearly a crore of its money there, and partly by the folly and impatience ot the shareholders who, in spite of the wise counsel of the directors, notably its chairman, Mr. Walter Cassels, another great name in the annals of Bombay Commerce, not to wind up the Company, wound it up to the detriment of all the interests concerned. But the history of that gigantic reclamation has already been fully narrated elsewhere by the present writer and need not be referred to here. Suffice to say, the fortunes of Mr. Premchand Roychand were indissolubly bound up with that house whose guiding star was Mr. Michael Scott. The firm was greatly crippled and eventually was reconstructed, till it was merged some years ago into another younger firm. Messrs. Leckie and Co. were also great merchants and bankers. They too were overwhelmed by the speculative mania and the aftermath that ensued. The other firms of 1836 either retired or were amalgamated with younger rivals, but the company named Gillanders, Ewart and Co. can be recognised in the firm of Ewart, Latham and Co., whose Calcutta branch is known as that of Gladstone, Wyllie and Co., and the London one as Gillanders, Arbuthnot and Co. Thus it has happened that the original firms which constituted the Bombay Chamber of Commerce in 1836 are gone. Their place knows them no more, and yet what magnificent work they did. Time no doubt rolls its ceaseless course, but we can never forget those sturdy traders from Caledonia who established that institution which after 84 years is flourishing in our midst, and to whom the civic and commercial world of Bombay equally owe a deep debt of gratitude. Honour be to those men.

CHAPTER XLI.—WHAT BOMBAY OWES TO THE CHAMBER OF THE FIFTIES.

A VARIETY of commercial topics of no little importance engaged the attention of the successive committees of the Chamber during the epoch-making period of Bombay in the fifties. The unsatisfactory service of the mail, the expediency of a bi-monthly service, the scarcity of shipping and the consequent dearness of freight, the crude system of haulage and transport, the desirability of stimulating mercantile produce, the postal service, the progress of the infant railways, the burden of transit duties, and other kindred topics were the subject matter of the annual report, not forgetting the ever-fresh topic of the extended cultivation of cotton. It is indeed a striking fact that, all through the history of the Chamber of

Commerce, *the* one subject of trade above all others which has continuously occupied the attention of that body is cotton. There is nothing surprising in it seeing that King Cotton has reigned supreme in the seaborne trade of Bombay. Whatever the ancient trade in this staple commodity and whatever travellers and others may have said and written about it, there is no doubt of the fact that it began to attract the attention of the merchants of the West in a very large degree from the seventeenth century. It must, however, be recognised that the systematic exports of the raw staple and some of its popular manufactured products, calicoes in particular, were owing to the enterprise of the British merchants trading to the East, who eventually established the Great East India Company. Milburn, who laboriously compiled those two ponderous volumes on Indian and Asiatic Trade, as back as 1812, gives an excellent narrative of Indian cotton. And so does another laborious compiler of that period, Mr. Macpherson. The latter gives a clear insight into the cotton trade by reproducing in the text samples of cotton invoices from Bombay. They are so interesting that they are worthy of study in the original as it is not possible to transcribe them in this place.

In those invoices the shipper of Bombay cotton to-day may learn for himself what the actual price of the best raw material, what the cost of transport and what the other charges were. He may compare notes as to freights and commission; also as to remittances and exchange, the latter being always at a premium and in favour of India.

Growth of the Cotton Trade.

But whatever was the cost of raw cotton at the commencement of the nineteenth century, there is no doubt, that in the early fifties the best Broach and Surat variety did not sell for more than Rs. 70 to Rs. 100 per candy. Cotton growing in the United States was not half so extensive as in this country till 1856. So that it is perfectly intelligible how persistent the Chamber was in its efforts to urge on the Bombay Government the importance and value of extended cultivation of cotton. But at this time of the day it is almost supererogatory to discourse on this subject, which is so familiar to every commercial man in Bombay, if not to the proverbial schoolboy of Thomas Babington Macaulay. But one name should not be omitted from mention in this place. How many are there in the city who not only extensively buy and sell cotton but recklessly speculate in it and even gamble themselves into ruin; who are aware of one of the pioneers who had had a great deal to do with improving the quality of Broach cotton in the fifties.

An honourable mention is made by the Chamber in one of its reports of that person, unknown to fame. He was Mr. J. M. Davis. There have, no doubt, been other Davises since; but this pioneer specially deserves mention, seeing that it was in the latter part of the fifties that the United States rose to the importance of extended cultivation of cotton, though the Civil War was yet remote and undreamt of. It was Liverpool which was so keen, and Liverpool was goaded by the Manchester factory—owners of the time, the early free traders of whom the most prominent were Bright and Cobden. The free traders, who were millowners, were greatly impressed by the necessity of importing as much as they promptly could of Broach and Surat cotton from year to year. It was a dire necessity with them. Manchester moved the Liverpool cotton merchants. These in their turn moved the Bombay Chamber who were themselves independently alive to the thriving trade in the commodity to the Presidency and bring ample grist to the treasury of the State. But the millowners of Manchester had another string to their bow. They were urging the magnates in Leadenhall Street to bring pressure on the Bombay Government. Thus it was the combined pressure of the two strong British interests which stimulated the larger cultivation of cotton. Private interests thus had a deep and solid foundation of the more extensive growth of cotton which of course the Civil War in America vastly stimulated. A public calamity in one country was the opportunity of another, exactly as we see to-day how, owing to the recent horrid war, more than one neutral State was able to forge ahead and capture the trade and industries, for the time, of the enemy. It may not be unnatural under the circumstances to question the Bombay millowners whether they would have been in the position they are situated to-day but for the initial steam and power applied from without. No doubt, India, or rather Bombay, *sui motu* could have considerably stimulated cotton cultivation. But it is a question whether the vast strides made in cotton cultivation would have been possible but for the two basic factors referred to.

CHAPTER XLII.—IMPROVEMENT IN THE MAIL SERVICE.

AS to the irregularity of the mails of those days one cannot but sympathise with the Chamber of the fifties, seeing how those of the present generation, since the opening of the Suez Canal, have been situated. The development of International Trade, which commenced soon after the opening of the Canal and the immense strides in steam navigation in consequence thereof, urgently demanded a regular bi-monthly service and that at a greater speed than was ever possible or thinkable during the age of the wooden walls and the early period of steam vessels. But the foreign trade took leaps and bounds, and as the need of speedier correspondence was firmly established, it became absolutely essential to have a weekly mail service, well regulated, well ordered, and withal punctual. In this respect all the foreign Chambers in the country set on foot a combined agitation, which eventually had its effects on the post office in London. Many indeed were the angry correspondence in the papers and many more were the well reasoned representations of the different Chambers, heartily supported by the Press, and by the members of the House of Commons in London interested in India's foreign trade. When all the difficulties were one by one smoothed down, it would appear that the one potential *lion* in the path of the reform was the autocrat at St. Martins Le Grand. Fortified by the British Navy at his back, the customary objection to increased salaries to carry the mails was brought forward. But it was proved to demonstration that that objection was untenable, having regard to the fact that there were good strong competive navigation companies ready and willing to carry the Indian mails. There was a periodic struggle, as each time the contract for subsidy had to be discussed in the House of Commons. And by a strange irony of fate it happened that, thanks to the many competing lines, the Monopolist Mail company had to climb down as to its subsidy. It was something over £70,000 a quarter of a century ago, and it is only half or less than half at present. The duration of the passage of the mails has from time to time been steadily curtailed in response to the reasonable agitation of the Chambers to speed the mails and to have them delivered on the thirteenth day from London. All these reforms in the regular and early mail service have been accomplished stage by stage, since the fifties and the men of the present generation owe a debt of gratitude to the Chamber in this respect. A more signal service to the Empire could not have been rendered. But just contrast the irregular, delayed and even vexatious mail services of the fifties. It would be deemed "intolerable" to wait to-day for a month to get letters, papers and periodicals, let alone "overland" goods. And yet further contrast the fact that for a time, a little earlier than the fifties, the monthly mail of the time was carried by the vessels of the Indian Navy, which necessarily steamed slower than the private merchant boats. Can anybody realise to-day the mental condition of merchants, when owing to the perils of the sea and unavoidable causes, the mail was late in arriving. There were no cables and no way of learning any news about a breakdown or other casualty, till 1865. When the Indo-European telegraph was established and till 1870 when the Great Eastern laid down the first submarine cable between Suez and Bombay, the landing of the mails at our antiquated bunders was one of a most primitive character, apart from the difficulties of the high monsoon seas at the Customs House. For a long time it was at the Customs House bunder that the mails were landed. It was somewhere in the eighties that they began to be landed at the Apollo Bunder. Even after landing, not till the middle of the seventies was there any efficient organisation at the Post Office to sort the letters. The earliest deliveries were made at the windows specially reserved at the Post Office. And hundreds of the genus hamal and peon crowded soon after the mail was signalled, with their window-delivery tickets, keeping a weary watch and waiting for their respective office letters. It was always an interesting sight, very suggestive, to see these crowds and muse awhile on the methods of delivery. The sea-sorting system did away with the primitive sorting, and Bombay, and for that matter all India, was gratified when letters came to hand within two hours of their landing. Contrast all the conditions of postal mail delivery to-day with those of the fifties. One cannot but thank the Bombay Chamber of Commerce in the first instance for all it did during the last half a century and more. Surely those sturdy stalwarts of the Chamber are the makers of the new Bombay, of the post, the cables, the docks and the railways. But for their persistent agitation made in all these respects we should never have got half the reforms.

CHAPTER XLIII.—RAILWAYS, TELEGRAPHS AND THE POST.

IN one of the foregoing chapters it has been observed that the fifties of the last century was, as far as Bombay was concerned, an epoch-making one in divers directions, especially in the matter of mercantile progress and mercantile facilities. Perhaps no public record offers more complete evidence of that fact than the comprehensive and elaborate reports of the Bombay Chamber of Commerce which, as has been previously observed, had had enormously to do with the making of Bombay as the great entrepot of commerce between Europe and Asia that it has been for thirty-five years and more. That position she had been able to attain chiefly on account of the pioneer work so admirably rendered by that body of English and Scotch merchants. It was the singular good fortune of India that, between 1844 and 1856, its supreme administration was presided over by two successive pro-consuls of the highest practical statesmanship. Lord Hardinge, the grandfather of our beloved and popular Ex-Viceroy, administered the affairs of this country from 1844 to 1848. No doubt the Governor-Generalship was practically characterised by war, owing to the political exigencies in the Punjab. Lord Hardinge was as much of a great soldier as a great statesman. In reality he was a man of peace and substantial economic progress. And it was during his administration that there was first laid the foundation of railway construction. He was only here for four years, part of which was occupied in the consolidation of the newly-acquired province of the Punjab. But whatever time he could otherwise spare was whole-heartedly devoted to the greater moral and material progress of the people. The railways in England were a quarter of a century old and their incalculable benefits were fairly realised Lord Hardinge strove to introduce railways in India and did most important spade work, so that when he laid down his exalted office there was before the Court of Directors his minute and matured scheme on the lines the construction should proceed. His successor, the Marquis of Dalhousie, came with the honourable ambition of bringing the railway project to a successful practical issue. Fresh from his experience as a Ministerat, specially at the Board of Trade, he was well-qualified to enter heartily into the greatest of all public works. He devoted the most minute attention to successfully launching the scheme. And thanks to his energy, undoubted ability and experience he had he satisfaction to see, at the close of his

Governor-General ship in 1856, that the East Indian Railway, the Great Indian Peninsula Railway and the Bombay, Baroda and Central India Railway had all made a respectable beginning. It is owing to these railways that much of the time and attention of the Bombay Chamber was occupied in suggesting and recommending alignments and routes which might greatly facilitate communications with the north-east as well as the south-east and also with the north-west. In 1854-55 that enterprising and energetic body of merchants was busy hammering away at opening Central India and Khandesh, with a view to developing the great cotton trade between the provinces and Bombay.

The Beginning of the G. I. P. R.

The Chamber did signal service to the city by recommending most earnestly to the Government the extreme value of the G. I. P. line being constructed in that direction, instead of allowing it, as was originally limned, to open these districts via Surat and the Tapti Valley. That talented engineer, Mr. Berkley, of the G. I. P. Railway Company, was heartily in accord with the recommendation of the Chamber. The Thull Ghat had to be pierced, but he was convinced that the opening of communications in the north-east lay by way of that Ghat and not by the Tapti Valley. So far the Bombay merchants, European and Indian, must thank their predecessors of the fifties that this sensible and most useful alignment was successfully urged. But for it it is doubtful whether during the Lancashire Cotton famine the Tapti Valley scheme could have been completed in order to supply as large a quantity of cotton as was wanted by the mills there. It was a great service rendered to the growing commerce of Bombay. On the other hand, the direct north-east route through Khandesh greatly quickened the construction of the line which ultimately connected Calcutta with Bombay. Of course, it was decided that the B. B. & C. I. line should take its own natural course in the north-westerly direction. In the south-easterly direction, on the way to Madras, the G. I. P. Company had completed the line as far as Campoolee. The old cart route was from Campoolee to the Bhore Ghat and Khandalla. For years together Campoolee was an important station and every monsoon time hundreds of pairs of bullocks were regularly kept in readiness to avoid all interruptions to passenger and goods traffic arising from accident by way of landslips on the Ghat incline. That practice was done away with when the Company felt fully confident of the safety of the Ghat during the monsoon. The Chamber was highly gratified when in 1855-56 this line as far as Campoolee was completed. Through communication with the Deccan was established for the first time. It was an event in the annals of Bombay.

The First Telegraph.

Next to the first railway construction which characterised the fifties was the opening of the first telegraphic wires. That, again, was an other event of the highest importance. What might have happened during the dark and bloody days of 1857 without the main lines of telegraph may be more easily imagined than described. The telegraph served as much as the army itself, such was its value. The wires between Bombay and Calcutta and Madras were completed in 1854-55, thanks to the excellent organisation of that able electrician of the Indian Government, Dr. O'Shaughnsey. It was indeed a marvellous public work at the time—being so new to India. I remember our elders of the family conversing on the subject and recalling the legendary lore of Hindu and Persian mythology just as much as previously in reference to the first balloon in which that intrepid aeronaut, Mr. Kyte (a suggestive name) flew. He was called in Gujarati the modern "Pavan Pavri," that is, he who in the legendary lore of the Aryans was known to achieve miracles by flying from the heavens to the earth in the twinkling of an eye. But like all new inventions of the civilisation of the nineteenth century introduced into sleepy or arcadian India the telegraphic signalling had to be done by semi-illiterates, whereas the organisation of intelligence to work them was a most difficult task. No wonder during the first twelve months a variety of misreadings, repetitions and all the rest of the bungles attendant on the new invention were largely in evidence. And the Chamber found that its mercantile messages were so often mutilated and misinterpreted that there was quite a litany of complaints from its members, and representations had to be made to the Government who, with exemplary patience, tried to remove them one after another. We, of to-day and yesterday, are so well and admirably served by telegraphs of all sorts, land, submarine, and wireless, that we can hardly realise the immense difficulties the Government had to overcome when first launching the telegraphic system. Let the reader stretch his imagination and ruminate on the condition of semi-darkness which was prevalent in all India in the middle of the nineteenth century in regard to railways and telegraphs, two marvels of applied science discovered by the occidental mind and implanted into Oriental soil. And yet we of to-day are never slow to whine and even denounce if the telegraph service is interrupted but for a few hours.

Such is the impatience of our go-ahead modern civilization. Anyhow, it is a fact that the general mismanagement during the first year of telegraphs created a great outcry among the mercantile community, while the mass of the population had no confidence in its success. Then there was further vexation owing to the extremely stringent character of the rules and regulations which were perhaps unavoidable or misconceived. Thanks to the persistent correspondence of the Chamber the public were able twelve months later to be satisfied with the tolerable regularity of the service every way and that body itself was not slow to express its gratification to Government.

A Glorious Evolution.

Another public service rendered by the Chamber was in connection with the postal service about which enough has already been said. The first comprehensive and practical legislation in postal administration was Act XVII of 1854. For the first time, the affixing of stamps on the covers came into vogue. That again was another event of the epoch-making fifties which greatly delighted the public, and none more appreciated the boon than the European mercantile community. But at first the charge was half an anna for a letter weighing ½ tola. Of course the stamp was for any distance within the four boundaries of the territory of the Honourable the East India Company. What a glorious evolution we have had within sixty years in the matter of postal service! Money orders, post savings banks and postal insurance were undreamt of. So, too, was the quarter-anna postal card which has revolutionised the entire system of correspondence, along with the vast progress in rudimentary education. And who had thought of half a dozen or more deliveries in 12 hours, at least in the big towns and cities? We were thankful if we had only one delivery at first during a working day. And yet one's appetite grows on what it feeds. Here we are in the year of grace 1920, clamouring for a bi-weekly mail and still further improvements and facilities by way of inland and foreign correspondence. In the matter of railways, docks, telegraphs and post we are veritable harpies. Perhaps a few years hence we shall have a daily aerial post and a direct telephonic system throughout the country which will enable us to hold conversation with the farthest corner of the green earth in about the same time that it takes light to travel to the Earth from the Sun.

Chapter XLIV.—THE WORK OF THE CHAMBER.

THE solid work in the interests of the city's trade and commerce which was achieved by the Bombay Chamber of Commerce in the epoch-making fifties, is certain to endure. But the interesting and instructive narrative of that good work is not yet exhausted. There yet remain some other references to be made for the merchant of to-day who being absorbed in the meticulous details of his daily work finds little or no time to make himself acquainted with the brilliant achievements of those merchants of the middle of the nineteenth century who were so greatly instrumental in the making of commercial Bombay.

The Customs House was yet a primitive institution, and it was the persistent effort of the Chamber to bring it up to date in more than one direction. Statistically it was in its infancy and every fresh suggestion that was made to place it on a systematised basis was at first opposed, only to be accepted in the end, after much superfluous correspondence. One of such important improvements suggested was the proper method of valuation of goods imported for the purposes of revenue duty. The publication of tariff values was deemed absolutely essential to the trade. It is astonishing to men of the present day that the Customs House of 1853-54 was so supremely indifferent as to hold secretly to itself the tariff and put the importers to frequent trouble and vexation for the purposes of appraisement. But the Chamber was a patient and forbearing body of commercial men. They knew how step by step the authorities could be brought round and made to see matters eye to eye with them. If we say that in the fifties the Chamber was a great instructor of the Customs authorities and taught them very many things necessary for their own guidance and for the interests of the merchants, we should in no way be exaggerating the valuable work it was then rendering. The merchants had also complained of differential tariff. There was one duty for the same class of goods in Calcutta and another in Bombay. Many indeed were the wranglings on this subject. The value of the publication of a uniform tariff applicable to all Indian ports could not be gainsaid. And the Bombay Chamber by its persistence and patience was eventually able to secure both.

Navigation Charts.

Navigation charts are a *sine qua non* of merchant vessels; and yet so deficient were the harbour authorities of the day that the Chamber had to goad on these officials to construct charts of navigation of the Arabian Sea and the Indian Ocean and reserve for public distribution a fairly good number of copies at a reasonable fee. The Indian Navy officers had done ample spade work in this direction as the various papers now and again read before the Geographical Society testify. Then there were the Admiralty and other charts. It should be remembered that ship accidents of running aground or sinking while entering the harbour, with very imperfect or deficient beacons or light-houses, were numerous. Not a year passed by without wreckages either at the harbour entrance or in the Arabian Sea. Socotra, for centuries, was known as the storm centre of the monsoon. And it was the constant efforts of those daring navigators belonging to the Indian Navy to take surveys of the lines and curves of that storm. Thus the preparation of navigation charts to help the merchant vessels was imperative. By dint of perseverance the Chamber's efforts were crowned with success in this direction also.

Construction of Wet Docks.

Then the construction of wet docks greatly engrossed the attention of the Chamber. It was mooted as early as the forties when the Government contemplated a dock in Mody Bay. But it did not come to any head. Correspondence ensued off and on. Committees would be appointed; reports would be made. The reports would lie in the pigeon-hole of the Public Works Secretariat to be one day dragged out, shaken of the accumulated dust and re-opened for reference. Situated as the Government of India then was in point of revenue, it was impossible for it to take on hand the construction of a wet dock even on a modest scale. There was the consensus of opinion that private enterprise could alone cope with the matter. But where was that enterprise? It meant capital on a large scale. And so they discussed and rediscussed the dock question, the dock site, and so forth from time to time till the first small dock was built at Colaba under the auspices of the Sassoons in the Seventies. Even that was a corollary of the bold, venturesome, but strictly sound, scheme of the original United Colaba Land and Reclamation Company, which was promoted in those halcyon days of 1863-64 only to come to grief during the general debacle of 1865—72. But the Sassoons showed the way. At last the persistent agitation of the Chamber headed by the longheaded, cool and calculating Mr. J.K. Bythell, of Messrs. Gaddum and Co., brought the matter to a head in 1869-70, with the active support of Mr. James Maclean, Editor of the

"Bombay Gazette." Then was mooted the purchase of the Elphinstone Land and Press Company, launched in 1856 by Messrs. W. Nicol and Co., and of the dozen private bunders, from Carnac Bunder to Sivree, which finally resulted in the creation of the Bombay Port Trust. How time rolls on and how we find to-day that, with the expanding commerce, even the three large docks we possess are held by some sagacious merchants to be inadequate to accom modate the future trade unless the Euphrates Valley Railway and Karachi between them take away a part of the trade to Karachi. Yes, time rolls on, and one of the memorable events in the career of the intrepid Mr. J. K. Bythell is that, with the experience gained in the construction of the Prince's Dock, he was able to agitate in that whole-hearted way of his for giving Manchester a canal whereby her shipping may find that room for expansion which was such a crying necessity for years., Mr. Bythell now deceased, lived to see how his great canal scheme was an accomplished fact besides being a financial success. He lived to see how his great scheme which he engineered and piloted for so many years midst the greatest difficulties and obstruction had become such an invaluable asset to the people of Lancashire.

The Abyssinian Campaign.

But to hark back to the proposed scheme of a wet dock. In 1854-55 it was resuscitated and Mody Bay or Bori Bunder were poimted out as the best localities. A Committee was appointed on which two members of the Chamber were represented. Mr. Ritchie was its Chairman, and later on Mr. Graham. It was about this time that a public spirited citizen, Mr. Edwin

Heycock, afterwards Sheriff of Bombay, mooted the scheme of reclaiming the Mody Bay foreshore, a work which was eventually taken in hand in 1866 and completed some few years later. The ground reclaimed in the vicinity of the Mint became most useful to the Government during the period of the Abyssinian War of 1867-68. The Apollo Street dock was overbusy with the embarkation of troops in the transport vessels and equipment for putting out to sea, under the direction and guidance of that great generalissimo of the forces, Sir Robert Napier, who eventually captured Magdala and was created a peer for his brilliant engineering strategy all the way on the march from Zulla Bay to that fortress. An excellent diary of the Abyssinian campaign was written by the facile Mr. A. W. Shepherd, the then Assistant Editor of the "Times of India," but long since gathered to the majority. But what a long stretch of years from

1845 to 1915 is it when we recall the fact that the Mody Bay or Bori Bunder Docks considered and reconsidered in the forties of the nineteeth century were not practically carried into execution till the beginning of the twentieth, of course, with the immense light, of experience and knowledge acquired in the interval. The foundation of the Alexandra Dock was laid in November, 1905, by His Majesty King George the Fifth, then Prince of Wales, and completed and opened for use nine years later by Lord Hardinge, Viceroy of India (21st March 1914).

Another Great Service.

Lastly, another public service of a most valuable character which the Bombay Chamber of Commerce had rendered in the middle of the fifties was in reference to public finance and public borrowings. It happened that in March 1855 the

Government of India suddenly launched a Public Works Loan bearing interest at 5 per cent. when the mercantile community was in the beginning of its busy season and money had greatly endeared, as was usual, in those days when no State currency existed and the rupees in hard cash were scarce. The effect of the launching of that loan at a most inconvenient time greatly disturbed the monetary market, with the result that Government paper already in circulation went down 10 per cent. The Bombay Chamber was greatly, but not unreasonably, agitated at this disturbance. Similarly were those of Madras and Calcutta. The chief grievance of all the three mercantile bodies was the total absence of any kind of publicity in the matter of State finance and the progress of the annual revenue and expenditure from time to time. Such secrecy was observed that it was very difficult for the merchants and bankers in the capital cities to carry on their monetary transactions arising from their trade!

The Chamber's Remonstrance.

Greatly perturbed, the Bombay Chamber was constrained on 28th July, 1855, to address a letter of remonstrance to the President of the Board of Commissioners for the Affairs of India, no other than Mr. Vernon Smith, who was afterwards raised to the peerage. Here is the preliminary paragraph:

> "By desire of the Committee of the Bombay Chamber of Commerce I have the honour to address you regarding the unsettled state of the money market throughout India which has lately been the subject of earnest and general complaint. In the middle of March last Government securities suddenly declined in value 10 per cent. It has since

continued in a state of unhealthy fluctuation. The shares of the Joint Stock Companies of the highest character have been saleable at a great reduction of price. The supply of capital for the ordinary purposes of commerce has been greatly restricted and subjected to rates of interest almost prohibitive. This unsatisfactory position of affairs, with its attendant evils and inconveniences, is attributed and, it is to be feared, with too much reason, to what must be regarded as the defect of the financial arrangements of the Indian Government, namely, the secrecy in which they are enveloped. Its immediate cause was the unexpected opening of the new 5 per cent. loan under the designation of a Bluebooks Loan, the origin and necessity of which have only within a few days past been disclosed to the public of India through the medium of papers laid before Parliament."

The Chamber's remonstrance on this subject ended with the practical suggestion that the Indian Government should publish a quarterly or half-yearly statement of the progress of revenue and expenditure and also issue a Budget. But on this subject another chapter will be needed. Sufficient to say at the conclusion here that this most important public representation was signed by Mr. James Graham, who was then the Chairman of the Chamber, a name still held in Bombay in the greatest esteem and regard.

CHAPTER XLV.—FURTHER MEMORABLE WORK OF THE CHAMBER.

THE fifties was really the age of adolescence for the Bombay Chamber of Commerce. Taking its birth in this city in 1836 it reached that age in 1857, the year of the greatest anxiety to the British authorities in the country and especially to the British residents. But while on the one hand the British arms were slowly and successfully coping with the Sepoy's Revolt in the disturbed localities in the northern parts of India, it is gratifying to notice the solid works of peace which were also prosecuted by the Government of that great statesman of unwearied patience and imperturbable serenity, Lord Canning. Railway construction which began during the Governor-Generalship of his immediate predecessor, was greatly accelerated. Lord

Dalhousie, a name reprobated by the loyal Indian feudatories for his mischievous policy of annexation, was the Governor-General who gave it the greatest impetus. So far his administration should be regarded with admiration. It was, he with his driving force who laid the sound foundation of those great twin public works, the railways and the telegraphs, which in fifty years and more have so magnificently revolutionised the economic and financial condition of India both for the State and the people. Not that some evils inseparable and inevitable from that policy have not arisen. But when the whole field relating to the railways, which have supplanted the old order of hack bullock conveyances and other modes of transport, so dear to the conservative mind of the unsophisticated and untutored Indian, is impartially surveyed, and the good and evil are justly weighed in the balance, it will be readily acknowledged that, on the whole, India has immeasurably benefited by the system. The telegraphs were an invention which never came into competition with the immemorial order of things and were therefore appreciated from the very commencement of their operation. The Indian, with his natural intelligence, was at once able to realise the incalculable utility and commercial value of the telegraphs. He, therefore, readily and kindly took to it from the very first. Nothing has come home to every unit of the teeming millions of the country more readily than the railways and the telegraphs as they began to demonstrate their respective utilities in their domestic economy.

The making of the G. I. P. Railway.

Enough has already been said in the previous chapter touching the fair progress the two lines of railways in this Presidency had made during their infancy. The G. I. P. R. system had vast engineering difficulties to surmount by way of piercing the Ghats, both in the south-easterly and in the north-easterly directions. The tunnelling operations were not of so highly a scientific character as those which accompanied the piercing of the St. Gothard and Simplon Passes in the last days of the nineteenth century. But there were very few labour-saving machines and Western civilisation had not so far materialised as to utilise nature to the purpose of humanity as to-day with a hundred-and-one resources. And yet we cannot but admire the genius of the great railway engineers of those days who amidst many difficulties were thoroughly successful in completing the tunnels. The talents of Mr. Berkley have long since been recognised. Labour, too, was not only dear but very unskilful. The men of commerce who were keenly interested in the speedy linking up of Bombay with the Southern Presidency watched from afar how those titanic works were being handled and proceeded with. In their report for 1856-57, the Chamber observed as follows touching the labour problem for which there had prevailed not a little pessimism. "The extreme and unprecedented demand for labour has been on the whole much more satisfactorily responded to than was anticipated." There was to be handled the heavy iron tonnage required on the various spots where active construction was going on. As many as 46,000 hands were reported to be at work on the G. I. P. line alone. Before closing with the G. I. P. Railway it may not be uninteresting to state here the progress railways had made at the close of the fifties.

The open mileage totalled 193. The mileage under construction was 376; that of lines sanctioned but not commenced was 357; and that of land surveyed was 140. In the south, the line was ready and it was expected that Sholapur would be reached in another twelve months. Great expectations were raised that, when that was an accomplished fact, the Hyderabad Districts, so rich and fertile in cotton and agricultural produce, could be satisfactorily tapped. The coaching, which totalled in 1856-57 fully 58·5 lakh passengers, yielded nearly 8 lakhs and the tonnage of goods carried, which was in the same year 71,000 tons, yielded about fifteen per cent. more.

The B. B. & C. I. Railway.

With reference to the B. B. & C. I. line the section between Surat and Ahmedabad was completed, but as yet

Bombay had remained unconnected with Surat. The American Civil War in the early sixties greatly quickened that connection. The company had to cross large rivers like the Tapti and the Nerbadda, just as the eastern line had to cross the Bhore and the Thull Ghats. Iron bridges had to be imported and the foundations of the pillars sunk deep beyond the bottom of the rivers. Bridge making, too, was an incomplete science then, but the talented engineers bravely overcame the difficulties. Mr. Lane must be specially mentioned as the Resident Engineer.

The close of the fifties of the nineteenth century was also memorable for the arrangement made for the mails, by which Australia and Ceylon were brought together and so was Bombay with Ceylon. These arrangements served to give a kind of alternate weekly mail service which was greatly appreciated by the Indian and European merchants of the city. Again, a local service was established for mails between Aden and Mauritius and thus indirectly to Bombay and London.

The Telegraphic Service.

In 1858-59 telegraphic service between Calcutta, Bombay and Madras was thoroughly established, though, owing to the military revolt in Upper India, tranquillity had not been so thoroughly established as to cause the service between Calcutta on the one side and Madras and Bombay on the other, to proceed without interruptions now and again. But the inconvenience had to be endured. Much importance was attributed to the Bombay and Calcutta telegraphic service, as the mails from China were landed at the port of Calcutta whence advices of opium, silk, tea, etc., were wired to Bombay. The interruption in this service may be easily imagined. The Red Sea telegraph between Aden and Alexandria was also completed, but practical operations were not started before 1864-65. It may be interesting to notice that a mail route to Suez via Karachi was mooted by the P. & O. Co. Increased cost, however, of such a route led afterwards to the abandonment of the proposal. A weekly direct mail between Bombay and London was again proposed in 1858-59, but it shared no better fate. Later on came the American Civil War and the project was not again revived for really practical operations till some twenty years later.

Among minor public affairs to which the Chamber had drawn the attention of the Government may be mentioned the standardisation of weights and measures. The Chamber was exceedingly keen on the accomplishment of this object. The men of those days chafed.

as their successors chafe to this day, under the different systems of weights and measures all over the country. Here the Chamber only viewed the change from its own point of view, giving the go-bye altogether to the innumerable usages and customs prevailing in the different provinces and even in districts and talukas of the same province. During the fifty years and more that have elapsed since the proposal was first mooted, there have been at least half a dozen representations to the Central Government but without avail. And even the Commission which was called into existence some few years ago and wandered up and down the city, taking a mass of evidence, has been hardly able to make a unanimous report! Such were the differences of opinion encountered by that body at various stages. It seems that the labours of the Commission have proved abortive and their report "shelved" perhaps never again to be revived till there is a tolerable unanimity among the vast population to standardise some of the principal weights. Evidently the population is not advanced in this respect and the governing authorities seem distinctly to be of opinion that in this matter the let-alone policy is most expedient.

A robust protest.

Another notable event of minor interest was the robust protest of the Chamber touching the attempt to levy town duties on all articles of imports. There was a storm in a teapot. The foreign men of commerce could not brook the preposterous idea of dues on trade commodities. Their protest was successful and the trinity of the Municipal Commissioners ot the year of grace 1857-58 was told by Government to rest content with a small levy of duties on articles of consumption entering the town. The Chamber to a body were of free trade persuasion and they could not brook the idea of burdening trade, alleging that it was in the nature of a transit duty. Transit duty was like a red rag to the bulls of the Chamber. It exercised them for many a long year during which they never missed a single opportunity to proscribe it.

Lastly, the question of chartered accountants and auditors, which till late vexed the soul of corporate commercial bodies, was not absent in the closing days of the fifties. Then it was a question of having Government auditors for the Joint Stock Companies' Act of 1857 for the first time introduced into India. The Chamber viewed with disapproval the section in the Act which prescribed that shareholders alone should have the power to appoint auditors, a very sound and sensible regulation. The Chamber had ultimately to yield, and such is the soundness of the wisdom of the first legislators of Companies' Act that in spite of irregularities, laches, misfeasances by Directors and officers of companies, the audit system on the whole has proved efficient; and therefore it is still maintained in the latest Act. And it is a matter of congratulation that the character and qualifications of the auditors have been so prescribed as to minimise the committal of fraud of the character which disgraced Bombay a few years ago.

This prolonged notice of the memorable good work done by the Bombay Chamber in the interests of commerce and the general public would be incomplete without a passing mention of John Connon, a sturdy Scotchman, of the most Puritanic integrity, who for ten long years ably served the Chamber as its Secretary. His energy and enthusiasm were great, while his public spirit and independence made him a prime favourite with all classes of people. But more of him when we refer to the distinguished personalities of the epoch-making fifties.

CHAPTER XLVI.—GOLD AND SILVER.

IT remains now to refer as briefly as possible to the condition of commerce, coinage and currency, and next, to education. The solid and useful work achieved by the Bombay Chamber of Commerce in the memorable fifties has already been described in detail. Touching currency and coinage, it may be observed that both were in a transition state at the time. The history of coinage is, indeed, a chequered one, commencing from the date of the acquisition of Bombay. Trade was next to nothing save that by the native craft navigating the western and eastern coasts. Bombay in the seventeenth century was still a glorified fishing village as can be seen even to-day from half a dozen Koliwadas and more in the town from Colaba to Mahim. The localities where the fishermen pursued their humble avocation are still there and still bear the old names. There is the Colaba Koliwada, the Fort one, in a bylane running west of Borah Bazar Street next to the Mapla chawl shops. Then there is the Mandvi Koliwada, now greatly improved and cleared of its congestion by the Improvement Trust. Then we have the Mazagaon, Worli, and Mahim Koliwadas. Even agricultural industry was of a very negligible character. In the seventeenth and eighteenth centuries a variety of coins were current. There were the silver rupees of the Great Moghul and those of his big Viceroys at Ahmedabad and Hyderabad with their respective standard of fineness and alloy into the minuteness of which it is unnecessary to enter. There were subdivisions of the rupee in smaller silver and copper coins. There were also the pagoda and Xeraphin, coins belonging to the Portuguese dominions that had passed away. There were the Maria Theresa and Spanish dollars imported in return of goods sold in Europe. There were also the rupees of the Marathas, and so on. Bombay was the repository of a coinage museum in the last half of the seventeenth and the whole of the eighteenth century. Silver itself was a rare commodity and necessarily silver coins were at a great premium. As far back as the years 1729 and 1732 orders were issued by the Board of Trade that copper coins, the money of the masses, should not be sold, under pain of heavy penalty, at more than 1 per cent. discount. But the silver coins most current and popular were what were then known as Surat and Broach. These were exchangeable at 80 pice to the rupee and not 64 as at present. The Surat rupees were those either of the Great Moghul, or of the factory of the East India Company in that city. Broach rupees were smaller in size and had Persian inscription on both sides. These Broach rupees were not uncommon in the city, say up to 1864. The heavy influx of bullion during the period of the American Civil War was coined into British rupees with Queen Victoria's effigy surmounted by a crown. These were first current in 1862 and as their volume was actually poured out by the Mint, the old Broach rupees went out of circulation.

The drain of Silver to the East.

It is recorded in the annals of the East India Company that throughout the whole of the eighteenth and for the first half of the nineteenth century silver was a rare commodity in India. In the eighteenth century the Company had often to import silver from the United Kingdom, and many, indeed, were the objurgations of the mercantile classes as to the "drain of silver to the

East." Indeed, there were memorials to Parliament on the subject and there were even pamphlets published to prove how the drain was prejudicial to British trade! What a mighty change! From the latter half of the nineteenth century silver became a drug in the market, and there was the opposite cry of India being "the sink of silver!" The silver which for over a century used to be sold at 65 or 66 pence per ounce steadily diminished in price till by 1890 it was only 30 which alarmed the Imperial Government and led to the closure of mints to the private coinage of silver in 1893. Times were changed but we need not go into the history of the change which is so large writ on the walls of business men.

But just reflect on the irony of the metallic situation. While silver was everywhere in demand and greatly endeared, gold in the year 1765 was cheap, the ratio being less than 15½ to 1. The East India Company, in order to allay the grumblers in the United Kingdom against the exports of silver to India, ordered their factory agents at Surat to coin gold into gold rupees! A gold currency was established and the present ardent advocates of that currency may take heart of grace and never fail, in the next currency controversy which is certain to arise after the conclusion of the war, to adduce this historical fact in support of the establishment of a full gold currency. Sir James Begbie might usefully employ his leisure hours of retirement in London to ransack the magnificent library at the India Office and make an excellent collection which could be hurled at the right psychological hour at Sir Lionel Abrahams, who is his opponent.

The Gold Rupee of 1765.

This gold rupee of 1765 was ordered to contain 38 *vals* of pure Venetian gold and there were also coined half sovereigns and quarter sovereigns bearing a proportionate quantity of the yellow metal. But as the fates would have it, within six years, that is in 1771, gold was exhausted by reason of the moneys made from it having almost all been exported for the purchase of materials required by the Company's servants in Bombay for the new fortifications, the same which a hundred years later had to be levelled to the ground to provide accommodation for a growing population. So famished was the Treasury for remittance that paper currency by way of bills of exchange was suggested. But the purse-proud magnates in Leadenhall Street could not be persuaded to agree to that wise remedy. Yet another irony of Indian currency. In these days your Secretary of State, the lawful successor of the Chairman of the Honourable the Court of Directors, forges paper money by the millions in order to pay off his numerous liabilities including purchases of military stores and ordinance. Another gold distress episode of the latter period of the eighteenth century must be related. The gold crisis, so to say, had continued. The King's soldiers bitterly complained of being paid out in small gold coins. They wanted rupees and in 1778 the gold currency came to a full stop! Is it possible that another full stop may be reached after the present unhappy war is over, seeing how Ossa after Ossa is being heaped on by the belligerents by way of emergency paper money? Evidently between 1770 and 1780 the Company's factors here were put to the direst straits by reason of the condition of gold and silver. An export duty of 3 per cent. was put on silver going away to Western ports and later on the same duty was levied for silver exports to Singapore and China! Here is a third currency consideration for our gold bugs of this day!

The Changes of time.

We have had for some years past a duty of 5 per cent. and more on the import of all private silver! Yet a hundred and twenty-five years ago we tried to stop all silver going out of the country by a levy of 3 per cent. duty. But time changes and with it all currency nostrums which are pronounced by the shibboleth makers change too. And the so-called permanency is a mere misnomer. Nothing human is permanent, aye, neither gold, silver nor paper currency. Each, in its order and time, vanishes to make place for something new. So we sing the past of silver and gold and link it with the present. There is nothing new under the sun. Humanity only rings new changes on the old harp; and then it goes on singing from one generation to another. We all sing to one clear harp in diverse tones and rise on the stepping stones of our dead selves to higher things, which, though new in garb, are yet as old as the hills. All is vanity of vanities.

Chapter XLVII.—EVOLUTION OF THE METALLIC CURRENCY.

THE evolution of the metallic currency in Bombay is indeed, most interesting. What vicissitudes, not only the rupee and copper coins passed through from 1665 to 1800 are worth remembering, but also those of gold. The struggle for silver was the greatest and continually exercised the servants of the Company at Surat and Bombay. With a chequered history of coinage in India it may be not unuseful to employ some students of research to ransack the collection of coins scattered in museums and literary societies in the country and to give us a connected history in chronological order. The occasional finds of ancient coins from Greece and Rome, from Babylonia, Persia, Macedonia, Parthia and Scythia, say till the first or second century of Christ, conclusively inform us not only of conquests from South-Eastern Europe and Western and Northern Asia but of the trade that existed between those countries and India. Archæology and numismatics for the last half a century have been greatly modifying history, and no history more than that of India. After the second century of Christ there were the raids of the successors of the Khalifs of Bagdad, who used to overrun the Punjab and Gujarat. Then there came the Pathan Kings of Delhi and their successors, the Moghuls. South of Vindhya there were the powerful kings and dynasties who flourished in the Presidency of Madras and on the east coast of the Bay of Bengal. Then we come to the days of the Portuguese and the Dutch, the French and the English. No doubt experts in numismatics in Bengal, in the Punjab, in Bombay and Madras have in the past read, earned and elaborated papers on the finds of the various coins. What is now wanted is a succinct history of all these researches, collected and scattered over the principal museums in this country and in England and France. The work would form a most instructive compendium and in a way a calendar of Indian history as unique as illuminating. It must be the labour of a lifetime. But the labour would prove invaluable and a landmark, the importance of which cannot be belittled. In short, a standard history of coins from historic times to the close of the nineteenth century would be classic and monumental, and the expert who writes it will leave an imperishable name behind him. India nowadays badly wants able and qualified students of research in many a direction, in ancient politics and history, in numismatics, in arts, manufactures and industries, and in other branches of human activity. The new order of men and things must produce such research students in order that India may eventually find her true encyclopædic historian. Meanwhile let us relate a little more of our parochial narrative in respect of coins in Bombay.

A hundred years ago.

It may be useful to remember that a little more than a hundred years ago there obtained a variety of metallic currency, some of which have already been described. The eighteenth century was a century of transition, and nowhere more so than on the coast of Western India. The Portuguese were in occupation of the Island of Bombay till its cession to King Charles II in the sixties of the seventeenth century. Then came the British. But beyond the boundaries of Bombay there ruled Hindu Chiefs who had their own coins. The Mahomedan Empire of the Moghuls had also circulated a variety of Moghul coins, remnants of which were to be found at the beginning of the nineteenth century. Surat and Broach and Ahmedabad were the principal towns whence the different rupees, gold mohurs and minor coins gravitated and circulated in Bombay. Again, the old, old trade by the native craft with Arabia and East Africa brought in different kinds of coins, American dollars, Maria Therisa dollars and so on. Then the E. I. Company's own rupees and mohurs of diverse fineness were there. So that the currency at the commencement of the nineteenth century was a mixed one and the Company's efforts for the first thirty or forty years were to eliminate all foreign coins and establish an uniform metallic currency throughout India. The silver rupee of 1800 contained 179 grains of silver with 7·97 of alloy. But as silver was dear and much prized, the Company again resorted to gold, of which coins of the value of one rupee were minted. They have been racking their brains for some time past to introduce a gold coin of ten rupees. Why will they not memorialise the Imperial Government to follow the example of the E. I. Company and slowly eliminate the token rupee, so uneconomic in the eyes of Mr. Webb and others, by substituting for it the gold rupee? A trial on a large scale will tell the Government at once, whether the coin would prove popular and in great demand. But here is the Proclamation issued in Bombay in 1801, which will make instructive reading for our gold currency advocates: "Small gold coins have been stamped and issued from the Mint of Bombay equal in value to one silver rupee which gold coins it is hereby declared will be received in all payments at the treasury of Bombay and Surat and in all payments of revenue or purchases." What the sequel was to this order is buried in obscurity. But if such a gold rupee is anywhere to be found, it is certain to fetch a high value to-day, and even may be useful in giving a hint or two to our Mints in case a fresh attempt is to be made in view of popularising a gold currency.

Birth of the Bombay Mint.

But the struggles of the Company in reference to coinage continued. In the year of the Battle of Waterloo (exactly speaking, in October 1815), it was officially announced that the Surat Mint was abolished. The Mint at Bombay was proclaimed as the only one where all variety of legal coins were to be had. In 1824, however, there was a change in the weight of the fineness of the silver rupee. It was ordered that in future the rupee would contain 165 instead of 179 grains, and the alloy would be 15 grains. This rupee alone was declared to be legal tender, which was a very wise step, indeed, in the reform of a uniform currency. But the reform was not completed till 1835 when all India had the silver rupee of the standard weight just referred to. There is the Act 17 of 1835 of the Government of India, passed in September, which enjoined the coinage of Company's rupees weighing 180 grains, of which 165 were of the standard fineness, and the rest of alloy. In the interval say, in 1827, there was an ordinance regulating the weight and issue of copper coins to exchange for the rupee. Sixty-four dirkees (pice) were to exchange for sixteen annas or one rupee. The weight of the different small coins was also fixed. But how were the mercantile accounts kept? Mr. Milburn has given us a graphic description in his massive tome on the commerce of India in 1813. It seems at the time that there were some monetary measures of value of a meticulous character and which bore no corresponding coins in reality, just as the Chinese tael forms, even to-day, a measure of value but without any kind of coin in metal to represent it.

Measures of Money in 1802.

Milburn says that in 1802 the following measures of money were in vogue :—

2	Reas were equal to	1	Hurdhee or pie.
4	Reas	1	Dookanee or 2 pies
6	Reas	1	Doria or Dirkee.
8	Reas	1	Fadia or double Dirkee.
3½	Fadias	1	Anna.
12½	Paisa	4	Annas or ¼ Rupee.
16	Annas	1	Rupee.
15	Rupees	1	Gold Mohur.

The two reas was purely imaginary. There was no coin representing it. So, too, with four annas. Till then no quarter-anna piece as a coin was coined. At the same time bankers and merchants and all other traders kept their accounts in reas, quarters and rupees.

100 Reas were equal to	1	Quarter
4 quarters	1	Rupee

But after the uniform currency was established in 1835 the mercantile community gradually gave up the old nomenclature. It is a fact, however, that very old firms like those of Forbes's and Remington's and many others continued to keep their accounts in the orthodox way in vogue at the beginning of the nineteenth century till as late as the seventies. But there are Indian firms in the town, even to-day, who still cling to that nomenclature, as if it had been stereotyped like caste itself from father to son.

In the Fifties.

Anyhow, the rupee became a uniform legal tender throughout India after the Act of 1835. Only it has lost its former par value, since it was enacted to exchange for sixteen pence per rupee. The economic effects of the change were hardly tested when a gold crisis in New

York disturbed the course of exchange and Reverse Council Bills came for a time in vogue and now, as we revise these pages, there is the upheaval in silver and gold exchange stands at. 2/4 and more and it is impossible to say when Indian currency and exchange may be stable. Be that as it may, in the fifties the rupee was sound money and there was no divorce between its current value and the bullion value. A tola of silver actually meant a sound rupee. But even in the fifties silver was always in demand. There was no scarcity of the metal. So the rupee passed with the utmost confidence from hand to hand, and if it was buried and hoarded the possessor of it knew that its value remained unchanged. It was more so by reason of the fact that there was no paper currency to compete with it. The honest rupee of 16 annas, and not 10 as was till August 1919, greatly in requisition. Only after the establishment of the old

Bank of Bombay, which came to grief in 1866, was there an extremely limited circulation of the notes which the Indian Government had authorized it to issue. The State paper currency was first established in 1862, on the suggestion of India's first and ablest Finance Minister, Mr. J. Wilson, who had been the founder of the "Economist" in 1844 and was an economist of first class reputation. So that the circulation of the old Bank of Bombay notes went on for, say, twenty-one years. No doubt there was no further issue of it after that but it remained a legal tender for some years, till in 1869 the winding up of the Bank of Bombay led to its inconvertibility. This old Bank of Bombay note was very well printed and not easily forgeable. It had the portraits of two authorities on the right and left., My memory cannot recall the identity of those two important personages. The circulation, however, was extremely limited and chiefly confined to the city of Bombay. It was only popular among European merchants and bankers. A few wealthy Indian firms confided in it. The vast trading population in the heart of the town viewed it with no confidence, if not altogether looking askance at it. The Bank was viewed with suspicion, and it was not till the early sixties when cotton consignments and other produce were greatly on the increase that the notes found favour, and most specially during the fever of speculation. The Indian merchants and shroffs clung closely to their silver rupees, and it is an absolute fact that one of the duties of the mukadams in the fifties was to accompany the coolies carrying rupee bags of 2,000 each to pay either to the banks or to firms where drafts or hundies had matured. Where the payments extended to over 10,000 rupees the bags were conveyed in bullock carts, the mukadam sitting tight, literally, over them and delivering them to the right and proper persons safely, bringing a pucca receipt with him. That is the history of coins and paper currency in Bombay in the fifties.

CHAPTER XLVIII.—EVOLUTION OF TRADE IN THE NINETEENTH CENTURY.

IT has already been pointed out how insignificant was the import and export trade of Bombay at the opening of the nineteenth century. But let the progress made at every decennium, up to 1860, be marked.

MERCHANDISE IN CRORE RUPEES.

	Imports.	Exports.
1810-11	0·75	0·79
1820-21	1·90	1·55
1830-31	2·35	2·50
1840-41	3·50	4·35
1850-51	4·54	5·71
1860-61	9·20	15·47

It would seem that the balance of trade was equal, or almost negligible, till the forties. From 1840-41, however,

Bombay's exports exceeded her imports. This was specially the case in 1860-61 for which there is an intelligible explanation. The cotton trade was going on briskly, thanks partly to greater extent of cultivation and to a partial construction of the trunk railways. From 1861 to 1865, owing to the American Civil War, the exports of cotton were, of course, phenomenal. But these need not be referred to here. As already observed, the period of the fifties for Bombay was an epoch-making one. The progress in the sea-borne trade was as striking as the progress in other departments of Bombay activity during the decennium.

Four staple commodities.

It may, however, be interesting to relate how, during the first half of the nineteenth century, Bombay imported in larger and larger quantities four staple commodities, viz., sugar, metals, silk and cotton piece-goods. Take the imports of the last three decades only.

IN LAKHS OF RUPEES.

	1840-41.	1850-51.	1860-61.
Sugar ..	21	44	21
Metal ..	33	83	250
Silk ..	32	24	40
Cotton piece-goods ..	130	131	335

It will be seen that the imports of sugar, which, of course, came from Mauritius, fluctuated. So, too, silk which came from China. But there was a steady and satisfactory progress in metals and cotton picce-goods. It is a phenomenal fact in Indian economics that despite 250 mills in India at present which turn out 27·7 crore lbs. of cloth, she has still to import on an average 60 crore lbs. of a variety of Lancashire cotton goods. Swadeshi patriots should bear in mind this fact. As to exports during the same three decades, the two principal commodities were cotton for the United Kingdom and opium for China.

IN CRORE RUPEES.

		1840-41.	1850-51.	1860-61.
Cotton	..	1·89	2·94	6·96
Opium	..	1·14	2·30	6·60

The Opium Trade.

Evidently Lancashire mills, as they prospered, demanded more and more of Indian cotton, the growth of American being inadequate for her purposes. India was the dominant supplier. It was after the American War that the scales were turned and American cotton began steadily to supplant Indian. As to opium no words are necessary. The East India Company's most profitable trade was in that drug. Its appetite grew on what it fed. The larger the profits from year to year, the larger the acreage of Benares and Patna poppy Crores on crores of the Chinese wealth have been drained to India for well nigh a century from China, till at last that country awoke to the appalling enormity both of the physical and moral drain, and how the humanities of British civilisation have now rendered that trade negligible. Indeed the British Government has washed its hands of the unrighteous trade and it is well that that has been so. The extent of the trade may be seen in the figures of the enormous exports between 1840 and 1860. The recorded value rose from 1·14 crore to 5·16 crore rupees. And it is needful to remember that during the period mentioned the price of opium was a great deal cheaper than what it was at the close of the nineteenth century and for the first ten years of the twentieth. But before we leave the subject of exports it would be exceedingly instructive for the modern shipper of cotton to Liverpool to learn what were the charges of a consignment at that period. The faithful Mr. Milburn has recorded for information a copy of the *pro forma* invoice of 400 bales of the very best Surat cotton which was valued at Rs. 180 per candy. That was in the year 1810. The tare was taken at an average of 16½ lbs. per bale. A bale in gross weighed 20 lbs. less than the bale of the present day. The charges were as follows :—

Repacking at Re. 1 per bale.
Weighing, sewing, including twine, say, Rs. 3-9 per bale.
Cooly labour at 3 annas per bale.
Conveyance to Bunder and haulage, nearly one anna per bale.
Freight for 14 boats at Rs. 4 per boat, or say, 2 annas per bale.
Commission at 5 per cent.

Exchange at 2s. 6d.

Premium of Marine Insurance at 7 per cent.

Freight at £22 15s. 0d. per ton.

The bill for the value of consignment was drawn at 90 days after sight. That practically meant a usance of six months, three months being taken for the average duration of a voyage by ship.

The grip of Lancashire.

It may be mentioned in passing that the export of piece-goods from Bombay was diminishing as Lancashire increased her exports; specially having regard to the fact that many sumptuary laws were enacted for cotton stuffs going from India to London. The stuffs exported from Bombay were generally from Surat, Broach, Cambay, Karachi and so on. Sometimes cloths woven in Madras also used to come to Bombay via the Deccan for export. There were also cloths from

Broach and Ahmedabad. But they all went by the generic name of Surat piece-goods like all Gujarat and Kathiawar cotton. The goods were mostly coloured and coarse in quality. The following stuffs, though exported to London, could not be used for consumption in England itself! For that meant competition with the nascent Lancashire cotton mills manufacturers. There was a protective tariff of a prohibitive character. No wonder the exports ceased as Lancashire exercised a tighter grip through the Government. Thus the hand-loom manufactures of Surat and Broach steadily underwent great diminution. Here are the names of some of the principal species of these goods :—

Annabatchees.
Bairampats.
Bejutapats.
Nunsaris.
Neganepats.
Salimpores.

There were also exported varieties of chintz, dhotees and long cloths.

By the fifties the trade in these Surat goods had almost died out. The weavers confined themselves to the manufacture of only such quantities as were locally consumed, say, within a radius of 50 to 100 miles. Of course they grew poorer and poorer till at last their avocation was confined to pure agriculture. But even to-day in Surat, Broach, Cambay Ahmedabad and other outlying places, and specially in remote villages, may be noticed hand-loom weavers of the type of the beginning of the nineteenth century. Of silk goods weavers the types were to be largely noticed till, say, 1890. But the two silk factories established about the time in the city greatly crippled their trade. Many were drafted to the working of the power looms in the factories. Nay, some of the hereditary Parsi traders and foremen weavers in Surat silks were appointed managers and agents on a large remuneration to make silk piece-goods, most of which found their way to Burmah.

Cotton Mills in the Fifties.

Such, however, have been the vicissitudes of trade. Yet even in the fifties there was a considerable demand in the city for Surat silks, especially the varieties known as Khin Khab, Alicha, Musroo and so on. Hand-made silk sarees may still be seen and purchased. For there are yet a few hereditary weavers whose families have, despite all penury, stuck to their ancestral calling. In the fifties Bombay had just four or five cotton mills. The pioneer was that started by that enterprising Parsee merchant, Mr. Cowasji Nanabhai Davar, about 1854-55. This gentleman was akin in bold and new enterprise of a remunerative character to the late Mr. Tata. He was an ardent advocate both of "swadeshi" industries and banking. The first cotton mill which he started and worked was known as the Bombay Throstle Mill. Ring spinning frames were absolutely unknown till, say, 1888, when Mr. Tata was courageous enough to make a beginning with those made by Messrs. Brooks and Doxey in his Empress Mills at Nagpur. The mill of Mr. Davar still exists at Tardeo and is now known by the name of Shivlal Motilal. Sandy Seventy vividly recollects visiting it more than once in company with his father about 1858. About the same time a cotton mill on a small scale was started at Broach by a European named Mr. Landen. It is the same which bears to-day the name of Broach Cotton Mills which in years gone by was managed by Messrs.

Greaves, Cotton and Co. There survived at Broach till the other day a Parsi gentleman, an octogenarian, named Mr. Furdoonjee Munsiff, who started the first carding machine there.

Some well-known Firms of the Fifties.

But to return to the piece-goods trade in Bombay in the fifties. There were the well-known firms of Graham and Co., Ritchie, Stuart and Co., Finlay, Scott and Co., Peel, Cassels and Co., Grey and Co., who used to import large quantities of grey and bleached goods. There was also the firm of King and Co., of which Mr. Byramji Jeejibhoy of that time was a broker and which dealt in English yarn, known as " mediotwist." The Grahams were the most prominent in their imports of grey goods, while Messrs. Peel, Cassels and Co. in fine bleached goods, specially mulls, jacconets and shirtings. The Rallis were not there at the time. They established themselves in the city in 1864. Messrs. Finlay, Scott and Co. were also a firm largely dealing in bleached goods. Messrs. Lyon Bros. must also be mentioned. Curiously enough, from the early part of the nineteenth century English and Scottish importing firms employed rich Parsi merchants as guaranteed brokers on a very handsome remuneration. These brokers guaranteed the solvency of the constituents, and also advanced large sums on which the customary charge of interest was nine per cent. It was the case that the salesmen employed to sell goods were Parsis also, the average pay being Rs. 700 to Rs. 1,000 per month.

Famous Brokers.

Among the guaranteed brokers may be mentioned Messrs. Cowasji Jehangir Readymoney and his brother Hirji.

They were brokers to the well-known firm of Cardwell, Parsons and Co. and Messrs. Lyon Bros. Messrs. Cursedji Ardeshir and Co., of the well-known family of the Dadys, were brokers to Messrs. Peel, Cassels and Co. and Messrs. Grey and Co. The late Mr. Muncherji Framjee Cama was a broker to the house of Graham and Co., the late Mr. Framji Nusserwanji Patel was broker to the house of Frith and Co., till he became a partner in it when the house was called Frith, Sands and Co., the predecessors of the present house of Framji, Sons and Co. The Petits were brokers to Rennie, Scovell and Co. and Dirom, Hunter and Co. There were also first class Parsi and Hindu firms. Dadabhoy Wadia was the greatest of them all in the early fifties till unhappily he came to grief. Next may be mentioned the firm of Jehangir Wadia and Co., who had great connections with the French Government, the last of which firm was the great philanthropist, Mr. Nowroji Manekji Wadia, C.I.E. The firm of Messrs. B. and A. Hormasji was also well known. The great Camas had several firms both here and in China. And it was Mr. Byramji Hormusji Cama, that prince of cotton merchants, who founded a firm in the middle of the fifties in London, of which our late G. O. M., Mr. Dadabhai Naoroji, was also a partner. The brothers Framji and Cursetji Cowasji were linked with Messrs. Leckie and Co., there were the Allblesses who had confined their trade to China, and so too Messrs. Cursetji Bomanji and Co., a firm of well nigh a century, which still carries on business with the country. Goculdas Tejpal, Jewraj Baloo, Motichund and others were large Bania and Bhattia traders in cotton and opium. There were well known Marwari firms also dealing in opium. Many of them are still in existence. One wealthy Marwari, named

Ramlal, was both a merchant and philanthropist. So was Motichund who had partnership transactions with the firm of Jamsetji Jeejibhoy and Co., and who built the Pinjrapole at Bhuleshwar. Among the opium merchants was Mr. Ruttonji Edulji Bottlewalla, who had his place of business in Mopla Building in Borah Bazar Street till the vicissitudes of fortune brought down the old firm. How few indeed remain at present of the eminent European and Indian firms of wealth and reputation which flourished in the fifties! Most of them were ruined by the speculations of 1863-64. Some were voluntarily wound up, while the rest were reconstructed and rehabilitated on the wreck of their former fortunes. But, alas, one can never forget those great merchants and public-spirited citizens of the epoch-making fifties.

CHAPTER XLIX.—EDUCATION IN THE FIFTIES.

BEFORE closing this series of recollections of the decennium embraced between 1850 and 1860, it would not be either uninteresting or uninstructive to refer to the state of education in the city. It has already been observed more than once that the fifties were an epoch-making one in the annals of Bombay. Whether we look to administration, provincial or local, or to banking and foreign trade, or to railways, telegraphs and post, or to social and domestic affairs, it was, indeed, remarkable and marked a stage of no insignificant a character in our civic history. Educational progress was similarly well marked, specially owing to the reforms consequent on the great educational despatch of Sir Charles Wood, which Indians in all parts of the country have recognised as their Magna Charta of Public

Instruction. Sir Charles was then the President of the Board of Control of all affairs of the East India Company. Its last Charter was renewed by Parliament in 1853, and Sir Charles as a leading member of the House of Commons had heard a great deal of what had been said about the extremely disappointing progress made in educational matters during the twenty years since the Charter Act of 1833 was passed. The evidence taken by the Parliamentary Committee which sat for two years prior to the date of the renewal of the Charter of 1853 was also conclusive in reference to the extreme backwardness shown by the Company's servants in advancing education. The territorial magnates were so absorbed in their trade of opium, silk and tea from China and Lancashire piece-goods and other commodities of English manufacture from Great Britain that there were not found a few friends of India, who had inveighed in and out of the Houses of Parliament on the almost total neglect of holding the torch of knowledge before a people whose science and literature were the theme of praise in all Europe. The golden era of Indian civilisation dates back many centuries before the birth of Christ and many more before Pythagoras taught his mathematics, or Socrates, Plato and Aristotle their Hellenic philosophy. But, alas, for successive waves of conquests, dating from the first invasion of the Punjab by the great Persian King of Kings, Darius Hystaspes, arts, science and literature suffered continually, with only spasmodic intervals of indigenous intellectual activity, till the establishment of British power a hundred and fifty years ago. But even Clive and Hastings did precious little to revive the ancient civilisation and to link it with the modern one of their age. At the opening of the nineteenth century there was darkness in the land.

The indigenous literature was confined to the learned pandits and mullahs. The mass of the population was illiterate. It was the Parliamentary Committee of 1793 which had strongly recommended the education of the people. But no heed was paid to it for well nigh ten years. Eventually, the East India Company was goaded by sympathetic Parliamentarians into doing something. As a result a despatch went forth about 1801 to spend just the magnificent sum of one lakh on the elementary education of the Indian people, even then counted by crores! But such was the heedlessness or insouciance of the Company's servants in this country that it was not till 1812, after more than one reminder, that they could be spurred into activity and spend the lakh. Anyhow, the first match was applied to the torch of knowledge in that year.

That was the general situation as far as the illiterate mass was concerned. It should not, however, be supposed that the well-to-do were entirely innocent of their indigenous instruction either in the Vedas and other Sanskrit lore or the Koran. Both Hindu and Mahomedan kings have been known for their patronage of arts and letters. Stray European travellers who began visiting India, say, from the eleventh or twelfth century, either for purposes of trade or from a motive of curiosity have testified to the fact. Marco Polo may be mentioned as the earliest, and as the fame of Ormazd and Indies began to spread for their barbaric pearl and gold, the cupidity of European commercial travellers was greatly whetted. The Venetians and the Genoese were the most prominent in the twelfth and thirteenth centuries. Thereafter came the Portuguese in the fourteenth and fifteenth centuries. As Christians they used to have sometimes a couple of monks and friars of the different orders. It is not a rash statement to make that the earliest teachers of India were the Jesuit friars. They built first a church to God and then started a school which was to shed light on the darkness of the places where they planted themselves and at the same time to convert the heathen to the religion of Christ. And we have records to show that these friars and priests dotted their churches and schools in various parts of India specially in coast towns East and West. And some of the signs of those medieval churches, if not schools, are to be seen in Bombay, Madras and Bengal.

So far as Bombay is concerned it is on record, according to the official chronicler, that at the close of the sixteenth century the Franciscan fathers were known to have maintained their parochial schools in the island where elementary Latin and Portuguese were taught. One was attached to that old and venerated Church of Esperance; while another to an equally old church known as that of Santa de Gloria. The third was linked with the oldest church at Mahim. Of course, all these were Catholic institutions. The Holy See at Rome was intensely interested in the propagation of Catholicism which was then fighting its first great combat with the Lutherans and the Calvinists. The revolt was there and most conspicuous in England as first opened by Henry VIII. Venetian and other commercial travellers returning from their long voyages to India related how Paganism and the worship of idols, together with their strange and fantastic rites, ceremonials and pageants were rife and what a virgin field the East Indies offered to the successors of St. Peter to spread the primitive religion of the Great Master and thus find compensation for the growing loss in Central and Western Europe.

It is intelligible to understand how the zeal and piety of St. Francis Xavier was fired to propagate Christianity just as the lust for conquest led the prosperous and powerful Portuguese sovereigns to despatch the great Albuquerque and Vasco de Gama to discover the new route. And we know how the great friar travelled from Goa to the Dutch Indies and thence to distant Macao, in Southern China, and even to Japan. Thus it was the zeal of Catholicism at Rome that led to the institution of Christian schools in the Catholic settlements in India of which, of course, Bombay was one.

But it may be interesting to relate that at the close of the seventeenth and the commencement of the eighteenth century Protestantism was not behind. The fervour of a prelate, known as the Rev. Mr. Cobb, was instrumental in establishing a school for the children of the few European residents in the city. In 1718 Governor Boone placed himself at the head of the school movement. He raised a fund which came to about Rs. 6,000, of which Rs. 2,000 were generously contributed by himself—a fine example in the early history of social duty which the head of Government owed to the Christian population and also to the Indian. The school was maintained by voluntary contributions. The East India Company also donated just Rs. 600! But real vernacular education imparted by the territorial magnates was yet in the nebulous future. Meanwhile, exactly a hundred years ago two societies were established which had for their object the education of Protestants, both of the Church of England and of Scotland. They were known as the Bombay Education Society, a venerable name which is still familiar to us of the present day. There was a respected archdeacon named Barnes who flourished between 1815 and 1845. Scholarships were founded and the other society was known as the Native Education Society of which Mr. Framji Cowasji, the great philanthropist, was a generous patron. He presented to that body a portrait of the archdeacon for his valuable assistance in the founding and directing of this first important Indian society for the dissemination of education. The Bombay Education Society, it is recorded, was the first of its kind in India and liberally supported by the parent institution in London. But it should not be forgotten that between 1815 and 1845 was also established what was known as the Elphinstone Native Education Institute. It was started in 1820 and worthily bore the name of the Governor, who during his Governorship of Bombay laid the solid foundation both of elementary and higher education. This society did the first pioneer work by preparing and printing a series of elementary school books in the vernacular. With the progress of education the Native Education Society came to be merged in the institution, which the Government established, called the Board of Education. This Board did most excellent work till in 1855 when it ceased to exist owing to the great educational reform introduced under the despatch of 1854 of Sir Charles Wood. There is not the least doubt that Montstuart Elphinstone during his satrapy did not a little for the establishment and promotion of both vernacular and English education. He was the first president of the Society and Captain Jervis of the Engineering Department was its first Secretary. The latter's services were afterwards fittingly recognised and a fine life-size portrait of his was presented by the Society to the Elphinstone Institution. The portrait was painted in his uniform of an Engineer and it was a great attraction to all scholars attending that institution in the fifties, Sandy Seventy among the number.

CHAPTER L.—MISSIONARY PROPAGANDA IN THE FIFTIES.

THE earlier history of education in Bombay, say before the date of Sir Charles Wood's Despatch of 1854, is exceedingly interesting and instructive. But the student of that history must seek for all his necessary information in the reports of the Bombay Native Education Society and its successor, the Board of Education. Till 1854 those bodies one after the other shared the burden of all public instruction in the city along with the well managed schools of the Missionaries. These missionary schools were established as early as 1813 and 1818 and were mainly for the benefit of the Mahratta community, among which they were planted, specially in Girgaum and Khetwady, which were their habitat. These missionaries had also established a girls' school in

1824. By 1829 these had multiplied to nine with an attendance of 400 girls. One school founded by the Church Missionary Society in 1835 deserves notice. It bore the name of a distinguished Civil Servant, Robert Cotton Money, who was Secretary to Government in the Education Department. Presumably it was the great support afforded to the school by that officer that the school was named after him. It bespeaks volumes to the credit of the organisation of that well-known Society that that Academy still flourishes and has been well known to at least three generations of the people of Bombay. Within five years of its foundation the Institution numbered as many as 450 scholars, which was, indeed, an index, of its great popularity, bearing in mind that English instruction in the city was then at its very threshold. Before it was twenty years old the need was found to have for it a local habitation of its own. The growing number of pupils demanded extended accommodation. That was eventually found in the spacious and handsome premises on the plot of ground where stands at present a glorified chawl, which the financial genius of the jerry-builder of the opening twentieth century has reared in the city. Money School was really a modest architectural building, with a portico facing the north end of the Esplanade Road, with the Kalbadevi Road on its east and the Chandanwady or Girgaum Road on the west. To the lover of simple but handsome architecture it is a matter of profound regret that such a building, more than half a century old, was put to the hammer of the auctioneer and razed to the ground in order that the site may be disfigured by the ugly jerry-building just referred to. There was an excellent opportunity for the Government or the Municipality or some æsthetic philanthropist to erect a premises there which might have imparted an artistic vista and served as an object of admiration to every lover of the æsthetic. Even the town-planner of the day could have put up there a structure worthy of that central spot now dedicated to the vulgar votaries of Mammon. The American missionary societies were quickly followed by their counterparts of the Scotch nationality. Then came a prelate, whose remarkable ability and towering personality soon after made his name famous not only in the literary circle of Western India, but all through the country. He was the distinguished Rev. Dr. John Wilson, a zealous missionary, who in his early career was of an ardently proselytising tendency.

Proselytising Propaganda.

Judging by the facts of the past half a century and more, it must be ruefully observed that the ultimate aim and object of the various missionary societies which so well flourished in the forties and fifties, was undoubtedly to convert the heathen. The great Bishop Heber of Calcutta may be said to have crystallised for all times in ringing verses that aim and object as follows :—

> "From Greenland's icy mountains,
> From India's coral strand,
> To where the Afric fountains
> Roll down their golden sand ;
> From many an ancient river,
> From many a palmy plain,
> They call us to deliver
> Their land from heathen chain."

It is an historic fact that the first half of the nineteenth century was characterised by a great manifestation of missionary zeal on the part of the English, the Scotch and the American people. The exertions of one set of missionaries for the propagation of the Gospel on the entire surface of the globe where non-Christians congregated in their crores, stimulated and encouraged the spiritual fervour of other Christian societies, and since they were all richly supported by their wealthy patrons, it is intelligible to understand why missionaries were sent to India to found schools for educating Indian boys and girls in the English and vernacular languages, with the ultimate purpose of conversion to Christianity. It was, indeed, the good fortune of India that the first rudimentary knowledge imparted to our growing children came through these well-endowed mission schools, having regard to the central fact, to which reference has already been made, that the territorial lords of India, no other than the Honourable the East India Company, neglected to discharge their primary duty towards the people of the country. It was the missionaries who held aloft the torch of knowledge before the people and burnt much oil for their educational benefit. It was they who first irradiated the darkness of the educational horizon. It was they who strove with laudable zeal to drive away the debased superstitions of the land and to lift the people from the degradation they had sunk into for a thousand years and more. So far India can never forget her debt of gratitude to those pioneer missionaries who organized schools and even colleges in their midst. On the other hand, it must be confessed that they failed almost in their fundamental object of proselytising. India even after half a century of Universities and Colleges remains valiantly faithful to her old immemorial faith, however encrusted with degraded superstitions. The spiritualism of the land is as firm as a rock to-day as it was in the days of Buddha and Asoka, though modified with the environments of modern civilization with which she is surrounded. But to resume the narrative of the early missionaries in the forties and fifties.

Commotion among Parsis.

Their over-zeal to convert some of the scholars who attended their schools led to a great commotion in the population, particularly in the Parsi community. Two young Parsis, Messrs. Dhanjibhoy and Hormusji, embraced christianity and were baptized. Zoroastrian orthodoxy was up in arms. A bitter religious controversy ensued. Pamphlets, brochures, books and tracts were written. The controversialists vied with each other in putting their fingers on many an inconsistent statement in the Gospel. A bulky volume was written in Guzerati which "Sandy Seventy" as a boy had the curiosity to glance at. If he recollects rightly, it was called "Christie Dharamnu Khotaru" or the "Hollowness of Christianity." Another was written ostensibly by a Parsi Editor, but which was afterwards recognised as having come from the pen of the redoubtable Nowroji Fardunji, he who in the first twenty years of the Municipal life of Bombay was called the Tribune of the People. But the fire of the controversy was not quenched for at least a generation, during which spasmodic conversions had taken place. In the fifties one Byramji Kershaspji, a bright scholar of Elphinstone Institution, went over to Christianity, which created a great upheaval among the orthodox of the community. With him, as associates, were two other Parsi youths, but the influence of their parents was successful in bringing them back to the Zoroastrian fold. But over Mr. Byramji there was a regular law suit. An injunction was taken from the Supreme Court of Judicature on the Rev. Dr. Wilson to show cause why Byramji should not be restored to his parents. Ultimately, as Byramji was of the age of majority and altogether unwilling to return to Zoroastrianism, the attempt was abandoned. All these Parsi converts to Christianity took holy orders. Of these 'reverend' prelates, the veteran was Mr. Dhanjibhoy who died only a few years ago at an advanced age, greatly esteemed and respected not by the missionaries alone, but also by the more enlightened and tolerant class of the Parsi community. His was a venerable figure as he appeared at great public meetings or public institutions and impressed many with his sincerity, piety and true Christian benevolence. To the mind of this writer, who used to see him often pass by on the road, he struck him as a real man of God and great piety. The Reverend Messrs. Hormusji, Sorabji and Kershaspji have also been gathered to their majority, but Mr. Sorabji was for years a conspicuous figure in Poona as the founder of a school that bore his name. Mrs. Sorabji and her three daughters ably conducted it after his death and Miss Cornelia Sorabji is a well-known personage in Indian life and literature. Poor Kershaspji, who afterwards styled himself Kershaw, underwent several vicissitudes and was, a few years before his death, station-master of Ahmedabad. "Sandy Seventy" has a vivid rememberance of him as a normal scholar in the Elphinstone Institution in the early fifties. His appearance was pleasing and handsome, his intelligence great, but there was even then a certain volatility about him. It may however be mentioned that there is still surviving one Parsi convert to Christianity of that time. He is the Revd. Shapurji Edulji, a son of whose created a sensation some time ago in London in connection with a false charge against him of horse-maiming. Mr. Shapurji embraced Christianity in 1855 with a Mahomedan class fellow of his in the Elphinstone Institution, named Syed Hussein El Medini, who died in London after his retirement from the Judgeship of the Karachi Small Causes Court. Mr. Shapurji is the author of a useful Anglo-Gujarati Dictionary. The present writer was his class-fellow along with Mr. Medini at the time of their conversion. The commotion, however, of the fifties was the last of its kind. It killed missionary enterprise as far as the conversion of the Parsi was concerned, though the number of conversions from the Mahratta community are many.

Foundation of Wilson College.

But to return to Dr. Wilson. His schools prospered, thanks to the co-operation with him of Mrs. Wilson, so that by 1838 the first nucleus of amalgamation called the Free General Assembly's Institute was formed. At last the whirligig of time and progress led to the foundation of a college which bears the name of that great Christian prelate and distinguished scholar. Time assuaged all intolerance and the reverend gentleman himself was conscious of the comparative failure of the conversion of heathens to Christianity. The college had able professors and soon came to fame and now stands next to none in point of teaching, thanks to the present Principal, no other than the indefatigable and scholarly Dr. Mackichan,* and to Rev. Dr. Scott,* than whom there is not in all Bombay at present a more popular professor. The Reverend Dr. Wilson rose to be Vice-Chancellor of our local University, while his literary fame spread more and more. Many, indeed, are his literary contributions to the "Journal of the Royal Asiatic Society" and lectures in public. But his great monumental work are those massive volumes on the History of Castes in India. The next interesting work is that of "Cave Architecture in Western India." He is the last of the great Scotch divines, and lies buried in the old cemetery on Queen's Road, which though closed years ago, was by special dispensation of the Government, opened for his interment.

---

*Both have lately retired.

CHAPTER LI.—THE EARLY DAYS OF ELPHINSTONE INSTITUTION.

OF all the schools established in the city during the last half of the nineteenth century, and more, none enjoyed so great and deserving a reputation as a public school than that known as the Elphinstone Institution. That was the name which was given by the Committee of the Bombay Native Education Society. It was popularly called the "Society School." At the time it was called an "institution" as it embraced both school and college. The latter had no separate building of its own till 1856. In that year the college was under the orders of the local Government removed to a hired building in a bungalow belonging to the Sassoons, west of the existing Babula Tank. The despatch of 1854 of Sir Charles Wood led to extensive educational reforms on an organised basis. But prior to 1856 the college was accommodated in the same premises as the school. The Education Society leased a plot of ground on the Esplanade Cross-road, running from the corner where stands at present the Bible Society to the northwest, far down to the north-east where we have the head office of the Police Commissioner. Mr. Juggonath Sunkersett was a member, and a most active and indefatigable one, of the Society's Committee He willingly leased an extensive plot on which the institution was built on a very well laid out plan. The school was divided into lower and upper divisions. The last was for secondary education as we now call it, while the first was for primary instruction. Two large blocks with a roomy verandah divided the ground floor. That wing which faced north or north-east was for Gujarati-speaking scholars and that facing north-west for the

Marathi speaking boys. It was wholly a boys' school. The class rooms were so constructed as to run into each other, communication being made through a door in each class. Thus the lower school had four Gujarati and four Marathi classes in the two wings. They were well lighted and ventilated. But on the entrance facing the east, where there was a porch, there were two classes at right angles to the main blocks. These two were divided by a central common passage, whence entrance to the upper hall and other class rooms was effected by an excellent broad stair case. This was the main entrance. There was another, half way down the north-eastern wing, which was very convenient for common use. An open passage intervened between this north-east wing and the outhouses for Hindus and Parsis, separately, and so on. One of the two class rooms at the north-east entrance of the porch was the fifth and the highest class of the lower school, while that on the opposite side was the lowest class of the upper school. A fairly good play-ground was provided, but it would hardly be considered ample and convenient according to our modern notions. But then in the pre-Victorian period they in England were not even quite advanced in matters of school gymnastics and other sports. All the same, the sports and amusements at the school during recess hours were of a nature fairly to exercise the muscles of the young scholars. The *Gilee danda* which has been so successfully replaced by the healthy British national game of cricket, was exceedingly in vogue. The *gilee* was a round piece of wood about an inch or two in diameter and 3 inches long and the *danda*, or long stick of a cylindrical type, perhaps 3 inches in diameter and 15 to 18 inches long. Mr. Dadabhai Nowroji in his school days in the forties was considered a clever adept at the game. The play has not gone out of fashion. It may be still seen in the suburban places and in every rural village. It had very much in common with cricket, including the runs made, generally known as *Jugoo.*

The upper school, which was for instruction in secondary education, preparatory to the college classes, had four Gujarati and four Marathi classes, and save one, they were all accommodated on the upper floor. The hall of the institution occupied the whole eastern front of the school overlooking the Maidan and the Fort, and was spacious and stately. A life-size oil painting of Mountstuart Elphinstone was hung up on the west wall and that of Sir John Malcolm on the east. Both were by great masters. There were also smaller oil portraits of some of the professors,—Bell, Henderson and Green. When the scholars had gained their promotion to the first class of the upper school, they were further drafted into what was commonly known as the "Candidate class." This class during the fifties was taught by one Mr. Draper, and by Mr. C. A. Beyts in the latter part of the period. The last was from Bishop College, Calcutta, and a very able instructor of scholars preparing for the college. He resigned the teachership in order to take up the headmastership of the Bombay Proprietary School, the first of its kind in all India, well-organised and well-directed by an influential and experienced Committee of Management, among whom were some members of the Kama family, the great social reformers, and Mr. Jaggonath Sankersett, a most prominent Hindoo gentleman who was a member of the former Board of Education which ceased to exist after 1856. The hall of the institution had a magnificent and well equipped library with a long table and comfortable library chairs for the use of the Board meeting. Examiners, too, held their meetings in the hall, which was otherwise sacred to the Principal and Professors. To the scholar it was a *sanctum sanctorum*, where he need never enter.

The college department was not well endowed at the commencement, but on the retirement of Elphinstone, the grateful citizens of Bombay, recognizing the need of a great college for imparting higher education, on which that great statesman and popular Governor was himself very keen, raised a magnificent fund of 2½ lakhs of rupees to perpetuate his memory, and it took the form of the foundation of a college bearing his most distinguished name. Scholarships were afterwards established to perpetuate other eminent men of learning and law. Thus scholarships were founded known as West and Perry. The former was in honour of Sir Edward West, an able and erudite Chief Justice of Bombay directly appointed by the Crown. Sir Erskine Perry was another Chief Justice who had thoroughly identified himself with the education of Indians. A professorship of jurisprudence was founded in his honour which bears his name. Governor Clare's retirement led to a Clare scholarship. For purposes of training teachers there was established a Normal Class with sufficient scholarships. The Normal Class was a most necessary one as there was felt a great want of teachers of the English language of the requisite qualifications. To-day the great desideratum, at least in the Bombay Presidency, is the adequacy of trained teachers for primary schools. These are fast multiplying, thanks to the greater liberality of the State in reference to the annual grants to these schools, but there are not trained teachers enough. That is why training classes have been opened in different places. The normal scholars turned out by Elphinstone

College in the fifties were a band of exceedingly well-trained men under the early Professors. When permanent teachers for the lower schools specially were fewer these scholars used to be employed and they did their work most creditably. None of the class survives so far as the knowledge of the present writer goes. There was till very recently one survival in the person of Mr. Hormusji Dadabhoy, ex-judge of the Small Cause Court. He died only the other day but he was exceedingly well read, and scholars in the lower forms were always delighted when he took his turn for an hour to teach them. Mr. Hormasji was in the middle of the fifties a teacher. Sandy Seventy acknowledges with gratitude the training in English he gave to him in the class for some ten months in 1857/8. He was known as a brilliant English scholar of great eloquence, fine specimens of which were later on heard in public places, specially in the Town

Hall. It would be tedious to mention so many of the good and valued teachers of those days. Some three dozen and more could be recalled. But there is one who may here be named as he also lived in our midst till 1918. Mr. Cowasji Edulji Khambata, octogenarian, was a distinguished and brilliant scholar of Elphinstone College. He deserves special mention as so few really knew his intrinsic worth, though he was better known among his early contemporaries, of whom Mr. Dadabhai Naoroji was one. His English was so correct and idiomatic that he was better known through the "Telegraph and Courier" in the early fifties in which he used to give gleanings in English of salient articles appearing in the Gujarati Press. That journal was a bright one under the editorship of one Mr. Craig, who had a literary pen about him and sometimes gave lectures in the Town Hall in connection with the Bombay Mechanics' Institute.

When Mr. Dadabhai Naoroji founded the "Rast Goftar" in 1851, it was felt that a few columns of English matter would proud of invaluable service to the public. There were Messrs. K. R. Kama and Sorabji Bengali as associates in the work of editing that journal. The necessity became acute in 1857 owing to the anti-Indian spirit of the columns of the "Bombay Times" then edited by Dr. George Buist. He fell foul of the entire Indian community and calumniated them in no measured terms which eventually lost him the editorship. The "Rast Goftar" did signal service by giving rejoinders in English to the irate editor's fulminations, and Mr. Cowasji was specially selected to indite the English columns. He wrote such excellent English and with such sobriety of thought that when later on he left for England the "Telegraph and Courier" paid him a handsome compliment on his extensive erudition and his idiomatic and sober English. Mr. Cowasji was for many years editor of the English columns of "Native Opinion," founded by the late Mr. V. N. Mandik, till he left for Calcutta to take up the managership of the Port Canning Company But such was his love of journalism that he used, whenever in Bombay, to contribute economic and other articles to the "Times of India" and the "Bombay Gazette," the editors of which had the highest opinion of his literary abilities. But such is the whirligig of time that beyond a very limited circle of friends very few were aware of the existence of this retired literary but most unassuming octogenarian who was such an ornament of the Parsi community. But how strange is it that the community knew him not! Mr. Khambata was a gem of the purest ray serene who lived unknown and silent in his retirement at Tardeo till his death.

Chapter LII.—THE ELPHINSTONE INSTITUTION.

THE history of the Elphinstone Institution remains to be completed. The earliest English Professors brought down from London were Messrs. Bell and Henderson, and a little later on, in 1835, Mr. John (afterwards Dr.) Harkness. Mr. Bell taught mathematics and natural science, and Mr. Henderson history. Mr. Harkness taught English literature and philosophy. The very earliest alumni of Elphinstone College, among whom was Mr. Dadabhai Naoroji, were under the first two professors already named. The present writer has no personal knowledge of the first two as they had retired when he entered Elphinstone Institution, but they were said to be most excellent in their own branches of knowledge. Mr. Harkness was appointed Principal of the Institution. A little later there were Messrs. Orlebarr and Paton. The last did not stay long and the first was also superintendent of the Colaba Observatory. Mr. Orlebarr retired to take up a professorship in Australia. Mr. Paton's place was taken by Mr. Green, who was formerly head-master of the Government school at Surat. He was an advanced Liberal of those days and taught political economy at the college. As school-master he had made himself proficient in the Gujarati language and as he knew from his practical experience how often Indian school boys blundered in acquiring English idioms, he undertook to edit a book on English idiomatic sentences with their translation in Gujarati. Against each English sentence was given on the opposite column of the book the Gujarati version. The book was deemed exceedingly valuable to all Gujarati scholars and was recognised by the Education Society as an excellent text-book and it maintained its reputation as such for very many years. "Green's Phrases" was the most popular text-book for Gujarati speaking scholars learning English throughout the Presidency. But Mr. Green's economic teachings in the college were exceedingly valuable and he made himself a most popular professor. Mr. Harkness, whom Sandy Seventy had known both as the Principal of the Elphinstone Institution and afterwards as Principal and Professor of Logic and Moral Philosophy in the Elphinstone College, was an Aberdeen man, Scotch to the backbone and Scotch in his broad accents, besides being a man of stern discipline. He was exceedingly hot tempered and used often to fly in a rage for the most trumpery affair. But age had mellowed him, specially in his latter days before he retired in 1862. The grateful Elphinstonians voted him a marble bust, which is accommodated in the

Bombay Native General Library. While Principal of the Institution he had two Indian assistants for the upper and lower schools. Those were Messrs. Dadabhai Naoroji and Bomanji Pestonji Master, who was afterwards a member of the Bombay Municipal Corporation. He was the father of Dr. Dinshaw, who also is a Councillor. When the writer entered the Institution in July 1854 he had for his teachers the late Messrs. A. F. Moos and Pestonji Jehangir Talyarkhan, both able men. The former was well known for his studies in natural science and was the curator of a miniature museum. Afterwards he became a merchant. The late well-known superintendent of the Observatory, Dr. Nanabhoy, is one of his sons. Mr. P. J. Talyarkhan who died a few short years ago was known as an excellent English scholar, but very unassuming and retiring. He, too, was a martinet in matters of scholastic discipline. In 1856 he left the teachership to become a librarian of the College, which was removed in that year to a separate house. He afterwards entered the service of Government in the Inam Commission Department and did yeoman's service as an able revenue officer. The Government of Baroda afterwards invited him to place on a sound footing its land revenue system. which he did most creditably. He was rewarded by Government with a C. I. E.

Lord and Lady Canning's Visit.

It was while Sandy Seventy was in his class in March 1856 that it happened that Lord and Lady Canning, who were about to proceed to Calcutta, visited the Institution and hereby hangs a purely personal reminiscence. The writer, then 12 years old, was known to be the best reader in the class and was called upon to read a humorous lesson from the principal text book, "Series of Lessons" (Mr. Culloch's School Series). The passage read was an extract from one of the tales of the Arabian Nights. It was so well read that Lady Canning patted the reader on the back by way of compliment. Lord Canning was appointed Governor-General of India and before proceeding to Calcutta visited many places of interest in this city, including the Elphinstone Institution, whose fame had been wide spread. If the writer's memory be correct, Mr. Claude Erskine, who was the first Director of Public Instruction, accompanied him on this visit to the great school. By a curious coincidence it so happened that Sandy Seventy, who, after leaving College in 1861, had for a short time proceeded to his father's firm at Aden, had the pleasure of seeing his Lordship there once more. He had stayed at that settlement for a couple of days to view the fortifications which were about to be strengthened after the dark events of 1857. Accompanied by the Political Resident, he visited the camp. The writer had a glimpse of him as he passed by. But what a contrast to the hale and hearty statesman he had seen him in the school in 1856! What memories! What portentious events in the interval of six years! There was the deplorable Mutiny. There was the Queen's Proclamation of 1858 transferring the Government of India direct to the Crown. there was the hounding of the great statesman and saviour of India who had with exemplary patience borne the burden and heat of the day and the calumnies of his own countrymen for having so discreetly amnestied those who had been guilty of sharing in the Mutiny atrocities and, lastly, there was the sad death of her who had all through the long period of anxiety and trouble, stood courageously by him while the Empire was trembling in the balance. To Sandy Seventy Lord Canning in 1862 appeared in physique to be quite a different personage from what he had seen him in 1856! He seemed to be a wreck of his former self!

Separation of the College.

But to return to the Elphinstone Institution in 1855, Mr. Dadabhai left for England to join the great Parsi firm of Cama and Co., the first commercial Indian house established there. Meanwhile a great number of changes were on the tapis in consequence of the new educational policy laid down in the despatch of 1854 of Sir Charles Wood. The college was eventually separated from the Institution which was thereafter called the Elphinstone High School. Dr. Harkness was the Principal of the College with three new professors from England, namely, Messrs. Sydney Owen, J. P. Hughlings and H. Rawlinson. Mr. Owen came out as Professor of History; Mr. Hughlings as that of

English Literature and Mr. Rawlinson as that of Mathematics and Science. They were all able men, but Mr. Owen retired after a year's service owing to illness. He was the author of a little history he wrote, afterwards called "India on the eve of Conquest." Mr. Owen was said to be of a very hasty and impatient nature and was not quite satisfied with the students who read history with him. He would nickname some as "potato-headed," some as "cocoanut headed" and so on; and the anecdote is related that he was once so irritated by the answer of a dull student that he observed he would "pitch him out of the window!" Mr. Owen in London was for many years a tutor at Oxford and died about seven years ago at an advanced age. Mr. Rawlinson was a very courteous professor, extremely handsome in appearance, and would have been most popular, but unfortunately he died of cholera, though not without preparing a college text-book on Conic Sections, which was in vogue for several years at the colleges in the Presidency. Professor Hughlings was an Oxford man and made an ideal teacher. He was an "exact English scholar," and exceedingly popular with the students in whom he used to take parental interest. He opened at his own expense a reading room for the students where all the best London weeklies, the "Evening Mail" and the three well-known quarterlies of the day were subscribed, namely, "The Edinburgh," "The Quarterly" and "The Westminster." He also issued two annotated editions of standard classics, namely Gibbon's "Chapter on Roman Law" and two chapters of Hookers' "Ecclesiastical Polity." Sandy Seventy owes a deep debt of gratitude to that professor for inspiring him and instilling in him a thirst for economics and he remembers how often, when visiting the reading room, he would tarry awhile to explain difficult fiscal problems discussed in the "Economist" edited by Mr. James Wilson, who in 1860 became the first Finance Minister of India. Mr. Hughlings died in the latter part of the seventies in Australia, where he had gone for the benefit of his health. His grateful scholars of the past under the lead of the ever-to-be lamented Mr. Telang presented to the college a fine oil-painting of the deceased. Mr. R. Sharpe Sinclair was the Professor of Mathematics, an Irishman and a favourite scholar of Archbishop Whatley. He belonged to the Trinity College of Dublin. He was a very eccentric or erratic personage, and was the first Registrar of the University after its incorporation in 1857, the late Sir Joseph Arnold being the first Vice-Chancellor. In 1860 there was imported one Mr. Candy as Professor of Applied Sciences. He was a Cambridge Senior

Wrangler, but altogether absent minded. That defect disqualified him from being a professor at all. Many indeed were the jokes which the students of the day perpetrated on him. An erudite man he was but a burden on the College. Eventually he retired in 1873, when Professor Hawthornewaite succeeded him, an able proffessor, who rose afterwards to be the Principal of the College. The writer, when in England in 1897, happened to meet Mr. Candy at a meeting of the Indian National Association in the rooms of the Imperial Institute. He found him the same absent-minded personage he was in 1860 at the college and seemed to flourish like a green bay tree. In 1860-61 there was another Professor of History in the person of Mr. Edmund Burke, a bright young Oxford graduate. He was afterwards made Principal of the Elphinstone High School in succession to Mr. William Henry Smith, who was the first headmaster under the new arrangement of matters educational effected in 1856. Mr. Burke found school life distasteful and took up the appointment of Registrar on the Appellate Side of the High Court. He, poor fellow, died of small-pox very shortly afterwards.

Sir Alexander Grant.

Lastly, Sir Alexander Grant was appointed at the special instance of Mr. E. I. Howard, Director of Public Instruction, as Professor of Logic and Moral Philosophy with a reversion to the principalship of the college on the retirement of Dr. Harkness. Sir Alexander came with a European reputation as the translator of the Ethics of Aristotle. He had been defeated in his competition for the principalship of the Edinburgh University in 1858, which went to Sir David Brewster. So he came out to Madras as an educational inspector, but Mr. Howard fully knew of his great capacity and talents, both as a professor and as an administrator, and invited him to the professorship of Logic and Philosophy at the Elphinstone College. For a time he also gave lectures on Greek history and specially Greek democracy. Sandy Seventy was one of the scholars and he learned his Bacon's Novum Organon under him. Throughout the whole history of the college there never has been so excellent a professor of great reputation as Sir Alexander Grant. He became principal in 1862 and Director of Pubic Instruction in 1866 in succession to Mr. E. I. Howard, who returned to the Bar which then offered a most lucrative practice owing to the heavy litigation in consequence of the aftermath of 1865. Sir Alexander again contested the Edinburgh University Principalship in 1868, and this time successfully. On his retirement in 1868 he was presented with a valedictory address by the citizens at the F. C. Institute, at which function Sir Richard Couch, then a puisne judge of the High Court, presided. By a lucky coincidence it happened that on the very afternoon of the presentation day Mr. Pherozeshah Mehta arrived from England after having been qualified for the Bar "fresh from the atmosphere of Lincoln's Inn." He was present at the interesting gathering in honour of his beloved principal who in turn had predicted from the college days of that scholar that he would prove a brilliant man and an ornament to the city of his birth. Sir Alexander Grant was most instrumental in interesting two wealthy philanthropic gentlemen of Bombay in the early sixties to give princely donations for the building of a Senate Hall and Library for the University and a local habitation for the Elphinstone College. Thus it was that Sir Cowasji Jehanghir (the first of that name) donated two lakhs for the Elphinstone

College and two lakhs for the Senate Hall of the University, while Mr. Premchand Roychand donated two lakhs for the Clock Tower, which bears his revered mother's name (Rajabai), and which is a thing of beauty and joy. And it may be noted here that it was at the instance of Sir Alexander that Sir Gilbert Scott, the famous London artist and architect, designed the University Buildings, which are the gem of gems of all public edifices in Bombay. Sir Alexander was a contributor to our local dailies and the Bombay "Saturday Review," which was started by Mr. James Maclean, afterwards the editor and proprietor of the "Bombay Gazette.' Sir Alexander also read very learned papers on historical topics in connexion with the Mechanics Institute which were attended by a very large crowd of students besides the citizens of Bombay. A life-size portrait of Sir Alexander presented by subscribers to the fund raised in his honour hangs in the Elphinstone College. It is extremely doubtful that Elphinstone College will have another professor of the great ability and learning of Sir Alexander Grant. Principal Wordsworth who came later on, was the only exception.

The Great Educational Charter.

Between 1855 and 1860 great educational changes took place all over India thanks to the great educational charter of 1854 known as Sir Charles Wood's educational despatch. In common with the other Presidencies Bombay immensely benefited by the great changes effected in the whole system of education. And it was fortunate that she had Messrs. Claude Erskine and E. I. Howard as her first two Directors of Public Instruction. The latter was in office for well nigh ten years and the solid foundation of the new education which he laid has stood Bombay in good stead during the last half a century.

CHAPTER LIII.—THE BEGINNINGS OF SOCIAL REFORM.

A REFERENCE in brief to matters social in the fifties may not be out of place. First, then, as to social intercourse between communities. Though in matters of trade the different communities pursuing mercantile avocations freely mixed with each other, the intercourse may be said to have ended there. European merchants were exceedingly affable and were no doubt courteous in their mercantile relations with their Indian customers, constituents and guaranteed brokers. The last enjoyed their highest confidence, and their mutual regard and esteem were great. But beyond these relations there were none others or next to none. The Hindu or the Mussalman, whether orthodox or any other, could not intermingle freely with the European. At the best a few well-known European gentlemen of society would be invited to such functions as marriage festivities of the wealthy members of these communities. Sometimes they would be invited to a nautch party where they would put in an attendance of half an hour or so. At departing these European guests would be garlanded with flowers and rose water sprinkled on them, as is the custom even now. The host would be overpowering in his welcome and reception and the guests would most good-naturedly and whole-heartedly reciprocate the invitation and appreciate the good will. Beyond these amenities social matters did not go. There was a wide gulf fixed between the two communities and the Europeans. Not so as regards the Parsis. Free from the trammels of caste and custom indigenous to the country of their domicile, they were able to mix freely in European society. They dined with them and took a share in their sports and entertainments, though, of course, the last were not so common and frequent as are to be witnessed to-day. The wealthy guaranteed brokers would often give farewell entertainments of a magnificent character to their retiring "seignor," meaning the chief or some leading partner of the firm.

Some Leaders of Society.

The Wadias, the Dadys, the Banajis, the Readymoneys and the Jamsetji Jijibhoys were all well known for their hospitality. Dinners or refreshments, or entertainments would be given in honour of some departing worthy. Expense was no consideration. The mainspring was to do honour to the guest in the most friendly spirit. The Lowji Wadia family, that is the descendants of the great naval builders, were so far known to be most prominent as hosts at a variety of entertainments given at

Lowji Castle, the family seat, in the vicinity of the old Government House at Parel. The first Sir Jamsetji was the next, and his town seat, the same which is now occupied by Messrs. Evans, Fraser and Co., was the scene of many marriage festivities, whereat the Governor, Members of Council, other officials and many European citizens were invited. In the fifties, by the courtesy of the Governor, his band, then known as the "Garrison Band" was lent for playing at such festivities. It was deemed very high honour by the host. Besides these "shethias" other Parsis also, specially those in business, mixed freely with the Europeans. The only drawback was that Parsi ladies were not present at such festivities and entertainments as has been the case for the last forty years and more. Of course it goes without saying that in the fifties caste and custom among the Hindus and Mahomedans were a great deal sterner in matters social than they are to-day. Their women folk were all in "purdah" as far as such public festivities were concerned. There might have been on occasions a mixed gathering of Parsi and Hindu women. Of Mahomedans there was none. Again, some of the social customs of the Parsis owed their origin to their long settlement in India among the territories of Hindu Rajas and Chiefs. Other superstitions, mostly of Hindu origin, were greatly in vogue and special reform societies were founded in order to sweep away the non-Zoroastrian customs and practices and to purify the religious rites, ceremonies and other matters of foreign extraction. There was also a very animated agitation with regard to the correction of the Parsi calendar on account of the omission of counting the additional day in a leap year, since their settlement in India in the seventh century A. D.

Mr. Dadabhai Naoroji—The Pioneer Reformer.

The principal Parsi social reformers were the Kamas who greatly befriended Mr. Dadabhai Naoroji who in the fifties was known as the best Elphinstonian. Mr. Dadabhai founded the "Rast Goftar" for the purpose of educating the Parsis of those days both in the matter of the restoration of the purity of Zoroastrianism and for taking the first step in female education. It was in the fitness of things that he himself, who had immensely benefited by education, should unflinchingly hold the torch of knowledge before his own community and lift them to a higher level, while weaning them from all foreign practices encrusted with the conservatism of over a thousand years. Mr. Dadabhai himself set a good example by first becoming a voluntary teacher of girls at their own homes. The encouragement he received was most favourable, though, of course, there were not wanting the tribe of the orthodox who were alarmed at what education may lead their females to! But undeterred Mr. Dadabhai went on his way in company with other friends, equally warm advocates of female education and religious and social reform. Indeed, reform in general was in the air in the Parsi community. And it was a glad harbinger of the bright dawn —the day that the first Parsi girls' school was founded to teach the three R's in Gujarathi. It was an excellent beginning, the solid fruits of which are to be discerned in the educated Parsi girl of the day, both in English and the Vernacular. Anyhow, the seed was sown in the ground, which was certain in the fullness of time to give a rich harvest. The Hindus were not backward. They followed the lead of the Parsis, and schools in the Vernacular were established for girls, chiefly of the Maratha community. But the Mahomedan world was a world of cimmerian darkness, for at that date the number of Mahomedans educated fairly in English was exceedingly small. It might be counted on one's fingers. Two religious Parsi societies were formed, called the Rahnumai Mazdiasna and the Rahi Rast. These had their own dogmas and doxies to grind, though, fairly reviewing them after this long stretch of time, it appears that the differences were like tweedledee and tweedledum. But it is superfluous and even unentertaining to enter into details of the schisms and factions. They had their days and have ceased to be. The only echo, which is sometimes faintly heard, is that about the correction of the calendar, which for the omission of leap year days has gone wrong to the extent of over seven months since the first comers settled in the land of the Sanjan Chief twelve hundred years ago. The Parsi New Year's Day, according to the reformed chronology should fall on the day of the vernal equinox or the Jamshedi Naoroj, the 21st March. As a matter of fact, this year the New Year's Day fell on the 12th September! Orthodoxy, though yearly declining, is still tenacious and if the reformers of to-day work on the line of least resistance, it goes without saying that another quarter of a century may witness fruition of their labours.

The Lifting of the Purdah.

Going back to the fifties, it may be said that fair preliminary progress was made with female education among the Parsis during that period, and in 1858 the first Parsi journal for female instruction was published called the "Streebodh," chiefly owing to the efforts of Mr. Sorabji Shapurji Bengali. It was published by the "Duftur Ashkara Press" founded by the Murzbans, who are indissolubly associated with every liberal reform among the Parsis and who were ever ready by means of tracts and journals to help the cause of social and religious reform. The Parsis should ever be proud of their Murzbans and the "Duftur Ashkara Press," which is still with us and prospering. The "Rast Goftar" was the advanced liberal paper of the Parsis, there being two other journals, namely, the "Jame-Jamshed" and the "Chabook" which were Liberal conservative. So, too, was the "Samachar." The "Rast Goftar" may be compared to the London "Spectator", of its early halcyon days. But speaking about social reform, and specially of sweeping away the practice borrowed from the Hindus of never allowing the females to go about in public and mix freely with the malesi it may be observed that the Queen's Proclamation of 1858 brought the first, beneficent innovation which rejoiced the hearts of the reformers. The Proclamation was celebrated in the city with great eclat and demonstration. There were many brilliant illuminations in the principal streets in and out of the Fort. And the Parsi females were too keen on viewing them. Queen Victoria was a name to be conjured with. There were many songs and verses in her honour, and so some of the bolder ones made it a point to break the ice of isolation, so to say. The richer class of women used to go about in their carriages, mostly shigrams, with the venetians half closed. On the night of the Proclamation illuminations they were about in open carriages. The venetians were let down. More, those classes who could not afford to drive in carriages went on foot. And, sooth to say, there was to be witnessed in the localities referred to quite a remarkable bevy of Parsi females attired in their rich silk saris and bejewelled. The "purdah" was literally lifted, and well it was that the veil was torn. Thenceforward their movements were freer, but yet only a minority had taken the courage. But the leaven was leavening slowly the whole lump.

The Great Diwali of 1864.

Yet another historical event, six years later, happily offered itself. It was the great Diwali of 1864, when Bombay was overflowing with silver and gold and banking and financial institutions by the scores were daily springing in her midst. That Diwali was the best one known in the lifetime of the oldest inhabitant then living. The illuminations were then superb and on a lavish scale, never since known. It was a unique Diwali in every respect. The Parsi ladies of the city moved about freely both on foot and in carriages. The purdah was wholly lifted and since-then the intermingling of males and females in Parsi and European society became universal. Thus it was that the spark kindled in the fifties sent forth a lambent flame of social reform, which has since burned with a steady light of which the community is proud. Female education took long strides till in 1863 the first Parsi school for girls for teaching English was founded by the late Mr. Manockji Cursetji on the happy occasion of the marriage of Princess Alexandra of Denmark with Edward, Prince of Wales. The school, in memory of that occasion, was named the Alexandra School. It is a matter of rejoicing to see the school progressing and flourishing, thanks specially to Miss Manekji Cursetji and her brother Cursetji who are its life and soul. Vaster strides have been taken since 1863 in Parsi female education, and to-day we are glad to notice so many Parsi girls who are graduates of the University, some of whom have taken high medical honours even in the University of London. Happy are the nation and the community whose mothers are educated.

CHAPTER LIV.—SOCIAL RECREATIONS IN THE FIFTIES.

THOUGH the fifties were an epoch-making period in many respects including social reform, it may not be out of place to refer here to one social feature which a handful of the far-sighted of those days had greatly deplored. Nautch parties were exceedingly common. Dancing girls, both Hindu and Mahomedan, were invited to enliven every important domestic entertainment of a joyous character. They were all professionals and, from their point of view, did their best in order to advance their own prosperity. With dancing girls were singing girls also. Generally these professionals combined these two arts. And those who excelled in singing were, therefore, most in requisition. On festive occasions no entertainment would be deemed complete where a nautch party had not been provided. Indeed, it was held to be shabby on the part of the few who, from motives of saving money, failed to observe the universal custom. Such was, indeed, the deep hold of that custom that it was impossible to evade it, as impossible as to evade resorting to the temple for divine service. When a community is intensely imbued with such a conception of social duty it is quite intelligible to understand why nautch parties were held a *sine qua non* in every rich family, Hindu, Mahomedan or Parsi. So long as those parties were not accompanied by any impure ideas or sentiments, nothing could in all fairness be urged against the prevalent practice. The songs no doubt were more or less songs of love. As such it was impossible to condemn them. For who could deny the existence of love songs from old days forward, from the days of burning Sappho to those of our own times. Singing and dancing are a human institution connected with joyous and festive occasions. It is only the license of songs, unbridled, license which inspires impure thoughts, which could be deprecated.

Need of Discrimination.

It is one thing to dance and sing whether in praise of the Almighty or any king or hero or heroine, and it is another thing pure erotic songs which excite human passions. Even to-day with all our refined civilisation do we not notice dancing and singing at home, in public places and elsewhere in every variety and form? The moral philosopher, no doubt, came on the scene to decry them. But the philosopher ought to differentiate between dancing and singing, which is as innocent as the babe, and dancing and singing which excites lust and inculcates vice or sin. Anyhow, all India has been known for centuries for its nautch parties—from the king to the peasant. So that, if in the fifties nautch parties were a *sine qua non* none could be reproached for having them. It was the custom of the country. Puritan missionaries and other characters were supposed to be shocked or affected to be shocked, who first denounced them as heinous, though worse vices of a most degrading character are practised in the West of which India is even free to-day. Thus it came to pass that nautch parties came to be denounced wholesale. Those who denounced them seem to have made no distinction between professional dancing and singing with its poisonous virus and that which was innocent and free from any impure thoughts or gestures or any other indications. Wholesale denunciations of such a character are greatly to be deprecated, just as wholesale condemnations of caste as if it were a monster which bred evil only. How much there is of hypocrisy in this world of ours, wicked as it is in many ways! While the seemingly evil is decried, the truly evil of a most diabolical character, cunningly concealed, is seldom brought to light. The saint in crape is twice a saint in lawn. In every community hypocritical saints are to be met with in abundance. The only just condemnation against nautch girls is the one where concubines or mistresses go about in public places dancing and singing. The evil could be removed if society itself is genuinely moral. And so far as dancing and singing connected with professional prostitutes are concerned, society is right in trying to eradicate the evil. But in the fifties the people went on their way, continuing the custom of their ancestors and *per se* nothing could be said against it. Of course, with education, the latent evils arising from dancing and singing came to be rightly denounced.

Social Reformers.

Social reformers there were, a handful only, in the Hindu community who earnestly endeavoured to see that the practice was slowly abated. But in the fifties not only Hindus but Mahomedans practised the custom. The old Moghul Emperors, as we all know, had a regular menagerie of immoral dancing and singing women. And the wealthy noblemen and Mahomedans of the middle classes followed suit. The environments were there. And at the time about which we write, in the absence of any education, it was not possible to break away from the environments. All evil social customs are slow of eradication and it was, therefore, nothing uncommon that this custom, so attractive, so entertaining and yet so conservative, should take a longer time than others, which came to be quickly dropped. Even the Parsis were not behind in the fifties in giving nautch parties on festive occasions. At many a rich Parsi country-house, during Pateti, Diwali and Holi and other holidays, it was the *sine qua non* that a nautch party should conclude the day's entertainment. If education among the Parsis was earlier than among other communities and spread faster, it was a logical sequence that along with other borrowed customs this one should also quickly disappear. The social reformer like the school master, was abroad, and it is a matter of rejoicing that the Parsis were the first in the field in the abandonment of nautch parties. It should not be forgotten that in the fifties there were no innocent recreations and amusements. In their absence all the communities had to fall back on the available and time worn, so that, if at the date there was next to no reform in this respect, it is not a matter of surprise. Reformers of to-day are rather impatient and seem to be deficient in human psychology, otherwise they would not be so prone to denounce nautch parties indiscriminately. To lose sight of the human equation and human verities is to reveal the ignorance of the reformers. The social life of a people is to be judged from many a point and such practice has to be considered on its own merits before being condemned, if at all mischievous specially to the morals of a community.

Other Recreations.

Barring nautch parties there was little by way of evening recreation and amusement. There was the solitary Grant Road Theatre, which occasionally put a piece on the board, which was then deemed an event in the social life of Bombay ! Once in a way the first circus was a delightful source of enjoyment for a few days. It was, if Sandy Seventy's memory serves him right, called "Romani." He had twice gone to see it and still remembers the jests, the freaks and other oddities of the clown. Rope dancing was deemed a little novel amusement but it was the sport on horseback, which used to thrill the audience, adult and young. No doubt, there was some music at the bandstand twice or thrice a week. The Governor's band (Garrison as it was then called) played twice a week, but the lovers of music were Europeans only and a sprinkling of Parsis. The first massed band was played when the news of the victory of Sevastopol was brought by the mail. Thus the fifties were exceedingly barren, so far as public amusements and entertainments were concerned. Social life was dull and unenlivening. Of course, fairs there were and of an infinitely superior character to those held now. At those fairs a variety of English made toys were the greatest attraction; also Swiss musical boxes and concertinas. Their novelty was the chief attraction. There were no toys "made in Germany" to be noticed. Indigenous wooden toys of a variety of character were sold in abundance. But the novelty of fairs has worn out, and it is no wonder that the booths and stalls at fairs of the day are comparatively poor, especially in toys of indigenous labour.

CHAPTER LV.—SOME PERSONALITIES OF THE FIFTIES.

THE sands of the fifties in Bombay have now been fairly explored and we have picked up such shells as are likely to be of value or permanent use in the future to whoever may choose to write an accurate history of the epoch-making decennium of the fifties of the last century in the city. But this collection of shells may well be arranged so as to include therein some of the towering personalities of that memorable period so far as the writer can stretch his memory. First and foremost, let us refer to the t vo heads of the State who were in successi ›n Governors of Bombay. Those were L rds Falkland and Elphinstone. The fo ıer was here during the first three ·ars of the fifties, and Sandy Sevent had a glimpse, and a glimpse only, of him once just on the eve of his retirement. He was said to be a polished personage of great amiability and complaisance, and, moreover, most liberal-handed. So much so that, among the Indian community, the current phrase for the time for any gentleman with a spirit of liberality was "Lord Falkland." Lady Falkland, however, has left behind her a literary souvenir which seems to be almost forgotten. She related her reminiscences in a book called "Chowchow"—a most appropriate word for trifles light as air,—which for those days were deemed bright and sparkling. But they have an interest of their own which would delight a Justin McCarthy of Bombay. Elphinstone who was here for seven years was now and again seen driving through Churchgate Street on his way to the Secretariat in Apollo Street or to the Town Hall. He seemed, so far as the writer's memory can assist him, a tall handsome personage in the tall hat of the day. The bodyguard and outriders were clad in the uniform of the native lancers, which was in colour sky blue. The scarlet uniform was first introduced by Sir Bartle Frere, following the uniform of the bodyguard of the Governor-General Sandy Seventy has a tolerably vivid recollection of Lord Elphinstone as he stood on the spacious verandah of the Town Hall, surrounded by his staff in brilliant array, civil and military, and the notables of the town on the day that the Queen's Proclamation was read (1st November 1858). It was customary in those days, and for a long time after, for Indian gentlemen, whether Hindus, Mahomedans or Parsis, to appear at the Levee and other State occasions in their full dress, which was the snow white and flowing *Jama* and *pichoree* or kummarbund. When standing together in solemn array they made an imposing picture. Some of the elders wore brilliant shawls of great value. That heightened their picturesqueness and enhanced their dignified appearance. None looked most stately such as Mr. Juggannath Sunkersett among the Hindus and Mr. Rustomji Jamsetji Jijibhoy among the Parsis. The Parsis dropped this full dress somewhere in the nineties, as the generation of the period affected more and more the English costume. But here and there were to be seen till very late a solitary specimen or two. The late Mr. Byramji N. Servai was one of them. Mr. N. J. Gamadia was also seen clad in his flowing *Jama* and *pichoree* at the ceremony of laying the foundation stone of the Alexandra Docks by His Majesty King George (then the Prince of Wales) in 1905. But the head-priests of the two sects of the Parsis are still always to be seen in such dress in public. This flowing robe seems to be an interesting relic of the gorgeous dress of the great noblemen at the Court of the Mogul Emperors. Many portraits of those bejewelled royalties as painted by Indian artists clearly show this special Court costume. Even Shivaji may be seen in the portraits we have of him dressed similarly but hardly gorgeously. But this sartorial affair had better be left to be narrated by the experts of Indian national costumes.

Lord Elphinstone.

Lord Elphinstone left the shores of Bombay in 1860, highly eulogised for his judicious and statesmanlike administration, specially for having kept well under control the Indian troops in the Presidency throughout the dark days of 1857. He was fortunate in having such a capable Police Commissioner in the city as Mr. Charles Forjett, whose special services have already been related. Lord Elphinstone had been so far instrumental in pushing initial railway construction in Bombay that the Chamber of Commerce, who presented him with an address, made special mention of it and of the stimulus he also afforded to the development of Bombay's seaborne trade. It is curious that he was succeeded by Sir George Russel Clerk, who had acted as Governor of Bombay for two years in 1848 and 1849. He belonged to the Bengal Civil Service, of which he was considered an ornament. He had served in the Council of the great Lord Canning. Sir George was of middle height and of unprepossessing countenance, seemed weather beaten and otherwise was simple and homely in his dress. He wore grey whiskers. The writer as a student happened to see him very closely when in 1860 he visited Elphinstone College, then located in a hired bungalow on the Babula Tank Road. All these recollections of the three Governors of Bombay (1851 to 1860) here related must be deemed personal as they struck the writer, then a lad between 7 and 16. They may not be quite accurate or faithful. He only recalls the impression he received when having a few occasional glimpses of them. Elphinstone is said to have been so charmed with Matheran; which was first discovered by Mr. Malet, that he built a bungalow where he used to retire when fagged and worried with the cares of State. The bungalow, now in occupation of Mr. Herbert Greaves, still bears the name of Elphinstone Lodge, one of the finest on the Hill. The writer also remembers this Mr. Malet, at whose hands he received a school prize in 1855 or 1856. It was Thomson's Euclid for "proficiency in Arithmetic." The annual exhibition was then held in the Town Hall, which had at the time not even the solitary statue of Mountstuart Elphinstone. It was placed in the south of the hall somewhat later till it had to be removed to the opposite side when the magnificent organ, the gift of Sir Albert

Sassoon, came to be accommodated there. So far as the memory of the writer can be stretched Mr. Malet was a ruddy-faced, somewhat of a stout physique and wore an eyeglass. But of the other Councillors of the Government in the fifties he has no recollection.

Some other Personalities.

He, however, remembers the faces of the personalities most in evidence during the fifties. These were the Rev. Dr. Wilson, the Rev. Murray Mitchell, the Rev. Dr. Fraser, the first principal of the Sir J. J. Parsi Benevolent Institution; Mr. Berkley, the talented engineer of the G. I. P. Railway, who designed and built the Bhore and Thull Ghat tunnels; Dr. Buist, the editor in the earlier part of the fifties of the "Bombay Times"; and Robert Knight of the later fifties of the "Times and Standard" which eventually blossomed into the "Times of India"; Sir Joseph

Arnold, the great Puisne Judge of the Supreme Court of Judicature, and erudite scholar and author, a contributor to the "Saturday Review" and a boon friend of the poet Browning, Fellow of Wadham College and the first Vice-Chancellor of the Bombay University; Drs. Leith and Haines, two brilliant sanitarians who have written fairly comprehensively on the health conditions of the city in the fifties and all about overcrowding and fevers of the pestilential type in the slums, which are still such a discredit, despite the much vaunted Improvement Trust, which is really improving the city backwards. There were the towering medical personalities, Drs. Morehead and Peet of the Grant Medical College. There was Dr. Reid, a fine witty Irishman, Law Professor of Elphinstone College, and Perry Professor of Jurisprudence. There was Mr. Spooner, a short man, somewhat lame, —who was the Commissioner of Customs, very popular and amiable. There was Dr. Giraud, Professor of Chemistry,—quite a model of a Professor for beginners in chemistry and botany,—a man of fine physique, with a French moustache and a ringing voice. Dr. Haines was also a Professor of Chemistry. To hear his lecture was a pleasure and a treat,—a man of remarkable fluency and an accomplished English scholar. There was Advocate-General Lewis and Mr. Spencer Compton, the Prothonotary. There were Drs. Vandyke Carter and George Birdwood, the former a tall striking personality every way, who was Professor of Anatomy, and the latter a short man, of great brilliancy and high literary accomplishments, who was Professor of Materia Medica. Sir George, as he was years afterwards, was indeed a personality and survived almost all his contemporaries of the Grant Medical College till his death in June 1917. But of him a great deal will have to be said later on.

The catalogue of the public worthies of the day is not exhausted. It is a legion perhaps as long as the catalogue of the Homericships, and we may fittingly close this resume with naming two other gods of the journalistic line in the persons of John Connon and Mr. Craig, one of the "Bombay Gazette" and the other of the "Telegraph and Courier." We cannot forget the accomplished Mr. James MacLean who started in 1859 the Bombay "Saturday Review." And last, not the least, the ever-to-be remembered Mr. Thomas Chisholm Anstey, the most eminent and encyclopædic barrister, the like of whom Bombay has never known in her juridical history.

Chapter LVI.—SOME LEGAL REMINISCENCES.

Mr. Anstey was, of course, the *facile princeps* of the local bar throughout his career which came to an end in 1873. He was a devout Catholic. He was at the outset of his legal career a Member of the House of Commons for Youghall in Ireland. There it is recorded he was a dashing free lance, sparing none, not even Cabinet Ministers. Lord Palmerston was his *bete noir*. He had once a bout with the masterful Whig which was the subject of a political cartoon in "Punch" somewhere in 1848. It was observed that on one occasion Mr. Anstey discussed some constitutional question which prompted him to begin with the beginnings of the Constitutional history of England. "Punch" said he began with

A. D. 1! It is related that Lady Palmerston was most desirous of capturing him. But at first the fly could not be got to be enmeshed in the web of the spider. But she was a consummate social diplomatist and at last succeeded in capturing him. A few months later he was offered the post of Attorney-General at Hongkong. He accepted it and his departure from the House was a great relief to the noble lord whom he had teased; and heckled so much. However, there was in Mr. Anstey's constitution a serious defect, but for which he might have risen by his profound juridical lore to some of the highest legal prizes in the gift of the Crown. He was a very angry man. Only a spark was needed to kindle his rage. It was owing to this defect that he quarrelled with Governor Bowen of Hongkong in the Legislative Council there on some Bill connected with the Police. He resigned his post and came to

Bombay to practise in what was then called the Supreme Court of Judicature. An eminent lawyer of great forensic ability he fast grew into practice. He was head and shoulders above his contemporaries of the Bombay bar. No respecter of persons, even of the judges, he often used to be in hot water with them and numerous are the anecdotes of his wrangles. "Scenes in Court" was a familiar heading in the local dailies of the sixties and seventies. Mr. Justice Westropp, an Irishman, knew well his faults while recognising his great abilities. He used to handle him most cleverly, so that there was not much of sparring with him. But he had not much patience with the impatient Sir Charles Sargeant. Matters once reached such a stage that that judge who, during his early career, was known to be somewhat hasty, had to ask Mr. Anstey to unrobe himself. This was quite an extraordinary and drastic procedure. But Mr. Anstey was equal to the occasion. He doffed his robe the next moment and threw it on the table and vociferated "where was the bailiff" so that he may serve him formally with a judge's warrant! There was a great sensation in the court and the next day the papers came out with their latest "scene." Of course, this judicial discipline lasted only an hour or so. But it had no chastening effect on Mr. Anstey. Mr. Anstey was Mr. Anstey.

On another occasion he soundly belaboured Mr. Justice Bayley, of whom he had a poor opinion. It was a full bench appeal in a criminal case at which all the seven judges of the court sat on the bench, which was indeed a unique historic incident. One Pestonji Dinshaw, a solicitor, was sentenced to seven years' imprisonment by Mr. Bayley, sitting as a judge in one of the criminal sessions in the early seventies.

It was a case of aiding and abetting in a poison or magic case. The appeal had reference to points of law and misdirection to the jury. Mr. Anstey, on behalf of the convicted appellant, was elaborating his points, when he came to describe how the judge had misinterpreted the law. In a loud voice of contemptuous indignation, he exclaimed: "My Lords, the learned judge held my authorities cheap and my law cheaper still." The court was crowded and even the outer spacious corridor of the old court house in Apollo Street was full of outside public. The judges looked grave while the judge indicted seemed from his countenance to have been quite red with the smart point the learned counsel had scored. The writer was present at the hearing and his impressions of the trial are still fresh in his memory. Another great criminal trial in which he bearded Mr. Justice Green was that known as the Parsi

Tower of Silence Riot Case. But it would fill quite a moderate volume to recall all the great trials in which Anstey was engaged and in most of which he won his forensic laurels. Such was his legal renown that in the great Wahabi Trial at Calcutta he was able to carry a great point of constitutional law. He questioned the jurisdiction of the trying Court which brought about a deadlock. Mr. Anstey returned triumphant while the Government of India had immediately to introduce a Bill in the Legislative Council to enable them to proceed with that famous trial for conspiracy. His memory was phenomenal. He would quote chapter and verse of even the most obsolete Act and direct his juniors to turn to the page and the line for purposes of reference. He had a fund of wit and humour in which he would indulge with his brother counsel when in his lighter and gayer mood.

Anstey as a Judge.

As an acting Judge in the year 1865 he proved himself quite Draconian in his punishment of the insolvents who came before him, insolvents of the mad speculation of the two preceding years. His long experience in the Insolvency Court stood him in good stead. His keen and powerful legal talent would at once detect the slightest fraud and woe betide the insolvent who came under the fire of his cross-examination. Thus it came to pass that he established a regular reign of terror among the fraudulent insolvents who went about in large numbers in those days of dethroned credit and reckless commercial immorality. His immediate predecessor in the Insolvency Court, Mr. Justice Hoare, who had been Chief Judge of the Small Causes Court, was too lenient while the exceptional times demanded an exceptional treatment. Mr. Anstey was specially selected to act awhile on the bench, while Mr. Hoare went on furlough, and it must be said to his credit that by his drastic treatment of fraudulent insolvents from the Bench he greatly contributed to inspiring confidence in the honest section of the mercantile community. The Insolvency Court used to be inundated with cartloads of all sorts of large and small schedules filed by all classes and conditions of men, honest and dishonest, mostly the latter. It had the salutary effect of checking the latter from "taking the benefit" of the insolvency law. Two signal cases greatly struck terror among this class. One was a case in which two directors of one of the mushroom companies of the day were brought to book. Mr. Anstey's fulminations against their laches and malpractices were great. He sentenced the two delinquents to transportation for life and escheated their property to the Crown.

The other case was not of so flagrant a character. It was purely one of reckless speculation. But the insolvent happened to be a member of the family of Sir Jamshedji Jeejeebhoy. He was sentenced to four or six months' simple imprisonment for his reckless speculation. These two and other draconic punishments led to a strong agitation for the removal of Mr. Anstey from the Bench. An influential memorial was presented to Sir Bartle Frere who gave back a dignified but firm reply to the petitioners upholding the drastic judgments and vindicating them. The interests of commercial ethics demanded the sort of treatment the judge had meted out and he had discharged a great public duty by clearing the dishonest atmosphere of commercial Bombay. Mr. Anstey's acting appointment soon after terminated and the memorialists heaved a deep sigh of relief. All the same, it was recognised that the Court had greatly purified commercial immorality and the public paid a tribute of praise to the retiring Rhadamanthus. Some most talented counsel there had been before Mr. Anstey's time and many more have been since his death. But it may be said without exaggeration that Bombay has never seen the like of him and never will.

The Brothers Howard.

In the fifties there were two able counsel, one of whom was Mr. Lowndes, who was Advocate General, and in great requisition by litigants. There was another talented barrister in the person of Mr. Howard, the senior of the one who was Director of Public Instruction for well nigh ten years. It is a curious circumstance that both brothers sadly met their death by accident. The elder fell from his horse and died. The junior was returning from Poona where he had been engaged in a professional case, when a runaway engine from Lonavla collided with the train causing serious loss of life, including that of Mr. Howard. It was in 1856 that Lord Elphinstone appointed him Director of Public Instruction. He was known as an able Oxford man. Education in Bombay had to be thoroughly organised in conformity with the broad policy laid down in the despatch of Sir Charles Wood and Mr. Howard was deemed to be eminently qualified for the purpose. The speculations of 1863-64 embarrassed him and he had to give up his post to resume his practice at the Bar which came to be considerable. Among other counsel who had a large practice in the fifties was one Mr. Dunbar. But he had retired some years before the speculative mania set in. The aftermath introduced such extensive litigation that many a new counsel arrived in Bombay between 1866 and 1870. Mr. Dunbar returned here for a couple of years, amassed a large fortune, and again retired. There was also Mr. George Taylor, an able man who was Master in Equity. He was also a good commercial lawyer and a member of the local committee of what was then the Agra and Masterman's Bank. He, too, had to give up the official appointment as he became hopelessly involved in large debts owing to speculation with Atmaram Madhowji and Dr. Diver, two speculative stars of the second magnitude at the time. Taylor died a broken hearted man. The last that was heard of him was at Baroda. The other counsel of ability, who afterwards rose rapidly and shone on the High Court Bench, was Mr. Michael Westropp. It is said of him that he was so long briefless that he was on the point of returning to England, when Sir Charles Jackson, who acted for some months as a judge, dissuaded him from his purpose and advised him to stay, having seen in him all the making of a good barrister. Sir Charles had judged rightly.

Sir Michael Westropp.

In the latter end of the fifties Mr. Westropp came into practice and soon acquired a reputation as a sound lawyer, specially in Hindu and Mahomedan law. By 1860 his reputation was well established. He became Advocate General, and in 1863, when the High Court was established by Royal Charter, he was appointed one of the puisne judges on the Original Side of that court. On the retirement of Sir Richard Couch, who went to Calcutta to be Chief Justice there, Mr. Westropp was appointed Chief Justice. This post he filled with infinite credit to himself and great advantage to the public till his retirement in 1884. But Sir Michael Westropp's abilities are so well known, even to counsel practising to-day, and so many are his elaborate judgments, though given most tardily, to the point of provocation, that it is superfluous to refer to them in this place. As a striking instance of his dilatoriness in giving judgment it may be observed that the very last one he gave was a few hours before he retired from the Bench in the case of the notorious East India Bank, heard fully five years before. But it was a most remarkable judgment and a scathing one for the parties involved.

CHAPTER LVII.—LEGAL LUMINARIES OF THE FIFTIES AND SIXTIES.

THERE remains to be related the narrative of a few other luminaries who shed their lustre on the legal horizon of Bombay. Those were Mr. Pigott, a learned Chancery lawyer, and Mr. MacCulloch, a most brilliant and eloquent orator whom it was always a treat to hear in the Court when any case, civil or criminal, of importance was being heard. There were also Messrs. Latham and Green besides other mediocrities.

There were two Pigotts, the younger of whom, a clever young man, was in many respects quite unconventional both in law and politics. His free-thinking was more or less obnoxious to the opportunists who wished to rise in their profession and to win a handsome practice. He was boycotted and was suspected of having great sympathy with the Fenian movement of the time. But, though boycotted by his brother counsel here, he had influence enough at Home to obtain for himself a judgeship on the bench of the High Court at Calcutta. The senior brother was an elderly person but well-versed in the law of equity. He came here with a fair reputation acquired in the Chancery Court. He jumped very early into practice after his arrival. Civil cases of a variety of complicated character were being duly filed in the Court. Mr. Pigott's opinion was well sought after. No evening was without some important consultations. His written opinions were greatly valued for their soundness. But he was not a good-speaking barrister. He was very inaudible to those not very near him. He would plead well but none could easily make out what points he was driving home. The judges, however, greatly respected him for his equity law. He was more or less in feeble health. That, perhaps, was one of the reasons of his weak voice. He really minted money and retired in a few short years.

Mr. MacCulloch.

But the *facile princeps* of counsel of the day, next to Mr. Anstey, was Mr. MacCulloch. A short dapper man, always with a beaming and cheerful countenance, his amiability and complaisance were indeed a model. There was a kind of magnetic attraction in him and all his friends at the Bar and Bench trooped round him. His was a most fluent oratory of a pleasing character. Whether a case was weak or strong MacCulloch was always at his best, endeavouring to do full justice to his clients. With a good case he was in his element, and it afforded one pleasure to hear his eloquence, apart from his forensic lore. He, too, was a good counsel in common law. But he was also very quick in seizing the strong or weak points of the counsel arguing on the opposite side and shaping his course accordingly. He had the happy knack of always attracting the sympathy of the judge more or less. His tact and judgment were admirable and his law generally sound. Like Mr. Inverarity, he was a master of cross-examination and one could read in his countenance, how he would chuckle when he had drawn out a stubborn witness and scored a point with him, all the while frequently passing over his face a red silk handkerchief which was to him indispensable. Just as Anstey had his mannerism of twisting red tape or string all the time he was developing his argument, so would Mr. MacCulloch take, off and on, his silk handkerchief from his pocket and wipe his face in the midst of a great speech or argument. Unluckily for Bombay litigants MacCulloch died prematurely at a comparatively young age. But in and out of the Court he was the very idol of those who knew him. It would not be wrong to say that he was the very antithesis of the brusque and growling Anstey.

Messrs. Latham and Green.

Latham, like Pigott, was a good equity lawyer. Indeed, after the retirement of the latter the former came to be in great requisition. Well-versed in law, his opinion was much sought after. His law was sound and every year that he practised saw him in full swing with heavy briefs. Like Pigott his voice, too, was not strong though somewhat louder. Calm and collected, patient and thoughtful, Latham made an exceedingly reliable counsel. His opinions were well balanced as if adjusted by the most delicate scale. Though an excellent lawyer he was also a politician with Liberal ideas, some of which were to be clearly discerned in the legislative debates when he had the honour of holding the post of Advocate-General. Like Mr. White, he was fearless in offering his opinion and never cared for the bureaucracy with its pretentions intellectualism. His sense of uprightness was great. No counsel was more conscientious. Just to all, he did not care for the favour or the frown of the Executive, as unfortunately some of the Advocates-Generals of the last twenty years have been. In short, he was no opportunist and never trimmed his legal sails to suit the mighty. But gone, gone for ever, is the type of the counsel of Latham. Lastly, we may say a few words about Mr. J. P. Green who eventually rose to be a judge after having more than once acted in that capacity. Green may be said to be clever at drawing plaints and petitions involving great legal acumen. He wore a placid countenance which had a deal of dignity and gravity about it. He made on the whole a good judge but as counsel he was ever an unhappy pleader. He could not make an impression as MacCulloch. But there was one trait of his which made him exceedingly unpopular with the Indians. He was very unsympathetic. And oftener than not owing to this failing his judgments were warped in cases where the litigants were of the white and dark races. There was also a good deal of leaning on the side of the executive which not a little marred his impartiality. This failing and race bias were most strikingly discerned in the Parsi Tower of Silence riot case which he tried and in which Anstey defended a gang of Iranis who were the accused. He was more or less in a weak state of health and died while on sick leave at Naples.

Many other counsel came at the close of the sixties and in the seventies, the most prominent of whom was Mr. Inverarity who is happily still among us, the prince of counsel, at the Bombay Bar. The late Sir P. M. Mehta was his senior by a few months. But it would be gilding refined gold to say aught about Mr. Inverarity who is to-day head and shoulders above the generality of counsel of the day. Then there were Messrs. Lowndes and Macpherson, and Lang and Marriott and a host of others. But it is of no use going beyond the sixties. So that all those who needed mention have already been named. Mr. Lowndes returned five years ago to be the Law Member of the Imperial Executive Council. He has won his laurels by his great legal acumen and broad statesmanship. He has on him conferred the dignity of a K. C. and a K.C.S.I.

Some eminent Solicitors.

It may now be useful to deal with the eminent solicitors of the fifties and the sixties. It may be mentioned at the outset that the earliest Indian who was enrolled as a solicitor of the Supreme Court of Judicature was Mr. Khanderao Moroji. Mr. Cumroodin Tyabji, who had passed his solicitor's examination in London, was the next, Mr. Pestonji Dinshaw, who had been articled at the firm of Bickerseth and Cleveland, was the third. In all probability Shamrao Pandurang preceded him. Firms of English solicitors were limited during the period to which these recollections are confined. The University was not established till 1857 and the first LL.B.'s were not known till 1864 or 1865. So that in the fifties and sixties Indians hardly betook themselves to the avocation of a solicitor. In the first place the apprenticeship was for five years. In the second place the fee of Rs. 5,000 was deemed to be costly. The European firms the writer had known were those of

Acland and Prentis.
Dallas and Lynch.
Keir and Prescott.
C. and F. Stanger Leathes.
Bickerseth and Cleveland.
Green and Tyabji.
Kelly and Hore.
John Macfarlane.
H. Crawford.
Khanderao Moroji.
Shamrao Narayan.

There were a few others. It is, however, interesting to notice that every one of the firms abovenamed have changed their names, owing to the oldest partners retiring and passing on their business to newcomers. For instance, take the firm of Messrs. Acland and Prentis which then occupied a premier position, with the most wealthy clientele, European and Indian. As business increased, another partner had to be added and the firm went by the name of Acland, Prentis and Bishop. The senior, Mr. S. L. Acland, died in 1866 and later on, both Messrs. Prentis and Bishop retired. But there were other younger solicitors at the time in the firm of whom Mr. Craigie was the senior. The firm changed its name and was known as Craigie, Lynch and Owen. And though new partners came and went, till late it was styled Craigie, Blunt and Caroe. Similarly Dallas and Lynch became Dallas, Lynch and Langdale and afterwards Dallas and Co., whose successor was Mr. Roughton, to be followed by Mr. Byrne, whose present successors are Messrs. Byrne and Smeatham. Keir and Prescott were later on Keir, Prescott and Winter, and so on. But it would be tedious to record here the changes which the old and rich firms of solicitors underwent till very few can trace their genealogy so to say. Still it would be an interesting reading were some veteran solicitor like Mr. Leslie Crawford to recall the old names, say, from 1860 and bring down their transformations up-to-date. There is an interesting history attached to each. In the forties and the fifties there were solicitors like Patch, Walker, Boyer, Bone, Ayrton and others. Mr. H. Crawford, a brilliant solicitor, with whom Mr. Anstey used to have many "scenes" in the Small Causes Court, was the successor of Mr. Boyer. Mr. Crawtord died in 1866 having met with an accident at Matheran while riding. One Mr. Hurrell had joined him and the firm's name was Crawford and Hurrell. Mr. Hurrell was a lucky solicitor and retired with a fortune of nearly 4 lakhs earned within five years, owing to the exceedingly litigious times when banks and financial associations by the dozens were being wound up, besides well nigh a hundred firms which became bankrupt and took the benefit of Act 28 of 1865. And as to ordinary insolvencies their number was legion. All the solicitors between 1865 and 1875 minted money literally. There was a rich harvest for them to reap during the decade. Hurrell was joined by Mr. Manisty who was formerly in the firm known as Kelly, Hore and Manisty. Then the firm of Hurrell and Manisty changed to Manisty and Fletcher. On the retirement of the former the firm was called Fletcher and Smith and afterwards Smith and Frere, till at last an amalgamation was effected between the successors of the old and eminent house of Hearn, Cleveland and Peile, and this firm is known to us at present as Little & Co. Mention must be specially made of the firm of Messrs. C. and F. Stanger Leathes. There were two brothers Leathe who had been solicitors to the old board of Municipal Commissioners in the fifties. When the

Municipality of 1865 was constituted that firm was engaged to be its solicitors so as to keep continuity. The successors of that firm were first Messrs. Crawford and Boevey. They, too, have undergone a few transformations and have been carrying on business for some years as Crawford and Co. Thus both counsel and solicitors have been changing and changing during the last fifty years. But before closing this chapter it may be not unuseful to place on record the name of one solicitor who acquired fame after his retirement. That was Mr. Acton Smee Ayrton who was a partner in the older firm which came to be known later as Dallas and Co. This Ayrton rose to be the First Minister of Public Works in the early seventies under the Gladstone Cabinet. He was a member of the East India Finance Committee (1871-74), which was commonly called the Fawcett Committee owing to the late Professor Fawcett having been its strongest member. Ayrton took interest in education when here. He had in Mr. Dhunjibhoy Nuservanji Cama, a wealthy China merchant and an educational reformer, a fat client. At Ayrton's suggestion he started the first Anglo-Vernacular school in the city which was commonly known as "Ayrton School" where both Sir Pherozeshah Mehta and I had been educated in the early fifties. There was a single class-room at first in Mopla's Oart in Gunbow Street. But a new school-house was built, with three class-rooms well-ventilated and well-lighted in the Wady, known as Manekji Sett's. And there was an excellent English and Gujarati teacher in the person of one Mr. Harivalabdas, who was himself an old Elphinstonian and social reformer.

CHAPTER LVIII.—PROFESSIONS OTHER THAN LEGAL.

COMING to some of the well-known personalities of other than the legal profession, it may be mentioned that among the physicians and surgeons there were those connected with the Sir Jamsetji Jeejeebhoy Hospital. Dr. Morehead was the first physician and besides principal of the Grant Medical College. He was known to be an exceedingly able doctor and professor alike, most amiable and sympathetic and withal enthusiastic in encouraging the study of western science of medicine, theoretical and practical, among the people of Western India. The earliest students of the Medical College who passed out as graduates for practice spoke in terms of the highest admiration and affection of their eminent medical *guru*. As a consulting physician he was greatly in requisition among the Parsis, who, as in every other walk of social life, were first to avail themselves of the skill and practice of English physicians, and thus it was that Morehead's name was a household word among the leading Parsi families.

Needless to say that that good doctor and talented organiser left the city midst the regrets of students and patients alike, and with the cordial good wishes of the community, both European and Indian, for his long life and prosperity in his retirement. With Dr. Morehead was intimately associated his second assistant in the hospital, Dr. Peet. He too, was equally distinguished for his amiability and courtesy among his students and patients. When Morehead retired he succeeded him at the college as principal and at the hospital as the first physician. The names of both are still enshrined in the memory of the generation which flourished in the fifties. In those days the consultation fee was only Rs. 10. It was as moderate as that which prevailed for counsel in the Supreme Court. That modest fee is in striking contrast with Rs. 20 at first and Rs. 30 later on in vogue. Fees for important operations too which did not exceed 200 or 300 rupees are now mounted up to 500 and 700 or even 1,000 and more. It would seem that the present day doctors are more extravagantly remunerated than those of half a century ago. Ballingall was known to be a first-rate man in surgery. Indeed the three earliest physicians and surgeons made a brilliant trio whose names are still recalled by old families who had appreciated their medical treatment and their great professional urbanity. There was also Dr. Carter (not to be confounded with Dr. Van-dyke Carter) who was a skilled ophthalmic surgeon besides a literary man who had read many papers before the Bombay Geographical and Royal Asiatic Societies

Some Leading European Practitioners.

But apart from these there were at least four European non-official medical practitioners, namely Drs. Yuill, Bremner, Mackay and Fogerty. The first two had a very large practice among the Parsi community. The present writer has a vivid recollection of Dr. Bremner as a boy under his treatment. They were very capable physicians. Dr. Mackay was the superintendent of the Native Medical Dispensary which still flourishes and is of inestimable boon to the poorer classes of the Indian community. He was very popular among the middle classes, and so, too, was Dr. Fogerty. The latter was widely known for curing most difficult cases. It is said that his skill was such that many preferred his medical treatment to that of the distinguished hospital physicians. He had an imagination and a fertility of resource which were deemed exceptional. He had his own consulting rooms in Medows Street and other parts of the Fort, and it is said he minted money most speedily and amassed a large fortune, a greater part of which he lost in the share speculations of 1863-64. He was also extravagant and altogether unconventional in social life which led to his estrangement from the community to which he belonged. At the close of the sixties there was a famous case in the High Court in which he appeared as a plaintiff before Sir Joseph Arnold.

The first Sir Cowasji Jehangir was in a critical condition, so much so that one day he was announced to be either dead or dying. Dr. Fogerty was called for and the patient recovered under his treatment. Sir Cowasji had for a time remained unconscious and it was his brother Hirji who had called for Dr. Fogerty. That physician, knowing well that his patient was rich and generous, sent in his medical bill the amount of which flabbergasted Hirji. It was so exorbitant that Hirji resisted it and eventually the matter went to Court. The learned judge (Sir Joseph Arnould) pronounced the bill to be exorbitant and even unprofessional. He cut it down to a modest butifair figure and criticised the doctor's conduct in most unfavourable terms.

The Engineering Profession.

There were fewer professional engineers than doctors in the fifties. None of the activity in building to be noticed during the last 25 years and more was then evident. Public offices had yet to be constructed. Indeed the era for better class of private buildings (save Elphinstone Circle 1864/5.) and those owned by the State did not commence till 1866-67. The first public offices taken on hand were the General Post Office, and the other was the Public Works Office both in Churchgate Street. Engineers in private practice, among Europeans, were Messrs. Scott and MacLeland and Campbell and among Indians Nusserwanji Chandabhoy. Messrs. Morris and Gostling came later and so did Mr. Stephen. There were, of course, the great engineers of the two railway companies. Of Mr. Berkley, of the G. I. P. Ry. enough has already been observed. He was the *facile princeps* of railway engineers, a regular genius, and no mistake. Then there were Messrs. Lane, Slater and Forde who belonged to the B. B. & C. I. Company, besides others of lesser distinction. Mr. Forde was a man who thoroughly knew Gujarat. During the share speculation, when reclamation projects were rife, he was appointed Chief Engineer to a Company called the Frere Land and Reclamation Company, of which Mr. Lyttleton Holyoake Bayley, afterwards a judge of the High Court, was the chairman. After the collapse of the share mania, Mr. Forde established himself as a private engineer and had an excellent practice. He was also appointed Consulting Engineer to the Municipality for a number of years and was the consultant at the time that the Tansa Water Works were first projected and being constructed.

Leading Bankers of the City.

Among European merchants and bankers some of the more well-known might be mentioned in this place. The Forbeses and the Remingtons were private bankers. The former were at one time the bankers of the East India Company and have been already referred to as regards the eminent public services they had rendered in that connexion. In the fifties and early sixties they were represented by Mr. R. Willis, Mr. Foggo, who rose to be a member of the Legislative Council, Mr. J. A. Forbes, the great municipal reformer, whose carriage was dragged in 1871 by enthusiastic ratepayers from the Town Hall to his office in Apollo Street and who was also honoured with a seat in the Legislative Council, and Mr. Percy Leith who was a high mason of his day. The Remingtons were also great bankers and enjoyed an equal reputation with the Forbeses. Their London house was known as that of Remington and Crawford, whose senior member was the uncle of Arthur Crawford, the Municipal Commissioner. There were Mr. Fogo, Mr. Hadow, and Mr. Lidderdale, the last of whom was intimately connected with the old Bank of Bombay and one of the important witnesses before the Bank of Bombay Commission of 1869 under the presidency of Sir Charles Jackson. In the great merchant's firm of William Nicol and Co. there were the two brothers, John and James Fleming, who were both very sagacious and enterprising and the founders of the original Elphinstone Land and Press Company in 1856 which was eventually bought up in the seventies by the Government when the Port Trust was established. This firm was really the earliest pioneer of British enterprise in great public works in India. And the firm steered most prosperously their company through the eventful financial crisis of 1865-66. Later on, there was the well-known Mr. Hamilton Maxwell who was such an active member of the first Bombay Municipal Corporation and the first to warn that body by declaring its financial bankruptcy under Arthur Crawford which eventually led to the thorough reform of the Municipality. Then there was the equally eminent house of Messrs. Ritchie, Stuart and Company of whom the most notable member was Mr. Michael Scott. This firm was the second in the matter of private enterprise of great works of public utility. It founded the Back

Bay Reclamation Company with a capital of a crore, the shares of which rose from 5,000 to 50,000 during the period of the speculation of 1863-64, and they were once deemed to be a gilt edged security. Mr. Tracey was another well-known member. The Grahams were the premier firm for Lancashire piece-goods. They had the elder Graham (James) in the fifties. Later there were Messrs. Hunter and Crum and Forbes Adam. The last named was four times Chairman of the Chamber of Commerce, and an active colaborateur with Messrs. Telang and Pherozeshah Mehta in 1887 in the Legislative Council during the passing of the great Municipal Act of 1888. There was the other big piece-goods importing firm of Grey and Co., whose two partners, Gavin Steel and Robert Hannay, were closely associated with the directors of the old Bank of Bombay. This firm, as well as that of the great house of Peel, Cassels and Co., had for their brokers the wealthy firm of Messrs. Cursetji, Ardaser and Co., Mr. Walter Cassels, a gentleman of massive intellect in commerce and philosophy alike, was at the head of the Peels, and was the most distinguished merchant in the early sixties. He was honoured by Sir Bartle Frere's Government with the piloting of the first Municipal Bill of 1865 through the Legislative Council. There was the firm of Messrs. Campbell, Mitchell and Co. whose partner, Mr. Andrew Grant, was a conspicuous figure in public meetings and his eloquence was such as to attract large crowds. He, too, was a man of great sagacity and talent. Then there was John L. Scott of the distinguished house of Finlay Scott and Co., also importers of piece-goods. But it is sufficient to have mentioned the most prominent merchants of the last half a century whom the public knew so well. Of course there was the great and honoured firm of David Sassoon and Co., founded years before by a talented senior bearing that name. And with him in those days was associated his eldest son, Abdulla, who afterwards was made a baronet and assumed the name of Sir Albert Sassoon, the donor of that magnificent equestrian statue of King Edward who visited India in 1875-76 as the Prince of Wales. He was also the donor of that Grand Organ in the Town Hall. Elias was another son who, on the death of his father, established a separate firm at the head of which till late was Sir Jacob Sassoon. Lastly, there was Mr. Kittridge, of the firm of Stearns Hobart and Co., who was an active business man and took no little part in public affairs. He was one of the first Dock Trustees and the introducer of tramways in the city, of which till long he was its most able managing director.

Mr. John Stuart.

Among bankers there was Mr. John Stuart a name still held in remembrance by the old generation as the most cautious and sagacious manager of the first Bank of Bombay established in 1841. By a curious irony of fate he was recalled from his retirement to liquidate the old bank which he had reared and left so prosperous at the close of the fifties. During the share mania, the bank was managed by James Blair and Donald Robertson, the two men who brought it to grief. There was John Ryland who had retired early. In the Oriental Bank, there was Mr. Pringle, a well-known and cautious bank manager. There were Messrs. Douglas and Brodie at the Chartered Bank. There was also Mr. Anthony Morrison who joined his fortunes in 1863 with the Joint Stock Bank afterwards called the Asiatic Banking Corporation. The Mercantile Bank had Mr. Jackson who afterwards rose to high distinction at the head office. Mr. Angus was the manager of the popular Commercial Bank, which came to ruin afterwards under the management of Sir Michael Rosario de Quadros. Lastly, there was Edwin Heycock who was the manager of the Central Bank of Western India. He was a merchant and a great friend of the eminent captain of industry who preceded Mr. Tata —the late Mr. Cowasji Nanabhoy Davar. Mr. Heycock established the first ice factory in Bombay and was once Sheriff. At the Agra Bank there was Mr. David MacCulloch. The National and the Hongkong Banks were not established before 1864, but the former had an excellent first manager in Mr. Windram and the latter in Mr. Stephen. And here we bring to a close the well-known European personalities of the fifties and early sixties.

CHAPTER LIX.—CONCLUSION—SOME PROMINENT LOCAL INDIAN CELEBRITIES.

I HAVE now come to the end of my narrative, and it is in the fitness of things that I should make a brief reference to some of the most prominent of Indian celebrities in the city who flourished during the period embraced by these recollections. First and foremost, there was Sir Jamsetji Jeejeebhoy, a merchant prince and a princely philanthropist to boot. He was the first Indian who was knighted by his sovereign and the first also on whom was conferred the dignity of a baronet. The knighthood came to him in 1845 and the baronetcy in 1857. The recognition was wholly due to his beneficent philanthropy, still unsurpassed, and to his unswerving loyalty to the Crown of England. None better understood what the duties of a loyal citizen were than he; and none made himself a more confidential adviser of the Government in the troublous days of 1857. Elphinstone found him *the one* Indian, above all others, whose sage counsel and guidance he most appreciated. He was in the full enjoyment of the confidence of the many Governors of Bombay. Their respect and esteem for him were great. His name was conjured by his contemporaries of all races and creeds; and it is even now conjured as one of the greatest benefactors of humanity. The great hospital which bears his honoured name is a living proof of his benevolence in reference to the relief of suffering humanity. Millions of men, women and children have benefited and are still deriving benefit from that charity. Other merchant princes have flourished and shown their philanthropy in different directions; but it may be said with truth that none has surpassed him. His name will remain enshrined in the memory of generations yet unborn.

Another great name which was so prominent in those days is that of Mr. Framji Cowasji. In some of the previous chapters reference has been made to the beneficent works he projected and brought to completion for the good of the public. The Framji Cowasji Institute is his noblest handiwork and will ever remain a permanent memorial of his honoured name. Next to Sir Jamsetji Jeejeebhoy, his is the most cherished name among the citizens who were in the making of Bombay in the first half of the 19th century. The third great citizen whose name is a household word among all classes of the community is that of the great Juggonnath Sankersett—a statesman of rare political sagacity, a citizen of renown, of great constructive mind, and withal fired with the purest patriotism. He was the first Hindu gentleman who was honoured with a non-official seat in the Bombay Legislative Council in 1863 by Sir Bartle Frere. He died in 1866 mourned by all the communities of Bombay. Sir Bartle Frere was prompt in issuing an official gazette extraordinary announcing his death and appreciating the value of his many services as a loyal and dutiful citizen. Mr. Goculdas Tejpal was a philanthropic Bhatia merchant of those days who was well known to Europeans as much as to his own, countrymen engaged in the trade. Dr. Bhau Daji, an enlightened physician and a most esteemed citizen, was greatly instrumental in inspiring him to do deeds of benevolence which are now so well flourishing in our midst, specially the Tejpal Hospital and the Sanscrit College on the Govalia Tank Road. There was Nacoda Rogay, a Kokani Mahomedan and a great friend of Sir Jamsetji. A gentleman of means and most polished manners, he was most unobtrusive in his charities for the benefit of his own community. But he was not a little helpful in conjunction with Sir Jamsetji in making peace between the Parsis and the Musalmans during the first riot of 1851. I was a boy of seven but have a distinct recollection how that riot terrorised the people in the Fort and how my parents sent a servant to fetch me home with all speed from Ayrton's school. The riot originated from a trivial cause, namely, a life of the Mahomedan. prophet which appeared in a Gujarati Journal called "Chitra Dnyan" (Illustrated Knowledge) along with a portrait. That portrait seemed to have given unnecessary offence to a few Mahomedans who therefore created a riotous disturbance. The co-operation of Mr. Rogay with Sir Jamsetji was highly praised.

Of course, the Kama family had already carved out a name for themselves by their great commercial enterprise abroad, specially in China and London. They were great social reformers and took the keenest interest in the advancement of female education and the spread of the true tenets of Zoroaster among the community. They fully understood the value of an enlightened and liberal Press and were greatly instrumental in founding the *Rast Goftar*, edited by Dadabhoy Naoroji. Messrs. Cursetji and Dhunjibhoy Nusservanji Cama, along with Mr. Dosabhoy Framji Cama, were the most well-known in these respects. There were also Messrs. K. R. Kama, S. S. Bengalee, Naoroji Furdoonji, Jehanghir B. Wacha, A. F. Moos and Cowasji E. Khambata, quite a literary coterie of the Fifties who assembled in the Duftar Ashkara Press, owned by the Murzban family, and helped to make the *Rast Goftar* in their capacity as contributors, a powerful organ of Parsi Liberalism in politics, commerce and social reform. Messrs. Bengalee and Naoroji Furdoonji were greatly associated with the first Municipal reform agitation. Both were active as members of the first Municipal Corporation under Act I of 1865 and both rendered very valuable services to the citizens by their sterling independence and financial sagacity. Mr. Bengalee was one of the three members of what is known as the "Hope Committee" which made a report on the finances of the Municipality at the instance of the Government. Mr. K. R. Kama exclusively applied his attention to the development of Zend Avesta studies. Mr. Muncherji Hormusji Cama (generally nicknamed 'Senchi') published in English a translation of the Zend Avesta by Dr. Bleek which greatly stimulated the study of Zoroastrian ethics. About Mr. K. E. Khambata enough has been mentioned in some of the preceding chapters. He was a good English scholar and covered himself with praise as Editor of "Native Opinion". There was Mr. J. B. Wacha who was a Gujarati historian and Mr. B. P. Master, a witty gentleman who was greatly associated with the affairs of the Municipal Corporation, specially in connexion with the water supply of Bombay of which he once gave a most humorous description that greatly quickened the City Fathers to provide for an adequate supply of drinking water. There was old Dr. Blaney who lived like a recluse in Armenian Lane and thence fired off of letter after letter as "Q" or "Q in the corner" in the *Bombay Gazette* on the feverish speculation of 1863-64 and its ultimate consequences. He became exceedingly well-known as a leading member of the Municipal Corporation. In fact he was a leader in all sanitary matters as was

Sir P. M. Mehta in general and constitutional matters, As a popular citizen Dr. Blaney had the great satisfaction of seeing a statue erected in his honour by public subscriptions during his life time. He was also a philanthropist and used to give away hundreds every month to the indigent, distressed and lowly poor of all classes. His is a name still cherished by the older generation of Bombay. Next may be mentioned the name of Karsandas Mulji, the great Hindu social reformer, who instituted the paper called the "Satya Prakash" and exposed the many improprieties of the Vaishna tribe of Maharajas and their orgies. He became famous because of the libel case instituted by the Maharaja against him. The historical judgment of Sir Joseph Arnould in this case, reveals the depths of those improprieties. The judgment was a great shock to the orthodox party. But this case also brought in to prominence

Bhatia gentleman, Mr. Lakhmidas Khimji, who entertained the most liberal views on the subject. Mr. Lakhmidas, it has been generally recognised, helped Mr. Karsandas with the sinews of the litigation which is one of the celebrated causes of the Bombay High Court. Mr. (afterwards Sir) Mangaldas Nathoobhoy was also a strong supporter of the Hindu reformer. But during the period embraced by these recollections Mr. Mangaldas had not attained the great prominence which he afterwards did. The Aga Khan case, which was also heard before the same learned judge, was another *cause celebre*. It was also one in which orthodoxy was a great deal given a hard knock by the impartial judgment of the same erudite judge. But the old Aga Khan, the grand-father of the present one, was influential enough to retain his supremacy as the spiritual head of the Khojas. That community was not so sharply divided as the Bhatia community was by the Karsondas libel case. Two other Hindu names which were greatly known in those days need to be mentioned. They are of the two medical brothers, Bhau and Narayan Daji. They were the earliest Hindu medical graduates of the Grant Medical College. Both had extensive practice, but the elder, Dr. Bhau, had a great tendency towards research. He had an original mind which was incessantly cultivated to a good purpose. He was much keen on scientifically testing the efficacy of Indian drugs on specific diseases. Leprosy cure was his great aim and object. He had only partially succeeded in his attempt. But Dr. Bhau was also a politician and social reformer albeit of a moderate character. He was in favour of the remarriage of Hindu widows. Dr. Narayan more or less confined himself to medical practice. Both brothers were highly esteemed by the European medical faculty. The late Sir George Birdwood held them in the greatest regard for their ability. Among Mahomedans, there were no men of public prominence save Mr. Rogay. The only other person was Mr. Cumrudin Tyabji who practised as a solicitor after having passed his examination as attorney in London. He became a partner in the firm known as Green and Tyabji. There were men of less prominence among the three Indian communities in trade more or less, but so far their share in public affairs as citizens require no special mention. Of course, with the rapid spread of education and the institution of the University the men of the Seventees and after rapidly rose and earned public distinction, but their career cannot be incorporated in these recollections. It is however to be hoped that some literary scholar will undertake that arduous task so as to keep the memory green of those who in different walks of life have earned a name and fame since 1865 or 1870.

To complete the list it is needful to do justice to two other celebrities, the first Sir Cowasji Jehanghir Readymoney and Mr. Dosabhoy Framji Karaka. The last began his post-academic career with the *Jame Jamshed* as its assistant editor. That journal was the special organ of the orthodox Parsis, then an overwhelming majority, under the leadership, of course, of Sir Jamsetji Jeejeebhoy. Indeed Zoroastrian orthodoxy was rampant in the Sixties, being hardly illumined by the light shed on the true tenets of that ancient creed by the great scholars of the west. The Parsi reformers were then just rising and organising themselves to do their very best to disentangle the creed from the alien weeds with which it had been allowed to overgrow during wellnigh eleven centuries of their domicile in Gujerat.

Living in the midst of a population, mostly of Gujerati Hindus, the descendants of Darius and Xerses had adopted many of their religious rites and ceremonies. It was the set aim and purpose of the reformers by means of lectures, meetings and other methods to make the orthodox understand how the noble creed of their great prophet was encrusted with Hindu and other Indian superstitions and beliefs. Mr. Dosabhoy Framji belonged to that band of reformers, albeit he was generally known as a Liberal Conservative. Later on he rose to be a Municipal Assessor during the regime of the Municipal triumvirate, generally known as the three Municipal Commissioners who flourished from 1858 till 1865. In 1860 Mr. Dosabhoy was appointed one of the five men of the Advisory Committee which the Government appointed to assist the Income Tax collector in enforcing the Income Tax, the first of its kind imposed on all India. Mr. Dosabhoy's tact, judgment, and, above all, his sweet reasonableness were soon recognised. And when the tax came to be abolished the Government of Sir Bartle Frere wisely promoted him to one of the magistrateships of the city—an office which he filled with great credit to himself and to the satisfaction of the citizens till his retirement. Mr. Dosabhoy's most important public activity was to be seen in the Bombay Municipal Corporation from its institution in 1865 to 1890. Once he was fortunate enough to be elected President during the year which memorialised for the first time the visit of a Prince of Wales to India, he who afterwards was King Edward VII.

Sir Cowasji Jehanghir Readymoney was indeed the most prominent citizen of Bombay after Sir Jamsetji Jeejeebhoy. Belonging to one of the first wealthy families who had settled in the city at the opening of the nineteenth century and endowed from his youth with all the instincts of a great merchant and a sagacious but cautious financier, he came to be recognised at a very early age as the coming celebrity. With his elder brother, Mr. Hirji, he was a guaranteed brother to Messrs. Cardwell Parsons and Co., and one or two other English firms. Mr. Cowasji also was well known for his rare broad-mindedness, his ardent civic patriotism, his large hearted and catholic philanthropy and, above all, his deep spirit of humanity. So that as he flourished and prospered those special traits became more and more marked and recognised. Sagacious and shrewd in matters of banking and finance, without a spirit of speculation, he was invited to be a Director of the old Bank of Bombay, an office which he filled with such foresight and caution as to elicit the admiration of the trading and shroffing community. So much so that Sir Charles Jackson, President of the Commission which investigated into the failure of the old Bank of Bombay, 1869, has placed on record that so long as Mr. Cowasji was on the board of Directors he was too careful to see that the bank never incurred a bad debt of even a single Rupee! The present writer would unhesitatingly say, having intimately known him in his younger days, that not a single Indian has hitherto approached him in respect of commercial ethics and integrity. He was a sterling personality and unreservedly confided by those who came into contact with him in matters of trade and finance. It was unfortunate that a constitutional ailment, contracted at an early day, had crippled his movements and in many ways physically incapacitated him. He had to be taken up and down in a chair. But till the day of his death his mental faculties were as strong as they were in his youth. His love of education, specially Higher, was innate in him. It was greatly enhanced by his intimate contact with Sir Alexander Grant, at first (Principal of Elphinstone College, and, afterwards), Director of Public Instruction. It was he who gave the handsome donation of 2 lakhs for providing a local habitation for Elphinstone College and it was he also who gave another 2 lakhs for that magnificent Senate Hall of the University which bears his honoured name. And it is a satisfaction to record in this place that in gratitude for his many beneficent and utilitarian charities, specially in matters of education, the citizens of Bombay raised public funds and erected his statue which stands in the University Gardens. All honour to such a worthy person whose name will be remembered by generation after generation for his great civic spirit, his spirit of humanity, his high broadmindedness and his catholic philanthropy.

Now my task is done. I have narrated my personal reminiscences so far as I have been able to remember them with perfect fidelity and have tried to present the dry bones of the history of this great city prior to 1865. The task undertaken was a voluntary one. It was self imposed but one of love. How far I have succeeded in collecting the shells and giving the citizens of Bombay an account of men and things during my boyhood and sometime after must be left to my readers to judge. I began by saying that Time rolls its ceaseless course. It is rolling still and will roll on to eternity. Empire's rise and fall. So, too, great cities and towns. Let me fervently hope that my native Bombay, dear to me from every point of view, may have a better fate, that she may flourish for

BACK BAY VIEW, 1860.

ever more, that her name may live in history as that of a great city, a great emporium of trades and manufactures, of vast enterprise and of a cosmopolitan character and the high gateway of the Asiatic continent closely linking the West with the East.

Errata.

Page		Line		Read	
Page	1	Line	2	Read	"apostrophise"
,,	2	,,	9	,,	"takes its"
,,	5	,,	16	,,	"Customs"
,,	7	,,	6	,,	"primitive"
,,	,,	,,	7	,,	"the water"
,,	,,	,,	9	,,	"d'etre"
,,	14	,,	12	,,	"albeit tiny"
,,	16	,,	5	,,	"voices"
,,	21	,,	17	,,	"Hesperides"
,,	26	,,	13	,,	"record"
,,	27	,,	19	,,	"had"
,,	31	,,	18	,,	"magnitude"
,,	32	Foot note		,,	"Æschylus Ædipus"
,,	45	Line	14	,,	"old of it"
,,	52	,,	24	,,	"trepidation"
,,	60	,,	19	,,	"where are"
,,	61	,,	6	,,	"sentries"
,,	63	,,	16	,,	"admitted"
,,	64	,,	11	,,	"has been"
,,	66	Chapter VI. Heading read "Forjett"			
,,	75	Line 12 read "rifled"			
,,	80.	,, 22 ,, "blown to pieces"			
,,	83	,, 17 ,, "almost all"			
,,	87	,, 19 ,, "itinerants"			
,,	70	,, 20 ,, "crossed"			
,,	95	,, 3 ,, "gambolled"			

Besides other trivial ones here and there in the rest of the pages all of which will be corrected in another edition.